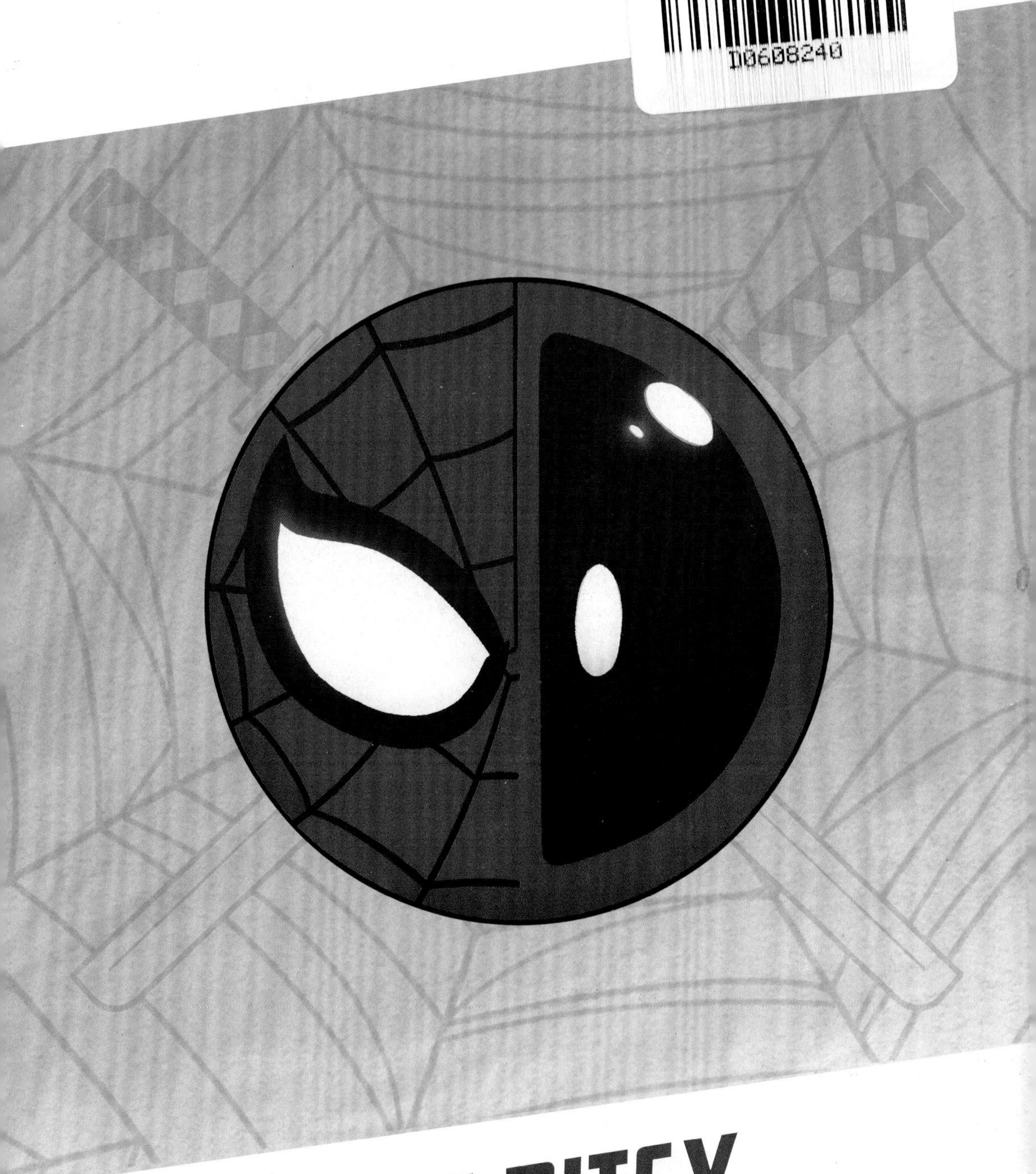

ITSY BITSY

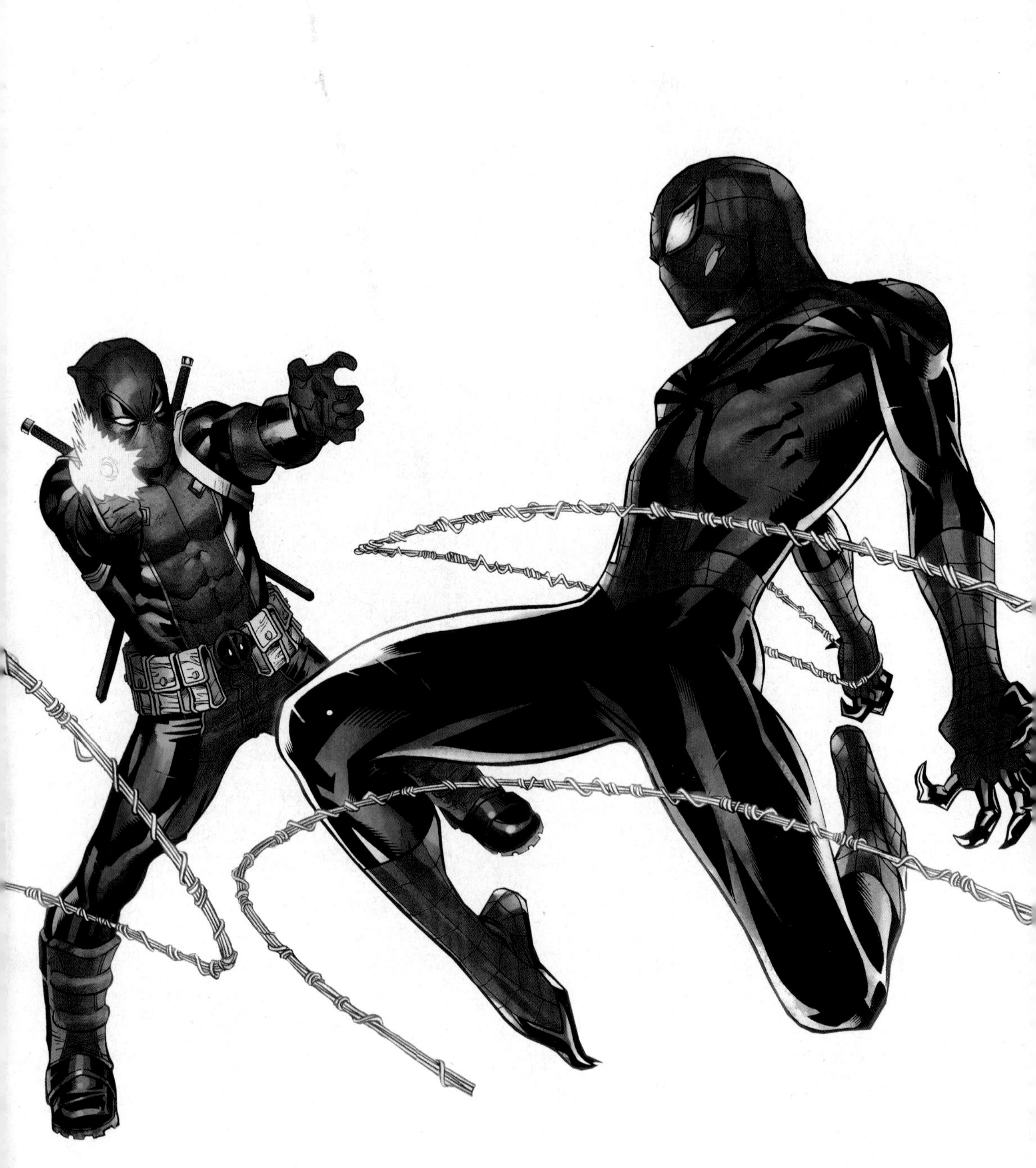

SPIDER-MAN CREATED BY
STAN LEE & **STEVE DITKO**

DEADPOOL CREATED BY
ROB LIEFELD & **FABIAN NICIEZA**

Collection Editor **JENNIFER GRÜNWALD**
Assistant Editor **CAITLIN O'CONNELL**
Associate Managing Editor **KATERI WOODY**
Editor, Special Projects **MARK D. BEAZLEY**
VP Production & Special Projects **JEFF YOUNGQUIST**
SVP Print, Sales & Marketing **DAVID GABRIEL**
Book Designer **ADAM DEL RE**

Editor In Chief **AXEL ALONSO**
Chief Creative Officer **JOE QUESADA**
President **DAN BUCKLEY**
Executive Producer **ALAN FINE**

SPIDER-MAN/DEADPOOL VOL. 3: ITSY BITSY. Contains material originally published in magazine form as SPIDER-MAN/DEADPOOL #9-10, #13-14 and #17-18. First printing 2017. ISBN# 978-0-7851-9787-4. Published by MARVEL WORLDWIDE, INC., a subsidiary of MARVEL ENTERTAINMENT, LLC. OFFICE OF PUBLICATION: 135 West 50th Street, New York, NY 10020. Copyright © 2017 MARVEL No similarity between any of the names, characters, persons, and/or institutions in this magazine with those of any living or dead person or institution is intended, and any such similarity which may exist is purely coincidental. **Printed in Canada.** DAN BUCKLEY, President, Marvel Entertainment; JOE QUESADA, Chief Creative Officer; TOM BREVOORT, SVP of Publishing; DAVID BOGART, SVP of Business Affairs & Operations, Publishing & Partnership; C.B. CEBULSKI, VP of Brand Management & Development, Asia; DAVID GABRIEL, SVP of Sales & Marketing, Publishing; JEFF YOUNGQUIST, VP of Production & Special Projects; DAN CARR, Executive Director of Publishing Technology; ALEX MORALES, Director of Publishing Operations; SUSAN CRESPI, Production Manager; STAN LEE, Chairman Emeritus. For information regarding advertising in Marvel Comics or on Marvel.com, please contact Vit DeBellis, Integrated Sales Manager, at vdebellis@marvel.com. For Marvel subscription inquiries, please call 888-511-5480. **Manufactured between 8/4/2017 and 9/5/2017 by SOLISCO PRINTERS, SCOTT, QC, CANADA.**

10 9 8 7 6 5 4 3 2 1

MARVEL COMICS
BEGRUDGINGLY PRESENTS...

PETER PARKER WAS BITTEN BY AN IRRADIATED SPIDER, GRANTING HIM AMAZING ABILITIES, INCLUDING THE PROPORTIONAL SPEED, STRENGTH AND AGILITY OF A SPIDER, AS WELL AS ADHESIVE FINGERTIPS AND TOES. AFTER LEARNING THAT WITH GREAT POWER, THERE MUST ALSO COME GREAT RESPONSIBILITY, HE BECAME THE WORLD'S GREATEST SUPER HERO! HE'S...

THE WORLD'S GREATEST SUPER HERO!

The AMAZING SPIDER-MAN

AVENGER...ASSASSIN...SUPERSTAR! WADE WILSON WAS CHOSEN FOR A TOP-SECRET GOVERNMENT PROGRAM THAT GAVE HIM A HEALING FACTOR THAT ALLOWS HIM TO HEAL FROM ANY WOUND. DESPITE EARNING A SMALL FORTUNE AS A GUN FOR HIRE, WADE HAS BECOME THE WORLD'S MOST BELOVED HERO. AND IS THE STAR OF THE WORLD'S GREATEST COMICS MAGAZINE (NO MATTER WHAT THAT JERK IN THE WEBS MAY THINK). CALL HIM THE MERC WITH THE MOUTH...CALL HIM THE REGENERATIN' DEGENERATE...CALL HIM...

DEADPOOL

LAST TIME:

DEADPOOL KILLED SPIDER-MAN! THAT IS, HE KILLED PETER PARKER, NOT REALIZING THAT HIS VICTIM WAS HIS NEW BESTEST BUDDY'S SECRET IDENTITY! TURNS OUT MYSTERIO WAS BEHIND IT ALL, HIRING DEADPOOL TO TAKE PARKER OUT SO HE COULD TAKE OVER AS THE C.E.O., PRESIDENT AND OTHERWISE BIG CHEESE OF PARKER INDUSTRIES.

BECAUSE HE'S COOL LIKE THAT, DEADPOOL RENEGED ON THE JOB AND LITERALLY DRAGGED PARKER BACK FROM PURGATORY. WHAT A GUY! HOWEVER, MYSTERIO'S PLAN TURNED OUT TO BE A RUSE TO DISTRACT OUR HEROES FROM THE REAL THREAT. THAT IS, PATIENT ZERO AND HIS UNINSPIRED PLAYLISTS ARE BACK AND JUST AS MANIC AS EVER! HE'S UP TO HIS OLD TRICKS AGAIN (HORRIFYING GENETIC MUTATIONS, DNA SPLICING... REAL DELIGHTFUL STUFF). HE ALSO HAS A BEAUTIFUL, MYSTERIOUS WOMAN HOLED UP IN A HIGH-RISE, AND HAS BEEN GIVING HER TRANSFUSIONS OF BOTH DEADPOOL AND SPIDER-MAN'S BLOOD. HMM...

HOWEVER, THAT'S ALL RIDICULOUSLY IRRELEVANT COMPARED TO THE REAL SHOCKER. DEADPOOL TOOK OFF HIS MASK... AND WAS DROP-DEAD HANDSOME AGAIN! NOT TO LOOK A GIFT MERC IN THE MOUTH, BUT...HUH??

JOE KELLY
Writer

ED McGUINNESS
Penciler

MARK MORALES WITH
ED McGUINNESS (#10, #13), JOHN DELL (#13) & WALDEN WONG (#17)
LIVESAY (#10), JAY LEISTEN (#10, #18),
Inkers

JASON KEITH WITH
MATT YACKEY (#17)
Color Artists

VC's JOE SABINO
Letterer

ED McGUINNESS, MARK MORALES & JASON KEITH
Cover Art

ALLISON STOCK
Assistant Editor

DEVIN LEWIS
Associate Editor

JORDAN D. WHITE & NICK LOWE
Editors

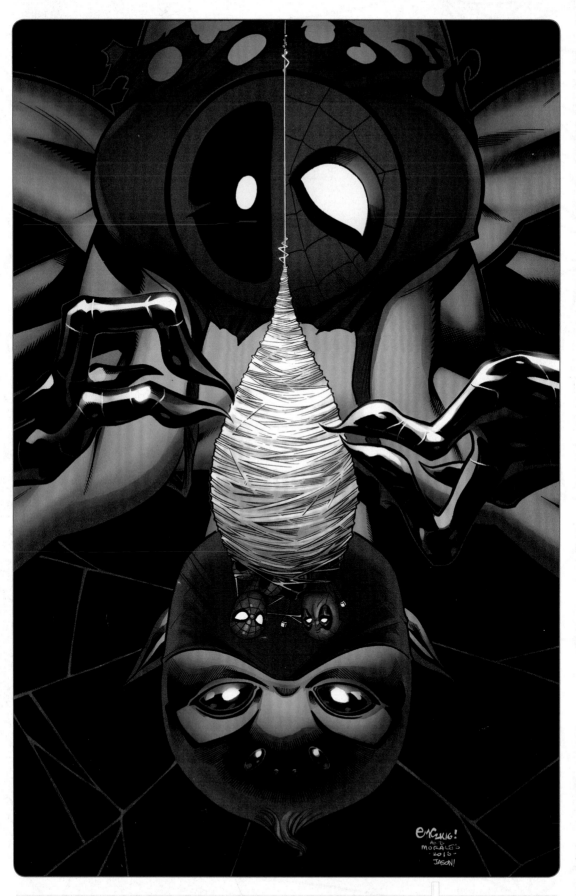

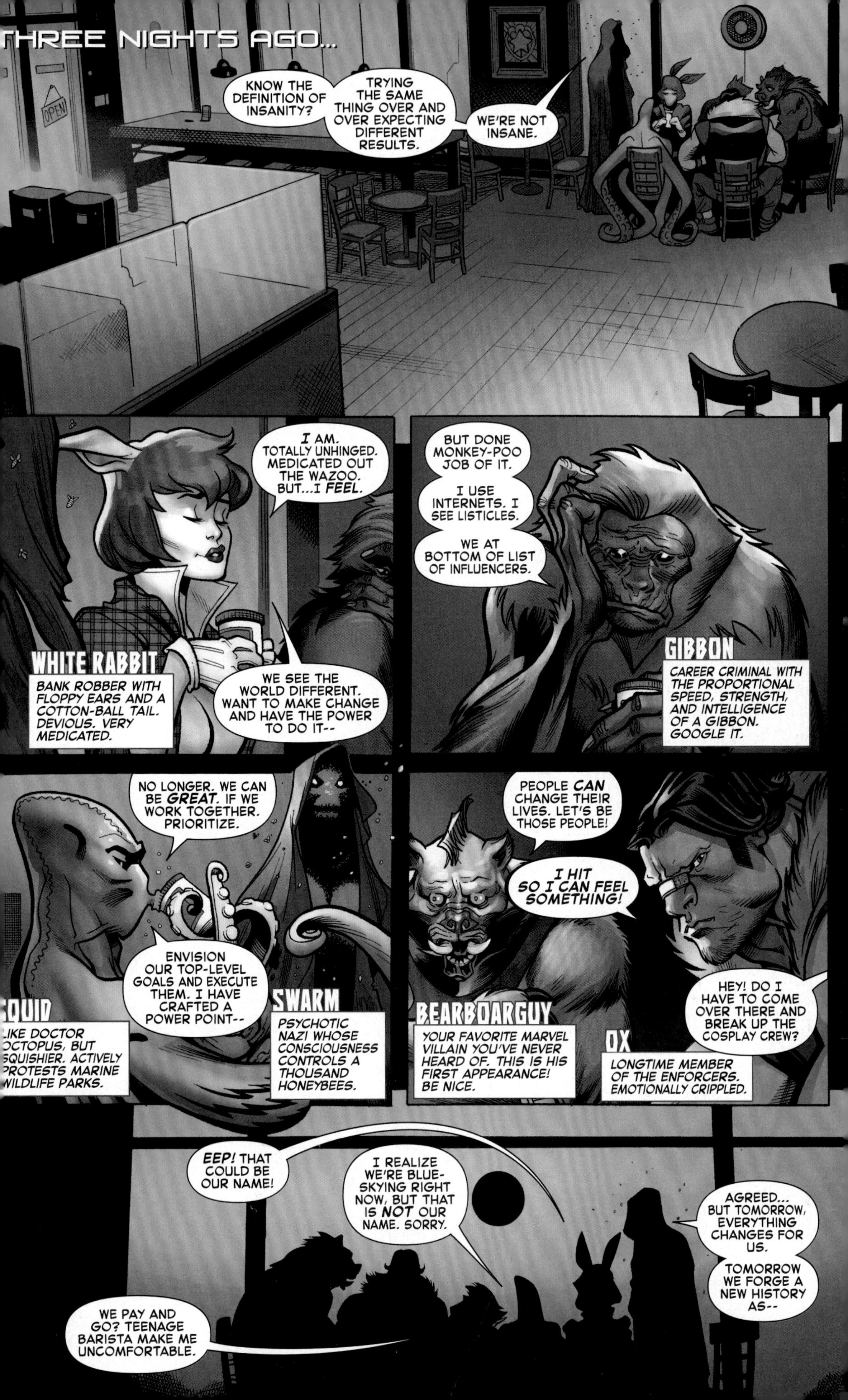
THREE NIGHTS AGO...
OPEN
KNOW THE DEFINITION OF INSANITY?
TRYING THE SAME THING OVER AND OVER EXPECTING DIFFERENT RESULTS.
WE'RE NOT INSANE.
I AM. TOTALLY UNHINGED. MEDICATED OUT THE WAZOO. BUT...I FEEL.
WHITE RABBIT
BANK ROBBER WITH FLOPPY EARS AND A COTTON-BALL TAIL. DEVIOUS. VERY MEDICATED.
WE SEE THE WORLD DIFFERENT. WANT TO MAKE CHANGE AND HAVE THE POWER TO DO IT--
BUT DONE MONKEY-POO JOB OF IT.
I USE INTERNETS. I SEE LISTICLES.
WE AT BOTTOM OF LIST OF INFLUENCERS.
GIBBON
CAREER CRIMINAL WITH THE PROPORTIONAL SPEED, STRENGTH, AND INTELLIGENCE OF A GIBBON. GOOGLE IT.
NO LONGER. WE CAN BE GREAT. IF WE WORK TOGETHER. PRIORITIZE.
ENVISION OUR TOP-LEVEL GOALS AND EXECUTE THEM. I HAVE CRAFTED A POWER POINT--
QUID
IKE DOCTOR OCTOPUS, BUT SQUISHIER. ACTIVELY PROTESTS MARINE WILDLIFE PARKS.
SWARM
PSYCHOTIC NAZI WHOSE CONSCIOUSNESS CONTROLS A THOUSAND HONEYBEES.
PEOPLE CAN CHANGE THEIR LIVES. LET'S BE THOSE PEOPLE!
I HIT SO I CAN FEEL SOMETHING!
BEARBOARGUY
YOUR FAVORITE MARVEL VILLAIN YOU'VE NEVER HEARD OF. THIS IS HIS FIRST APPEARANCE! BE NICE.
OX
LONGTIME MEMBER OF THE ENFORCERS. EMOTIONALLY CRIPPLED.
HEY! DO I HAVE TO COME OVER THERE AND BREAK UP THE COSPLAY CREW?
EEP! THAT COULD BE OUR NAME!
I REALIZE WE'RE BLUE-SKYING RIGHT NOW, BUT THAT IS NOT OUR NAME. SORRY.
AGREED... BUT TOMORROW, EVERYTHING CHANGES FOR US.
TOMORROW WE FORGE A NEW HISTORY AS--
WE PAY AND GO? TEENAGE BARISTA MAKE ME UNCOMFORTABLE.

TODAY.

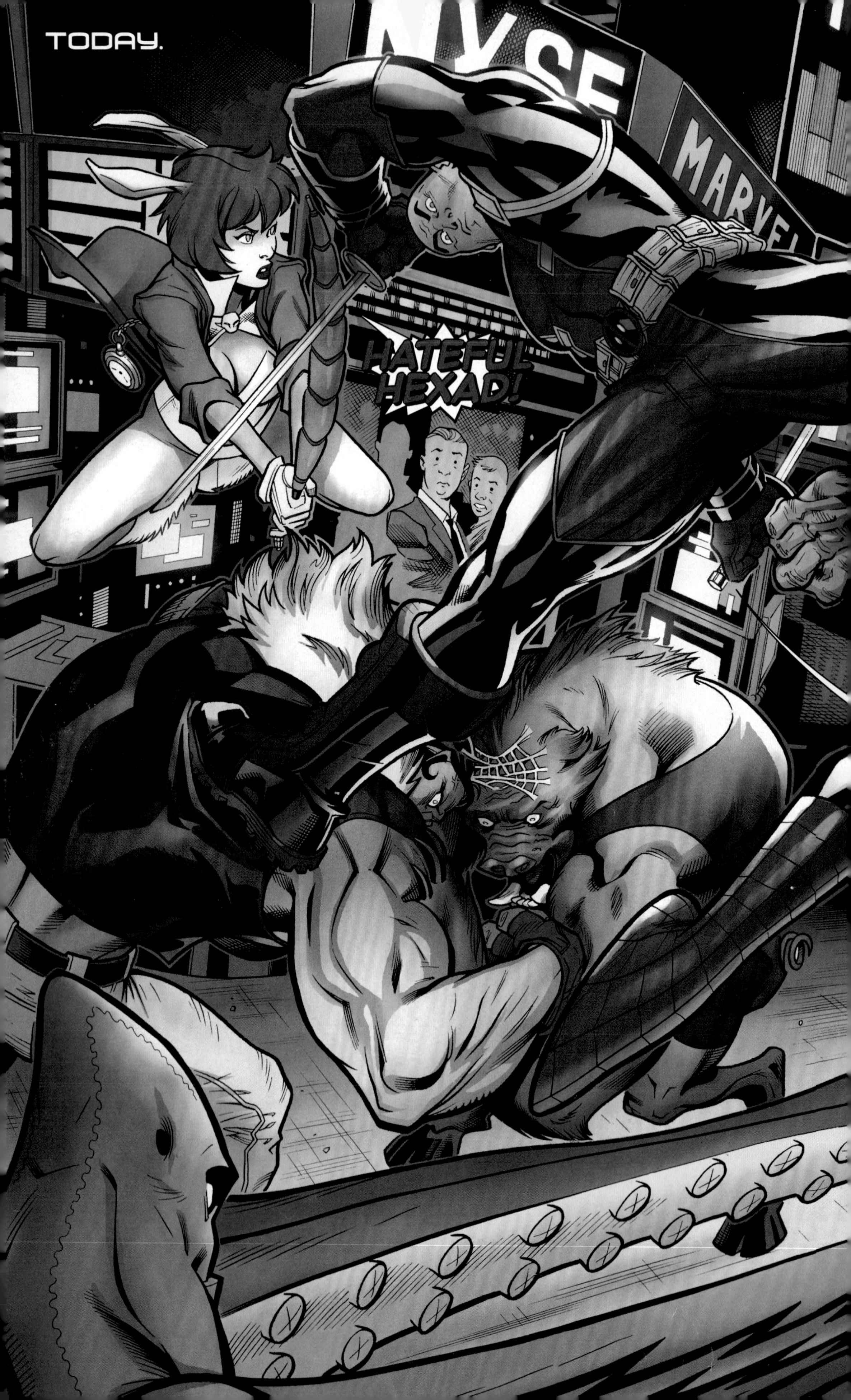

NYSE
MARVEL
HATEFUL HEXAD!

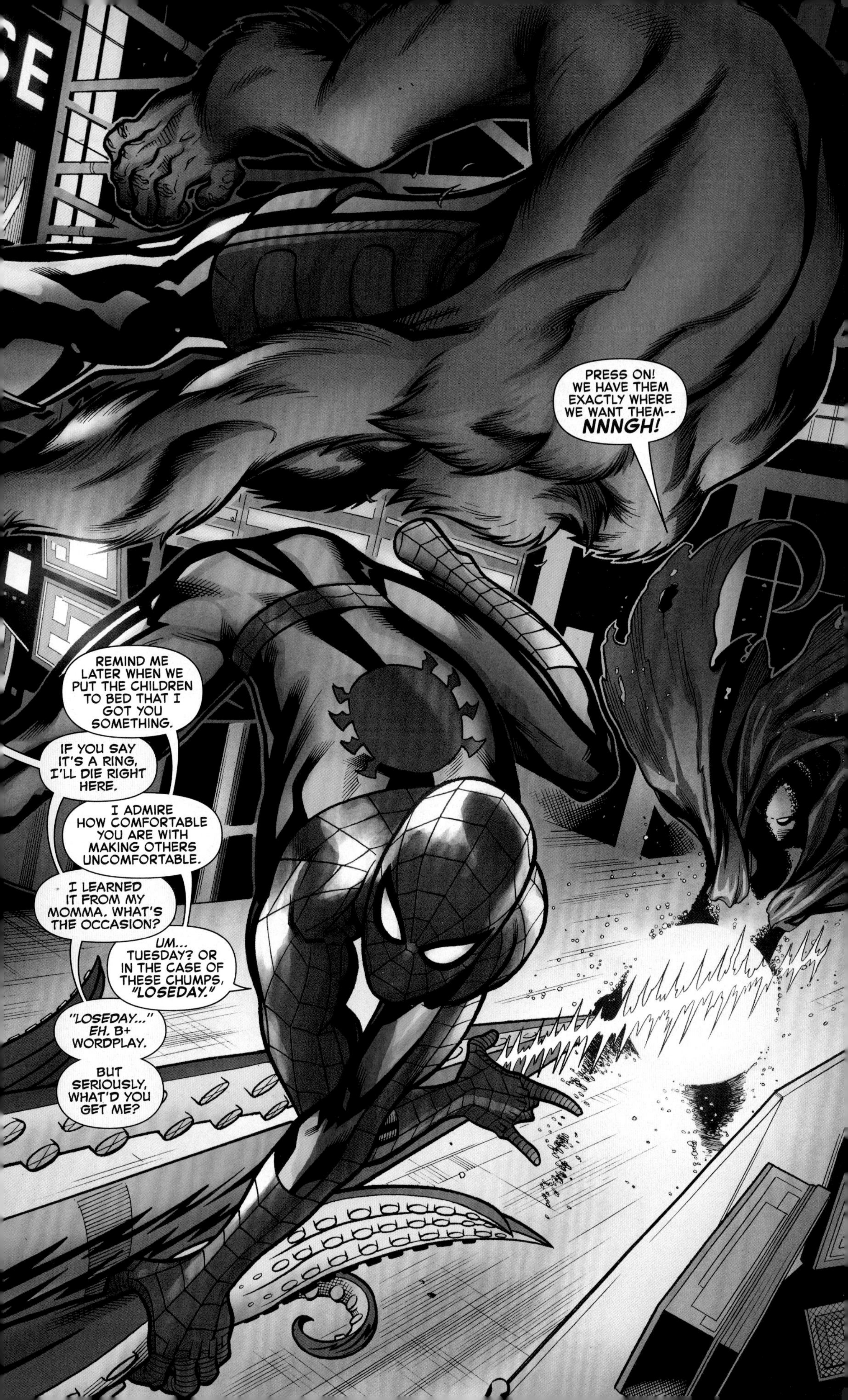
PRESS ON! WE HAVE THEM EXACTLY WHERE WE WANT THEM-- NNNGH!
REMIND ME LATER WHEN WE PUT THE CHILDREN TO BED THAT I GOT YOU SOMETHING.
IF YOU SAY IT'S A RING, I'LL DIE RIGHT HERE.
I ADMIRE HOW COMFORTABLE YOU ARE WITH MAKING OTHERS UNCOMFORTABLE.
I LEARNED IT FROM MY MOMMA. WHAT'S THE OCCASION?
UM... TUESDAY? OR IN THE CASE OF THESE CHUMPS, "LOSEDAY."
"LOSEDAY..." EH. B+ WORDPLAY.
BUT SERIOUSLY, WHAT'D YOU GET ME?

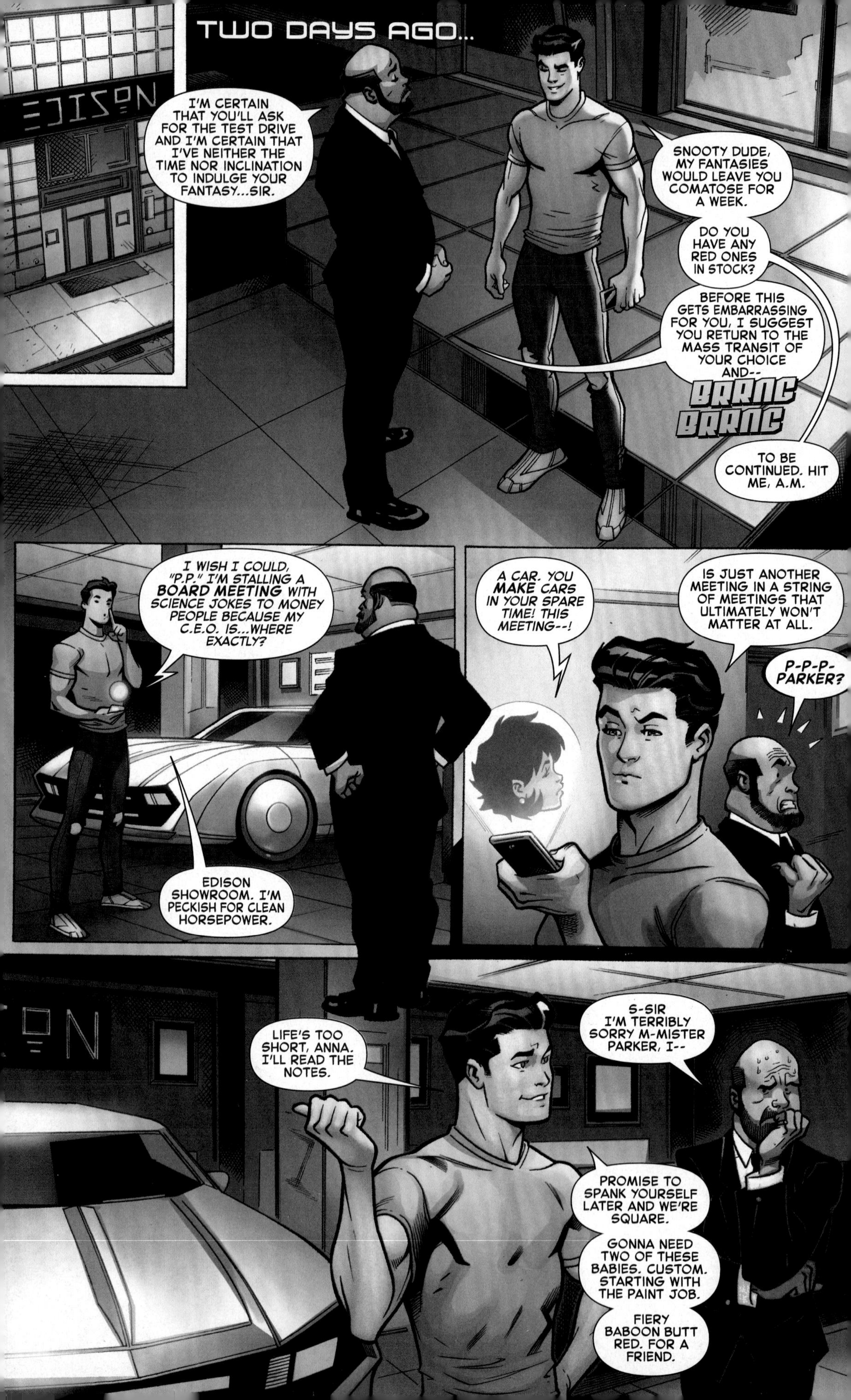
TWO DAYS AGO...
EDISON
I'M CERTAIN THAT YOU'LL ASK FOR THE TEST DRIVE AND I'M CERTAIN THAT I'VE NEITHER THE TIME NOR INCLINATION TO INDULGE YOUR FANTASY...SIR.
SNOOTY DUDE, MY FANTASIES WOULD LEAVE YOU COMATOSE FOR A WEEK.
DO YOU HAVE ANY RED ONES IN STOCK?
BEFORE THIS GETS EMBARRASSING FOR YOU, I SUGGEST YOU RETURN TO THE MASS TRANSIT OF YOUR CHOICE AND--
BRRNG BRRNG
TO BE CONTINUED. HIT ME, A.M.
I WISH I COULD, "P.P." I'M STALLING A BOARD MEETING WITH SCIENCE JOKES TO MONEY PEOPLE BECAUSE MY C.E.O. IS...WHERE EXACTLY?
EDISON SHOWROOM. I'M PECKISH FOR CLEAN HORSEPOWER.
A CAR. YOU MAKE CARS IN YOUR SPARE TIME! THIS MEETING--!
IS JUST ANOTHER MEETING IN A STRING OF MEETINGS THAT ULTIMATELY WON'T MATTER AT ALL.
P-P-P-PARKER?
LIFE'S TOO SHORT, ANNA. I'LL READ THE NOTES.
S-SIR I'M TERRIBLY SORRY M-MISTER PARKER, I--
PROMISE TO SPANK YOURSELF LATER AND WE'RE SQUARE.
GONNA NEED TWO OF THESE BABIES. CUSTOM. STARTING WITH THE PAINT JOB.
FIERY BABOON BUTT RED. FOR A FRIEND.

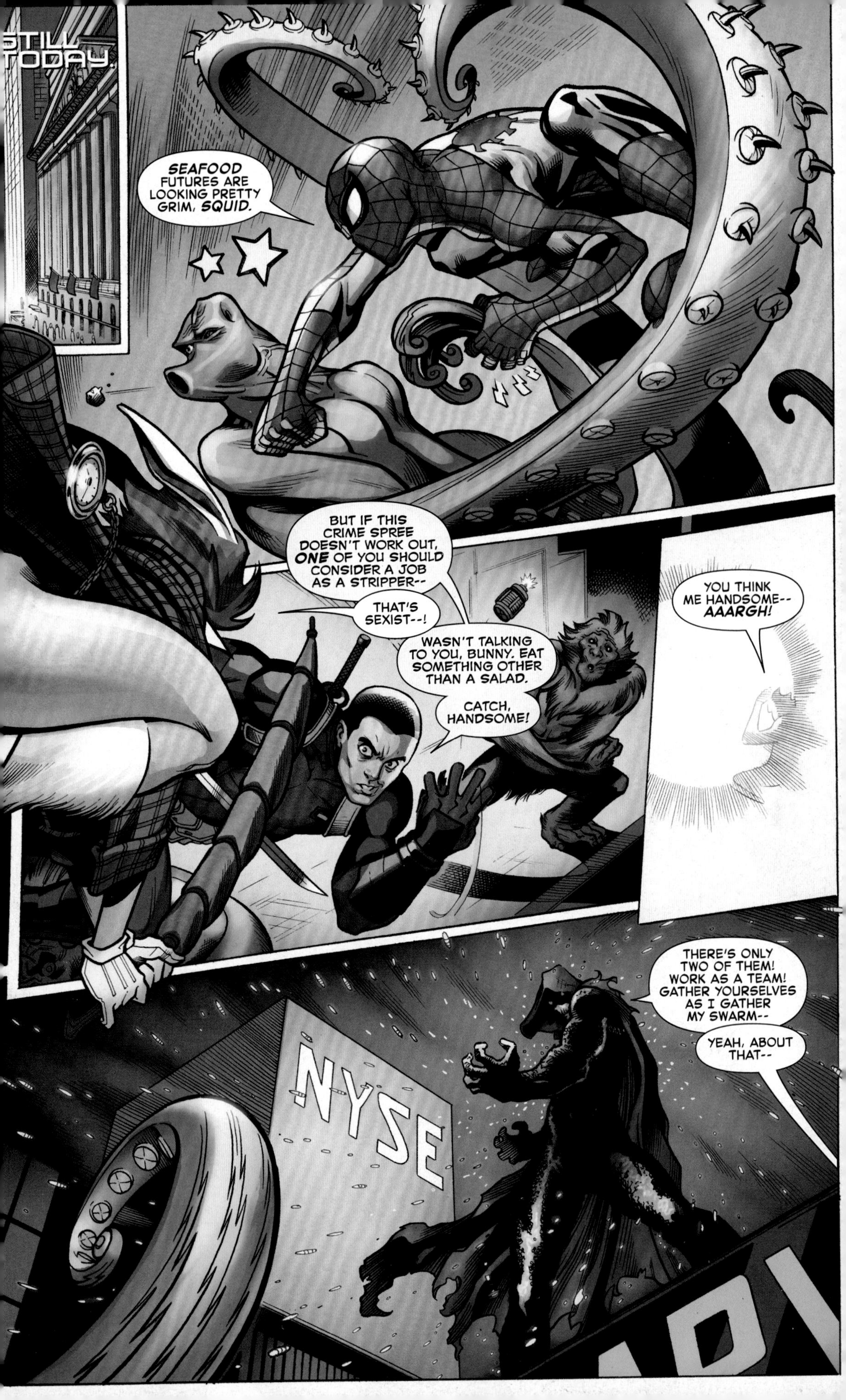
STILL TODAY.
SEAFOOD FUTURES ARE LOOKING PRETTY GRIM, SQUID.
BUT IF THIS CRIME SPREE DOESN'T WORK OUT, ONE OF YOU SHOULD CONSIDER A JOB AS A STRIPPER--
THAT'S SEXIST--!
WASN'T TALKING TO YOU, BUNNY. EAT SOMETHING OTHER THAN A SALAD.
CATCH, HANDSOME!
YOU THINK ME HANDSOME-- AAARGH!
THERE'S ONLY TWO OF THEM! WORK AS A TEAM! GATHER YOURSELVES AS I GATHER MY SWARM--
YEAH, ABOUT THAT--
NYSE

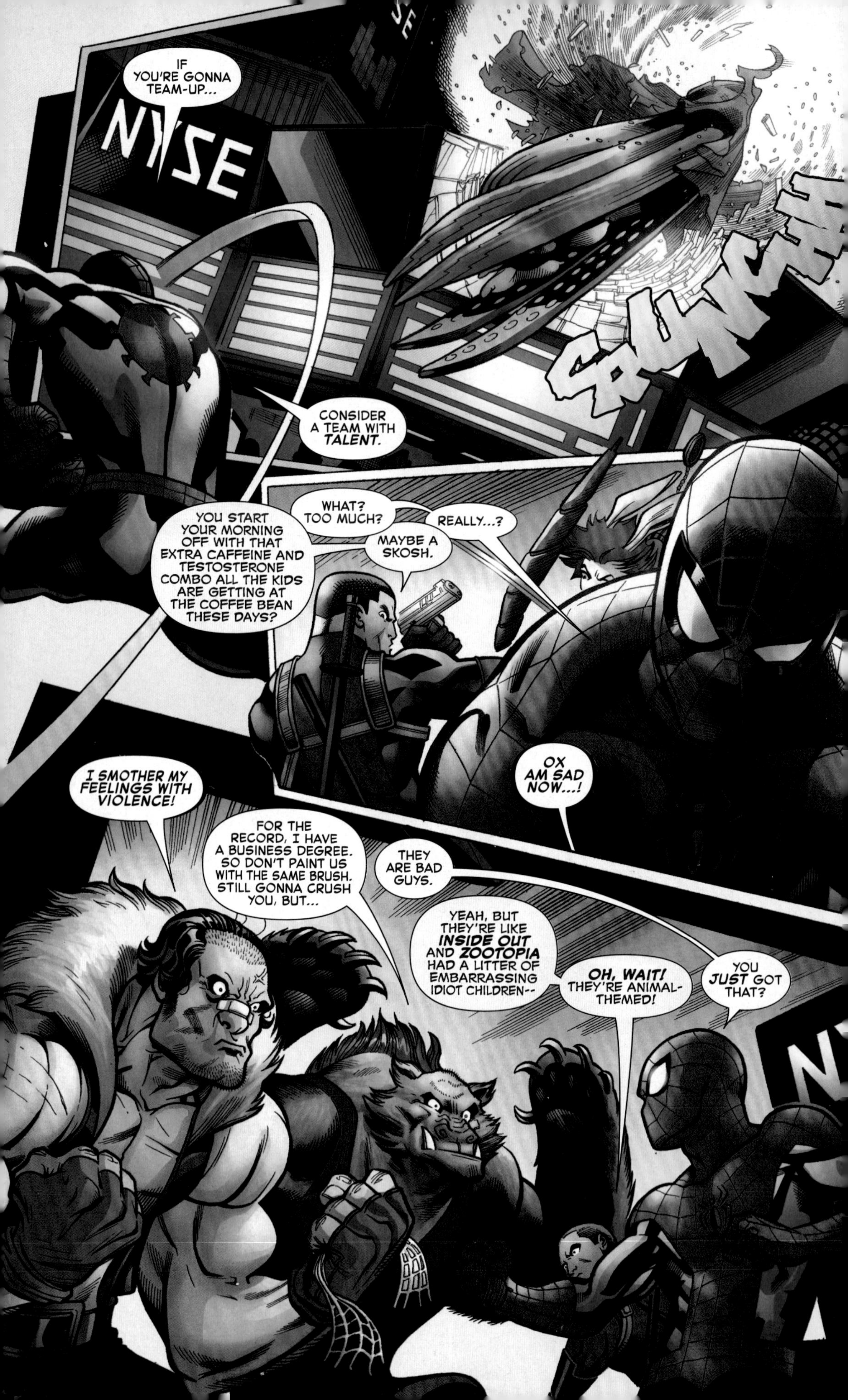
IF YOU'RE GONNA TEAM-UP...
NYSE
CRUNCH
CONSIDER A TEAM WITH *TALENT.*
YOU START YOUR MORNING OFF WITH THAT EXTRA CAFFEINE AND TESTOSTERONE COMBO ALL THE KIDS ARE GETTING AT THE COFFEE BEAN THESE DAYS?
WHAT? TOO MUCH?
REALLY...?
MAYBE A SKOSH.
OX AM SAD NOW...!
I SMOTHER MY FEELINGS WITH VIOLENCE!
FOR THE RECORD, I HAVE A BUSINESS DEGREE. SO DON'T PAINT US WITH THE SAME BRUSH. STILL GONNA CRUSH YOU, BUT...
THEY ARE BAD GUYS.
YEAH, BUT THEY'RE LIKE ***INSIDE OUT*** AND ***ZOOTOPIA*** HAD A LITTER OF EMBARRASSING IDIOT CHILDREN--
OH, WAIT! THEY'RE ANIMAL-THEMED!
YOU ***JUST*** GOT THAT?

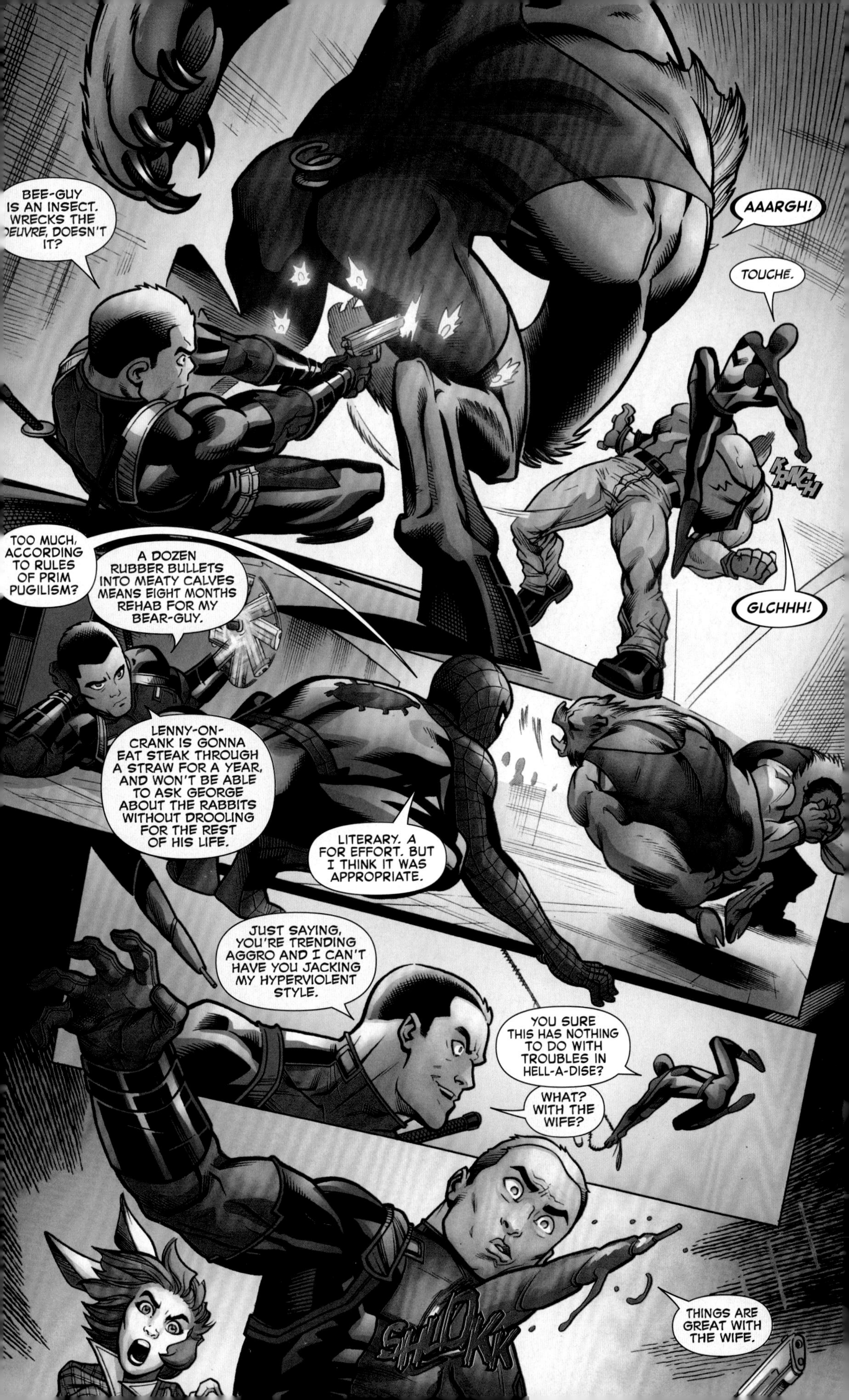
BEE-GUY IS AN INSECT. WRECKS THE OEUVRE, DOESN'T IT?
AAARGH!
TOUCHE.
KRNCH
GLCHHH!
TOO MUCH, ACCORDING TO RULES OF PRIM PUGILISM?
A DOZEN RUBBER BULLETS INTO MEATY CALVES MEANS EIGHT MONTHS REHAB FOR MY BEAR-GUY.
LENNY-ON-CRANK IS GONNA EAT STEAK THROUGH A STRAW FOR A YEAR, AND WON'T BE ABLE TO ASK GEORGE ABOUT THE RABBITS WITHOUT DROOLING FOR THE REST OF HIS LIFE.
LITERARY. A FOR EFFORT. BUT I THINK IT WAS APPROPRIATE.
JUST SAYING, YOU'RE TRENDING AGGRO AND I CAN'T HAVE YOU JACKING MY HYPERVIOLENT STYLE.
YOU SURE THIS HAS NOTHING TO DO WITH TROUBLES IN HELL-A-DISE?
WHAT? WITH THE WIFE?
THINGS ARE GREAT WITH THE WIFE.
SHUKK

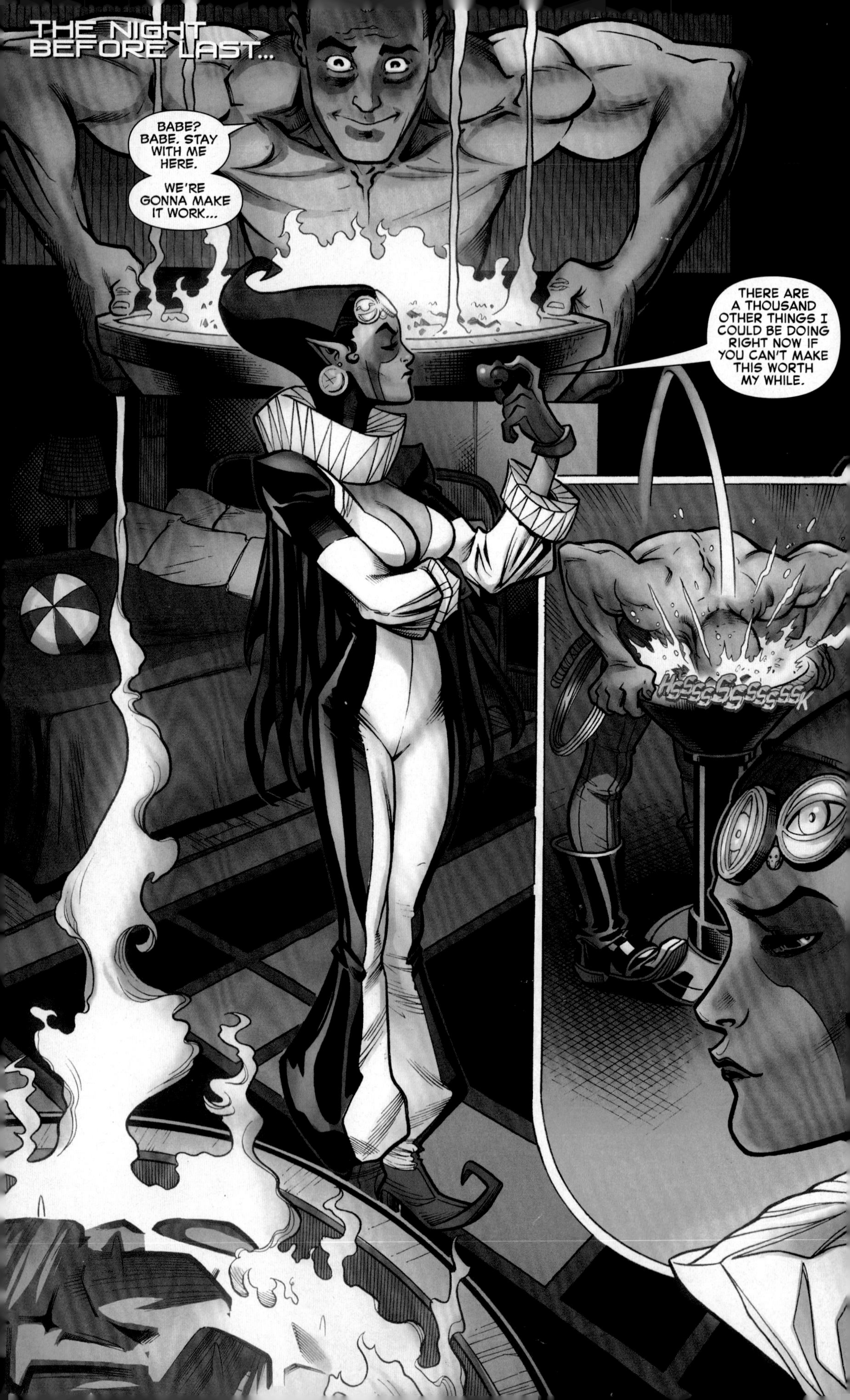
THE NIGHT BEFORE LAST...
BABE? BABE. STAY WITH ME HERE.
WE'RE GONNA MAKE IT WORK...
THERE ARE A THOUSAND OTHER THINGS I COULD BE DOING RIGHT NOW IF YOU CAN'T MAKE THIS WORTH MY WHILE.
HSSSSSSSSSSSSK

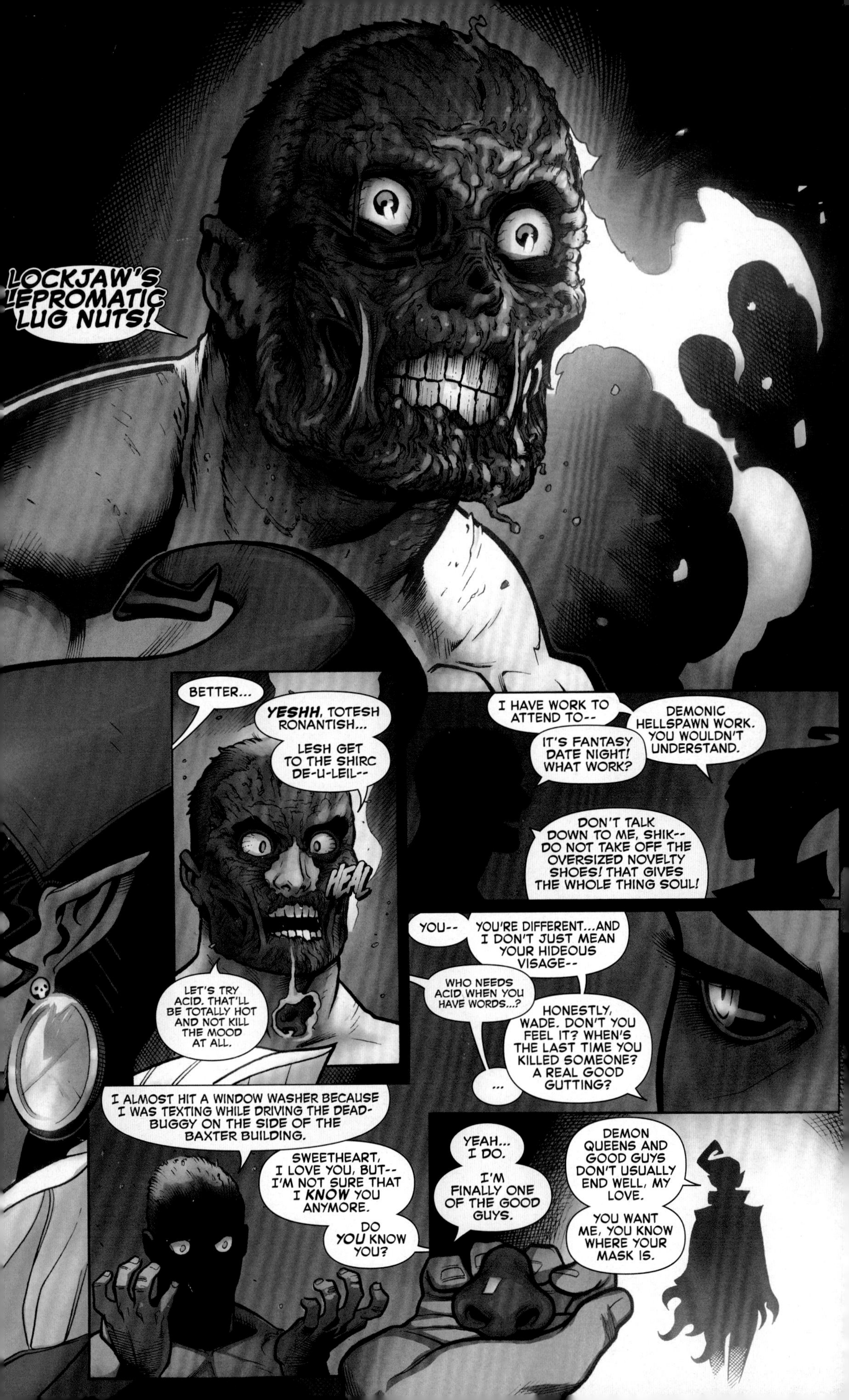
LOCKJAW'S
EPROMATIC
LUG NUTS!
BETTER...
YESHH, TOTESH RONANTISH...
LESH GET TO THE SHIRC DE-U-LEIL--
HEAL
LET'S TRY ACID. THAT'LL BE TOTALLY HOT AND NOT KILL THE MOOD AT ALL.
I HAVE WORK TO ATTEND TO--
IT'S FANTASY DATE NIGHT! WHAT WORK?
DEMONIC HELLSPAWN WORK. YOU WOULDN'T UNDERSTAND.
DON'T TALK DOWN TO ME, SHIK-- DO NOT TAKE OFF THE OVERSIZED NOVELTY SHOES! THAT GIVES THE WHOLE THING SOUL!
YOU--
YOU'RE DIFFERENT...AND I DON'T JUST MEAN YOUR HIDEOUS VISAGE--
WHO NEEDS ACID WHEN YOU HAVE WORDS...?
HONESTLY, WADE. DON'T YOU FEEL IT? WHEN'S THE LAST TIME YOU KILLED SOMEONE? A REAL GOOD GUTTING?
...
I ALMOST HIT A WINDOW WASHER BECAUSE I WAS TEXTING WHILE DRIVING THE DEAD-BUGGY ON THE SIDE OF THE BAXTER BUILDING.
SWEETHEART, I LOVE YOU, BUT-- I'M NOT SURE THAT I KNOW YOU ANYMORE.
DO YOU KNOW YOU?
YEAH... I DO.
I'M FINALLY ONE OF THE GOOD GUYS.
DEMON QUEENS AND GOOD GUYS DON'T USUALLY END WELL, MY LOVE.
YOU WANT ME, YOU KNOW WHERE YOUR MASK IS.

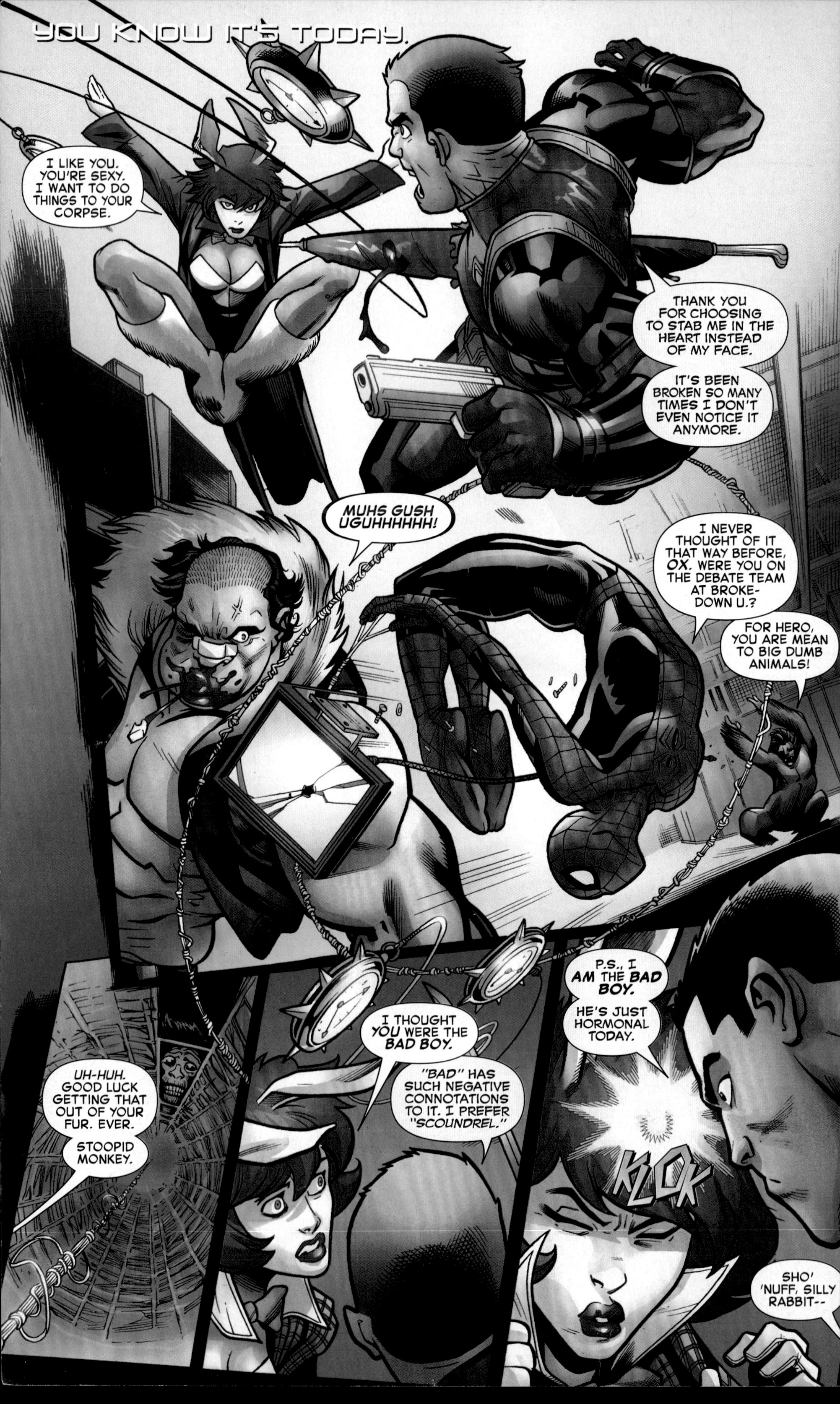
YOU KNOW IT'S TODAY.
I LIKE YOU. YOU'RE SEXY. I WANT TO DO THINGS TO YOUR CORPSE.
THANK YOU FOR CHOOSING TO STAB ME IN THE HEART INSTEAD OF MY FACE.
IT'S BEEN BROKEN SO MANY TIMES I DON'T EVEN NOTICE IT ANYMORE.
MUHS GUSH UGUHHHHHH!
I NEVER THOUGHT OF IT THAT WAY BEFORE, OX. WERE YOU ON THE DEBATE TEAM AT BROKE-DOWN U.?
FOR HERO, YOU ARE MEAN TO BIG DUMB ANIMALS!
UH-HUH. GOOD LUCK GETTING THAT OUT OF YOUR FUR. EVER.
STOOPID MONKEY.
I THOUGHT YOU WERE THE BAD BOY.
"BAD" HAS SUCH NEGATIVE CONNOTATIONS TO IT. I PREFER "SCOUNDREL."
P.S., I AM THE BAD BOY.
HE'S JUST HORMONAL TODAY.
KLOK
SHO' 'NUFF, SILLY RABBIT--

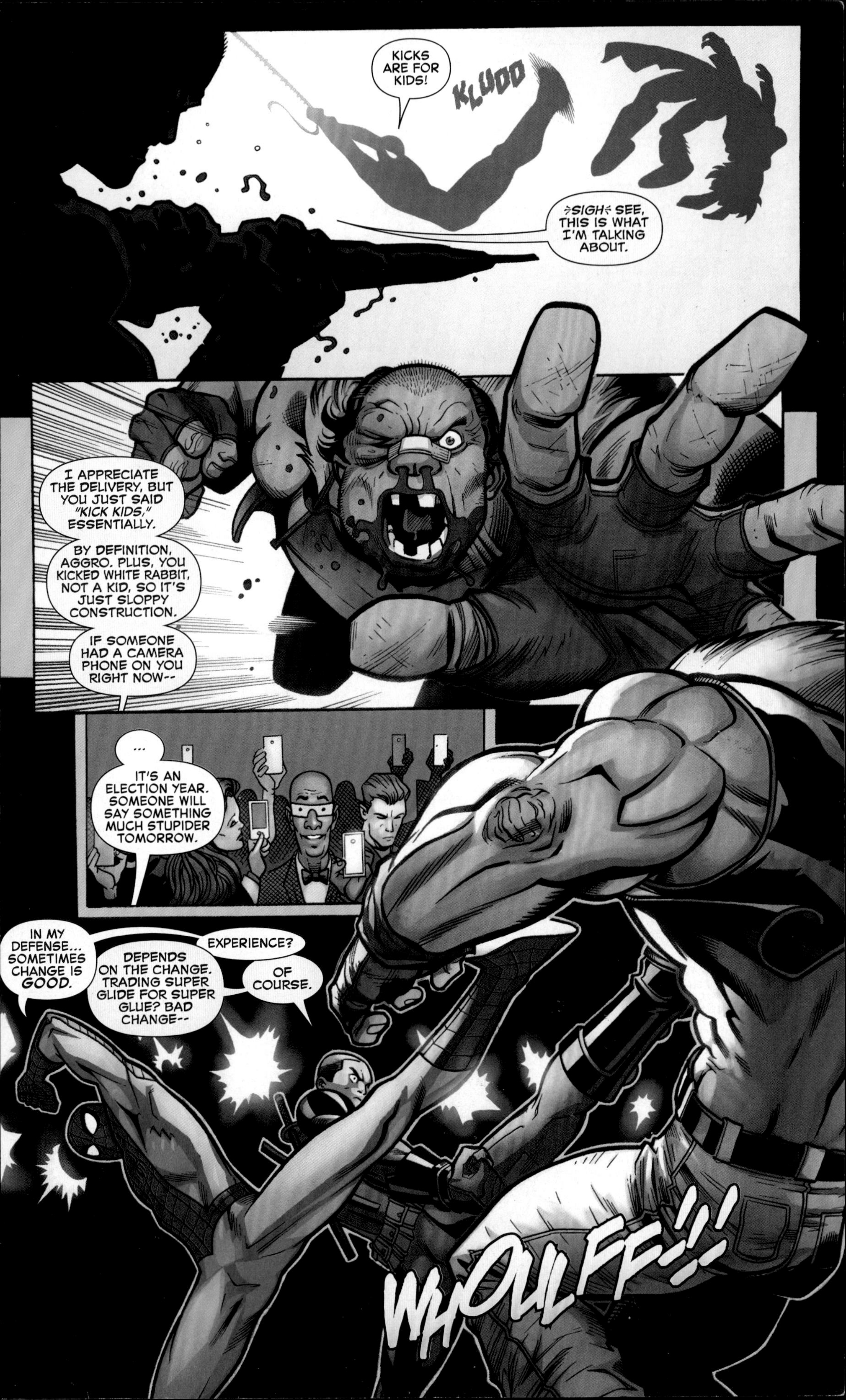
KICKS ARE FOR KIDS!
KLUDD
≈SIGH≈ SEE, THIS IS WHAT I'M TALKING ABOUT.
I APPRECIATE THE DELIVERY, BUT YOU JUST SAID "KICK KIDS," ESSENTIALLY.
BY DEFINITION, AGGRO. PLUS, YOU KICKED WHITE RABBIT, NOT A KID, SO IT'S JUST SLOPPY CONSTRUCTION.
IF SOMEONE HAD A CAMERA PHONE ON YOU RIGHT NOW--
...
IT'S AN ELECTION YEAR. SOMEONE WILL SAY SOMETHING MUCH STUPIDER TOMORROW.
IN MY DEFENSE... SOMETIMES CHANGE IS GOOD.
EXPERIENCE?
DEPENDS ON THE CHANGE. TRADING SUPER GLIDE FOR SUPER GLUE? BAD CHANGE--
OF COURSE.
WHOULFF-!!!

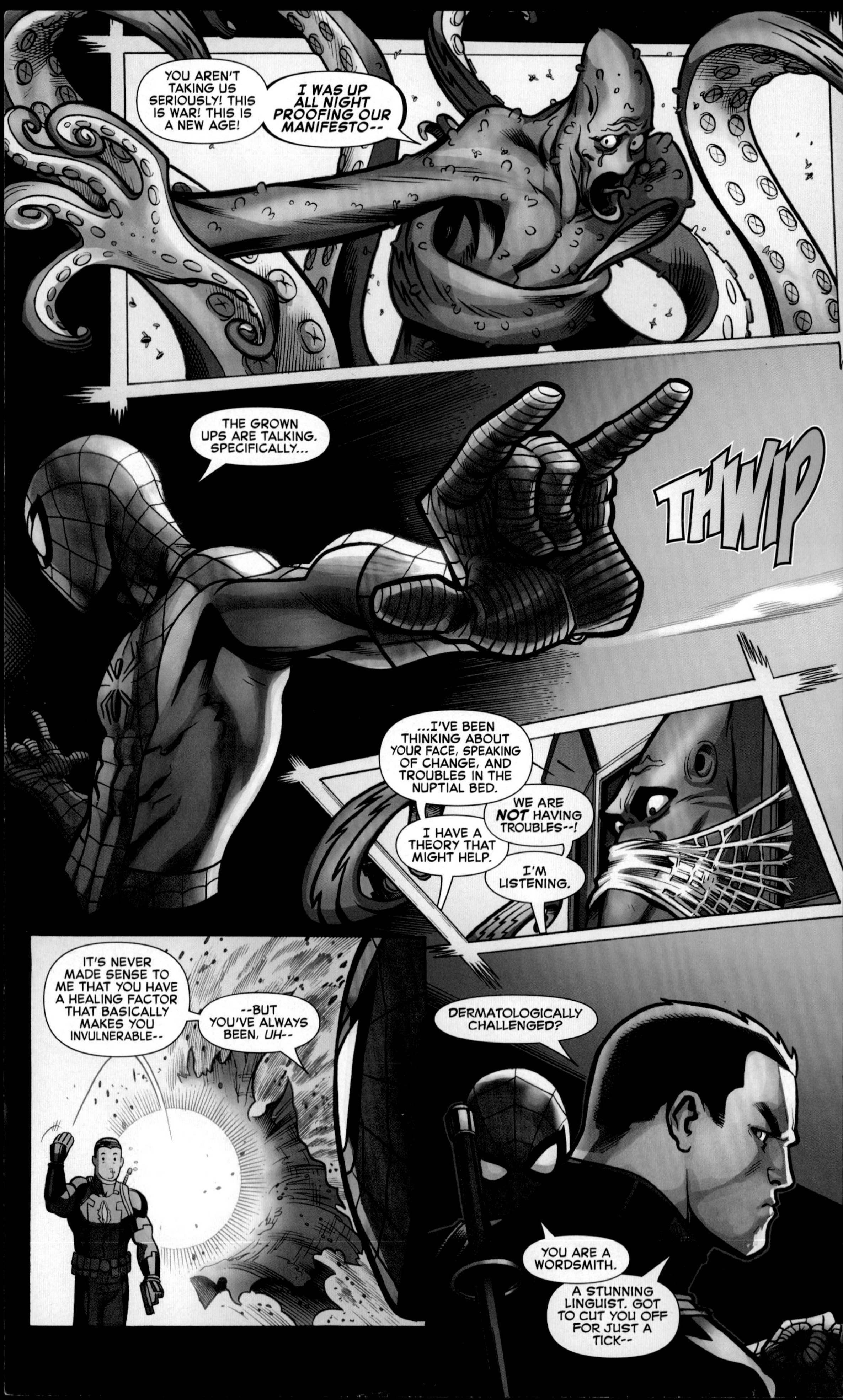
YOU AREN'T TAKING US SERIOUSLY! THIS IS WAR! THIS IS A NEW AGE!
I WAS UP ALL NIGHT PROOFING OUR MANIFESTO--
THE GROWN UPS ARE TALKING. SPECIFICALLY...
THWIP
...I'VE BEEN THINKING ABOUT YOUR FACE, SPEAKING OF CHANGE, AND TROUBLES IN THE NUPTIAL BED.
WE ARE NOT HAVING TROUBLES--!
I HAVE A THEORY THAT MIGHT HELP.
I'M LISTENING.
IT'S NEVER MADE SENSE TO ME THAT YOU HAVE A HEALING FACTOR THAT BASICALLY MAKES YOU INVULNERABLE--
--BUT YOU'VE ALWAYS BEEN, UH--
DERMATOLOGICALLY CHALLENGED?
YOU ARE A WORDSMITH.
A STUNNING LINGUIST. GOT TO CUT YOU OFF FOR JUST A TICK--

YELP!

AS YOU WERE.

IT'S JUST A THEORY, BUT MAYBE, HAVING A FACE LIKE SALAMI SAUTÉED IN ELEPHANT SNOT WASN'T SOME CRUEL TWIST OF FATE...

...BUT PSYCHOLOGY.

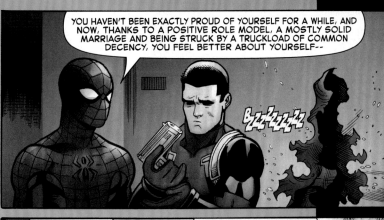

YOU HAVEN'T BEEN EXACTLY PROUD OF YOURSELF FOR A WHILE, AND NOW, THANKS TO A POSITIVE ROLE MODEL, A MOSTLY SOLID MARRIAGE AND BEING STRUCK BY A TRUCKLOAD OF COMMON DECENCY, YOU FEEL BETTER ABOUT YOURSELF--

BZZZZZZZZZZ

THANKS, OPRAH SPINFREY.

DO YOU HAVE A BETTER THEORY?

YEAH, "I WOKE UP LIKE THIS." MEANWHILE, LET'S PIVOT BACK TO YOUR BEHAVIOR--

CURSEZZZZZ...

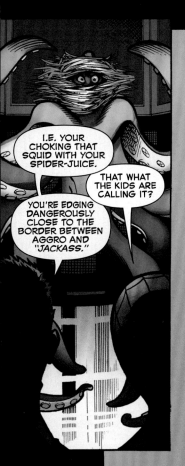

I.E. YOUR CHOKING THAT SQUID WITH YOUR SPIDER-JUICE.

THAT WHAT THE KIDS ARE CALLING IT?

YOU'RE EDGING DANGEROUSLY CLOSE TO THE BORDER BETWEEN AGGRO AND "JACKASS."

EASY FELLA. I GOT YOU. SOMETIMES THE WEB SHOOTERS ARE A HAIR OFF.

HOW OFTEN DOES THAT HAPPEN?

NEVER. BUT, FIRST TIME FOR EVERYTHING! HENCE WEB-SOLVENT!

MMMFM! MMMMMM!

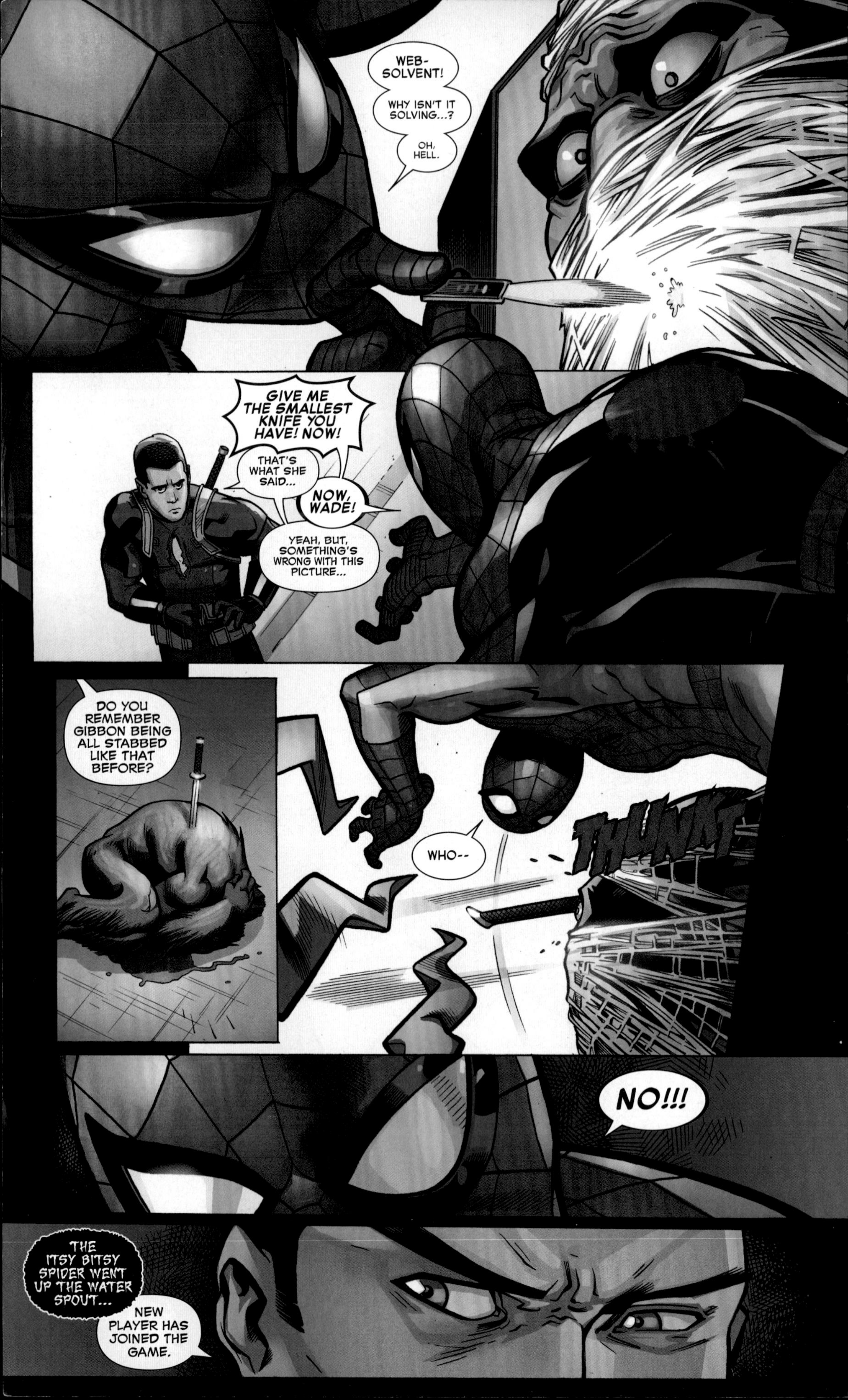
WEB-SOLVENT!
WHY ISN'T IT SOLVING...?
OH, HELL.
GIVE ME THE SMALLEST KNIFE YOU HAVE! NOW!
THAT'S WHAT SHE SAID...
NOW, WADE!
YEAH, BUT, SOMETHING'S WRONG WITH THIS PICTURE...
DO YOU REMEMBER GIBBON BEING ALL STABBED LIKE THAT BEFORE?
WHO--
THUNK!
NO!!!
THE ITSY BITSY SPIDER WENT UP THE WATER SPOUT...
NEW PLAYER HAS JOINED THE GAME.

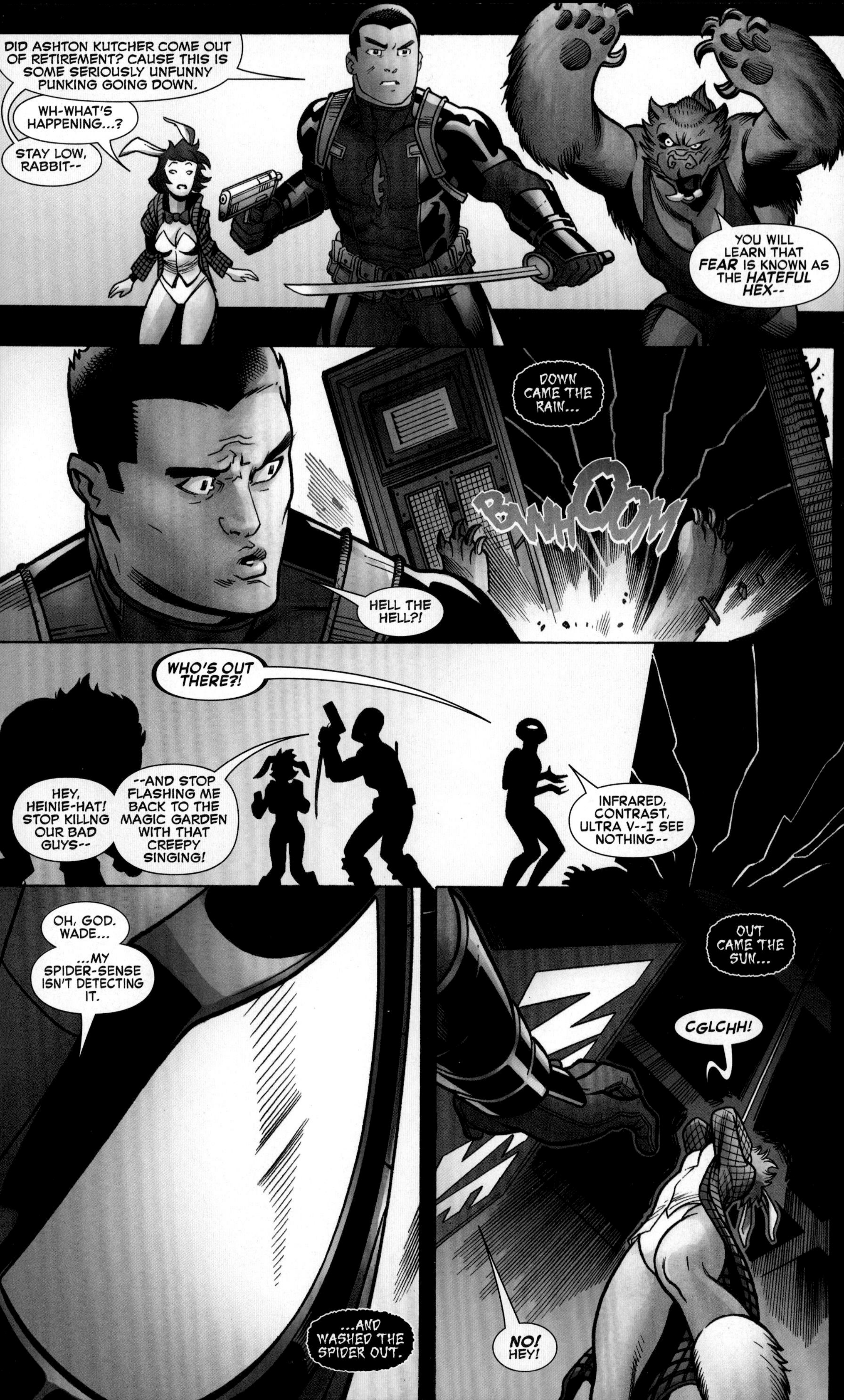
DID ASHTON KUTCHER COME OUT OF RETIREMENT? CAUSE THIS IS SOME SERIOUSLY UNFUNNY PUNKING GOING DOWN.
WH-WHAT'S HAPPENING...?
STAY LOW, RABBIT--
YOU WILL LEARN THAT FEAR IS KNOWN AS THE HATEFUL HEX--
DOWN CAME THE RAIN...
BWHOOOM
HELL THE HELL?!
WHO'S OUT THERE?!
HEY, HEINIE-HAT! STOP KILLNG OUR BAD GUYS--
--AND STOP FLASHING ME BACK TO THE MAGIC GARDEN WITH THAT CREEPY SINGING!
INFRARED, CONTRAST, ULTRA V--I SEE NOTHING--
OH, GOD. WADE...
...MY SPIDER-SENSE ISN'T DETECTING IT.
OUT CAME THE SUN...
CGLCHH!
NO! HEY!
...AND WASHED THE SPIDER OUT.

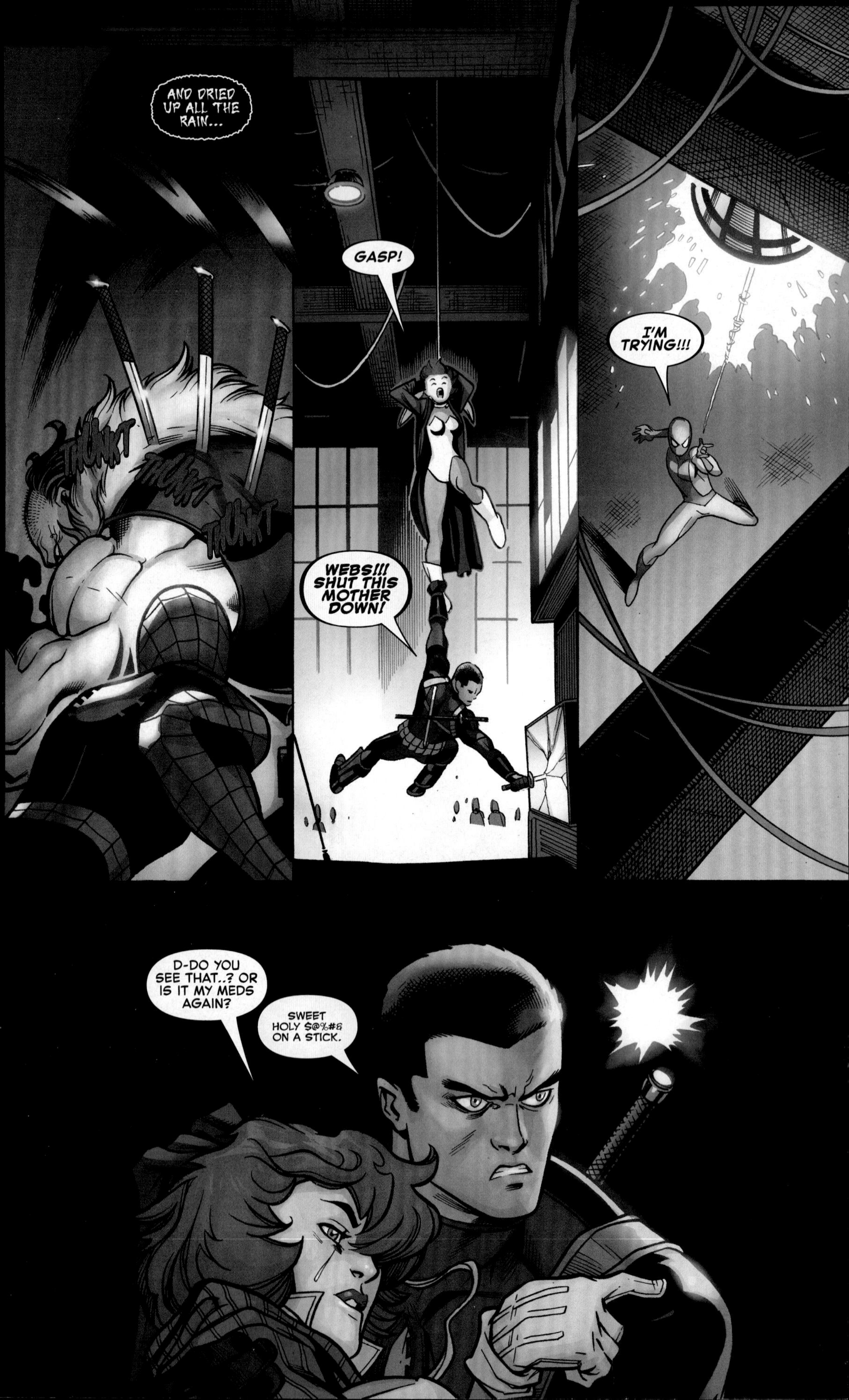
AND DRIED UP ALL THE RAIN...
THUNKT
THUNKT
THUNKT
GASP!
WEBS!!! SHUT THIS MOTHER DOWN!
I'M TRYING!!!
D-DO YOU SEE THAT..? OR IS IT MY MEDS AGAIN?
SWEET HOLY $@%#& ON A STICK.

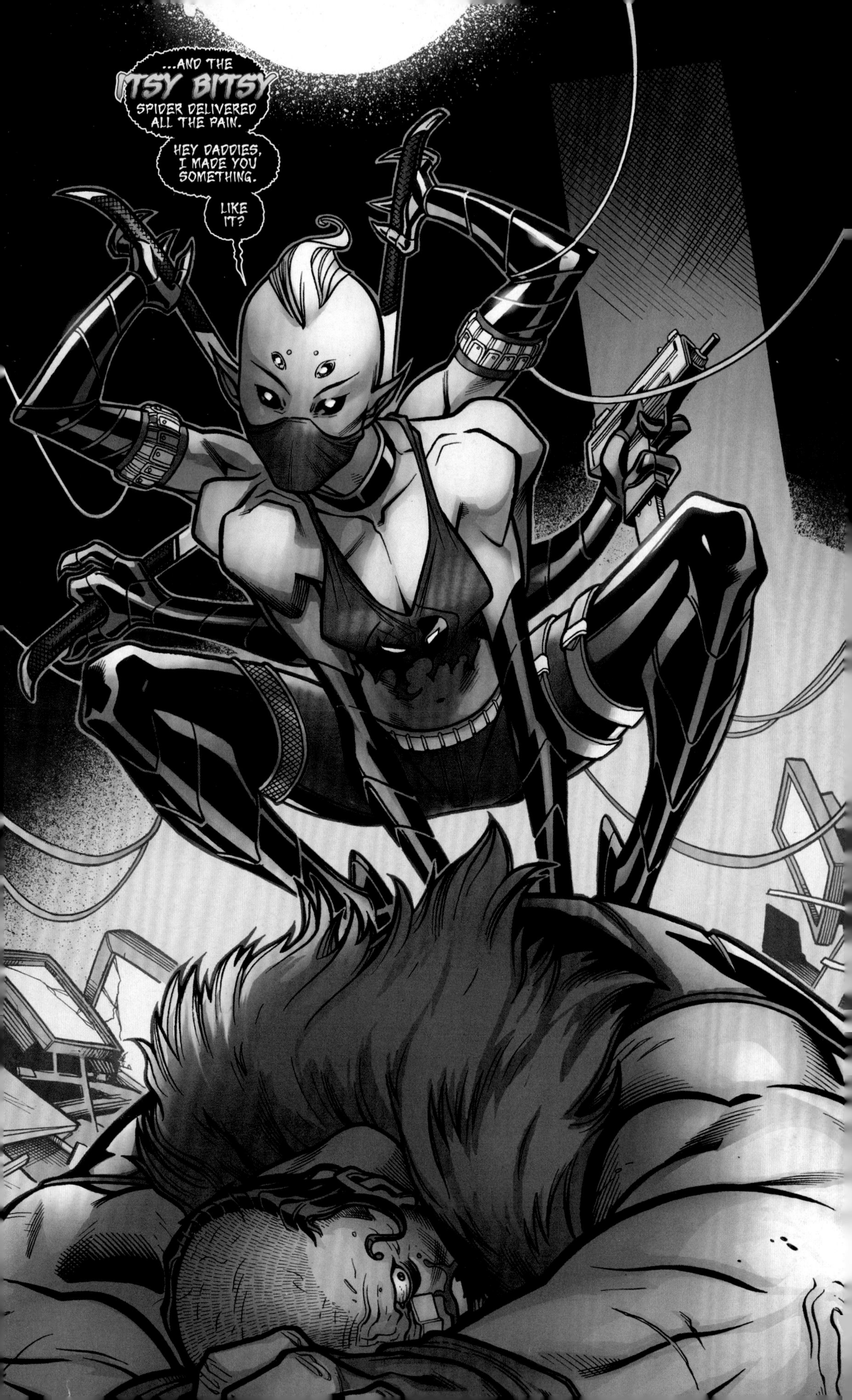
...AND THE ITSY BITSY SPIDER DELIVERED ALL THE PAIN.
HEY DADDIES, I MADE YOU SOMETHING.
LIKE IT?

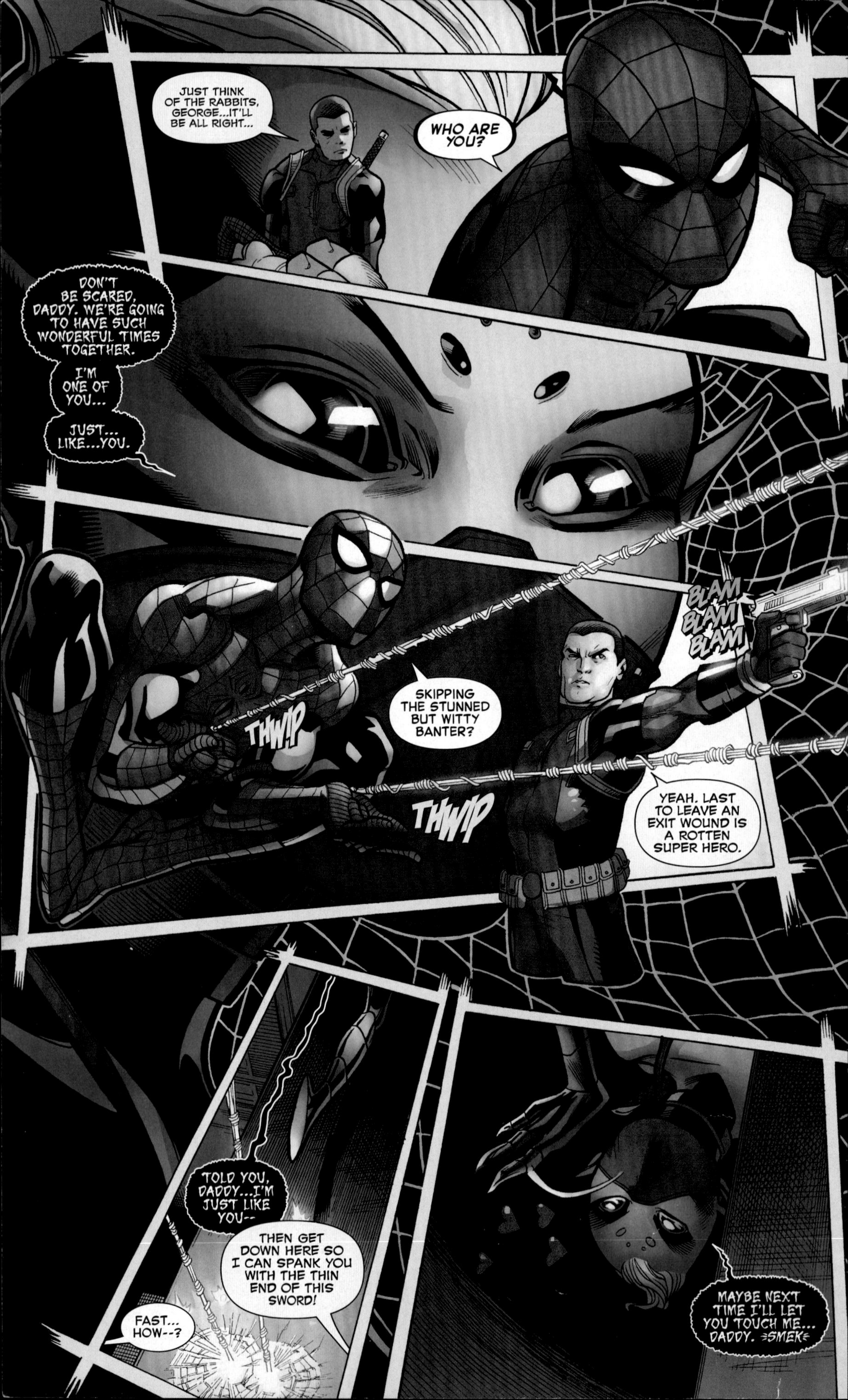
JUST THINK OF THE RABBITS, GEORGE...IT'LL BE ALL RIGHT...
WHO ARE YOU?
DON'T BE SCARED, DADDY. WE'RE GOING TO HAVE SUCH WONDERFUL TIMES TOGETHER.
I'M ONE OF YOU...
JUST... LIKE...YOU.
BLAM BLAM BLAM
THWIP
SKIPPING THE STUNNED BUT WITTY BANTER?
THWIP
YEAH. LAST TO LEAVE AN EXIT WOUND IS A ROTTEN SUPER HERO.
TOLD YOU, DADDY...I'M JUST LIKE YOU--
THEN GET DOWN HERE SO I CAN SPANK YOU WITH THE THIN END OF THIS SWORD!
FAST... HOW--?
MAYBE NEXT TIME I'LL LET YOU TOUCH ME... DADDY. SMEK

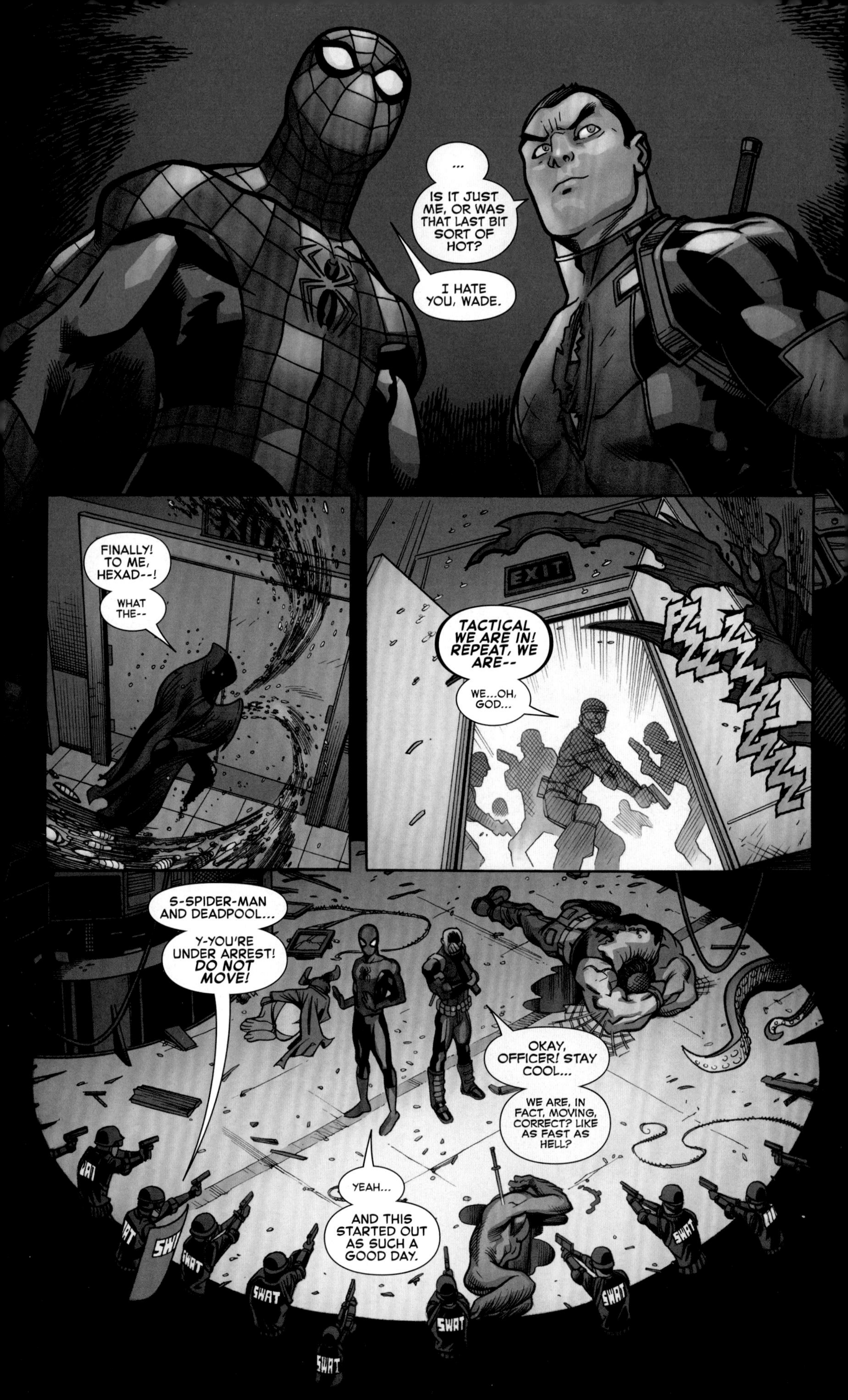
...
IS IT JUST ME, OR WAS THAT LAST BIT SORT OF HOT?
I HATE YOU, WADE.
FINALLY! TO ME, HEXAD--!
WHAT THE--
EXIT
TACTICAL WE ARE IN! REPEAT, WE ARE--
WE...OH, GOD...
S-SPIDER-MAN AND DEADPOOL...
Y-YOU'RE UNDER ARREST! DO NOT MOVE!
OKAY, OFFICER! STAY COOL...
WE ARE, IN FACT, MOVING, CORRECT? LIKE AS FAST AS HELL?
YEAH...
AND THIS STARTED OUT AS SUCH A GOOD DAY.
SWAT

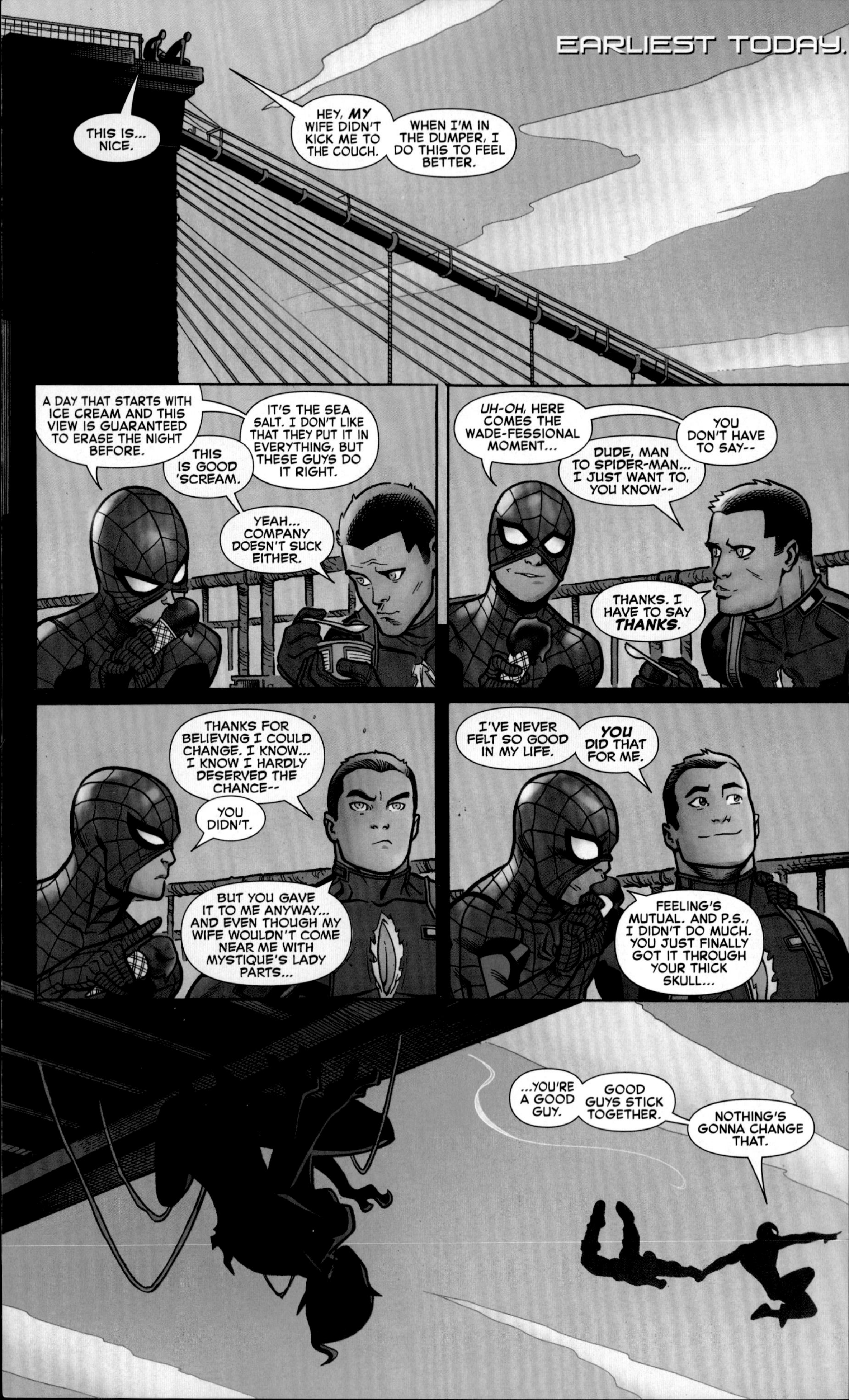
EARLIEST TODAY.
THIS IS... NICE.
HEY, MY WIFE DIDN'T KICK ME TO THE COUCH.
WHEN I'M IN THE DUMPER, I DO THIS TO FEEL BETTER.
A DAY THAT STARTS WITH ICE CREAM AND THIS VIEW IS GUARANTEED TO ERASE THE NIGHT BEFORE.
IT'S THE SEA SALT. I DON'T LIKE THAT THEY PUT IT IN EVERYTHING, BUT THESE GUYS DO IT RIGHT.
THIS IS GOOD 'SCREAM.
YEAH... COMPANY DOESN'T SUCK EITHER.
UH-OH, HERE COMES THE WADE-FESSIONAL MOMENT...
YOU DON'T HAVE TO SAY--
DUDE, MAN TO SPIDER-MAN... I JUST WANT TO, YOU KNOW--
THANKS. I HAVE TO SAY THANKS.
THANKS FOR BELIEVING I COULD CHANGE. I KNOW... I KNOW I HARDLY DESERVED THE CHANCE--
YOU DIDN'T.
BUT YOU GAVE IT TO ME ANYWAY... AND EVEN THOUGH MY WIFE WOULDN'T COME NEAR ME WITH MYSTIQUE'S LADY PARTS...
I'VE NEVER FELT SO GOOD IN MY LIFE.
YOU DID THAT FOR ME.
FEELING'S MUTUAL. AND P.S., I DIDN'T DO MUCH. YOU JUST FINALLY GOT IT THROUGH YOUR THICK SKULL...
...YOU'RE A GOOD GUY.
GOOD GUYS STICK TOGETHER.
NOTHING'S GONNA CHANGE THAT.

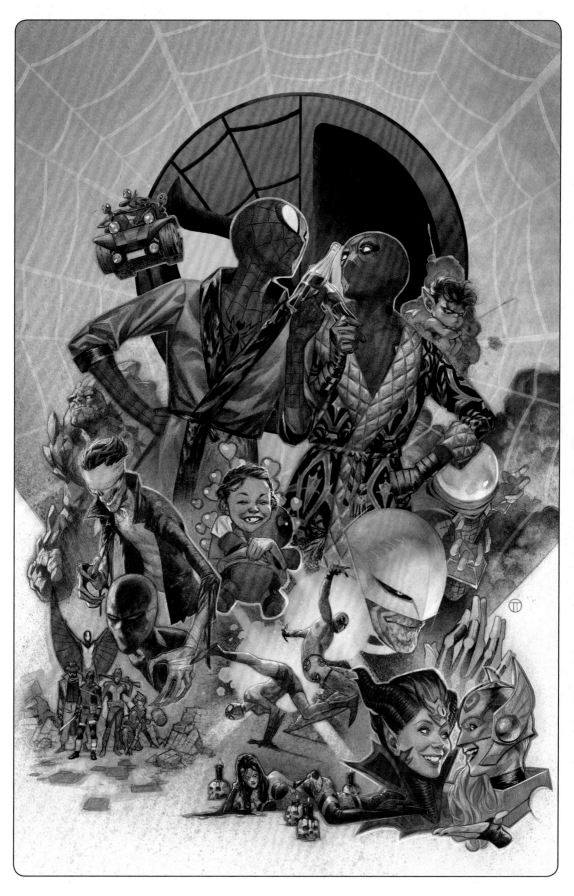

9 STORY THUS FAR VARIANT BY
JULIAN TOTINO TEDESCO

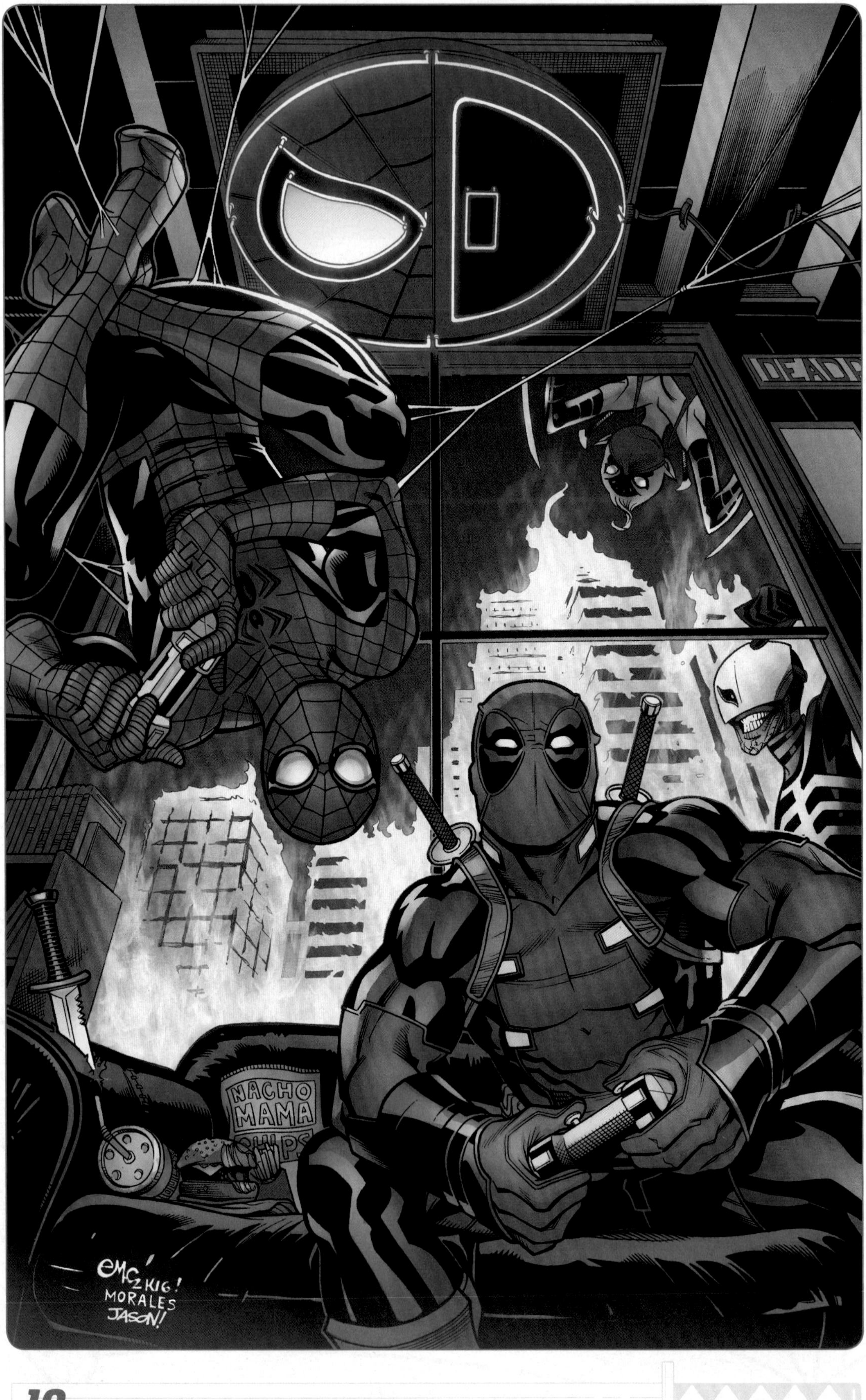
DEADP
NACHO
MAMA
CHIPS
eMc2KIG!
MORALES
JASON!

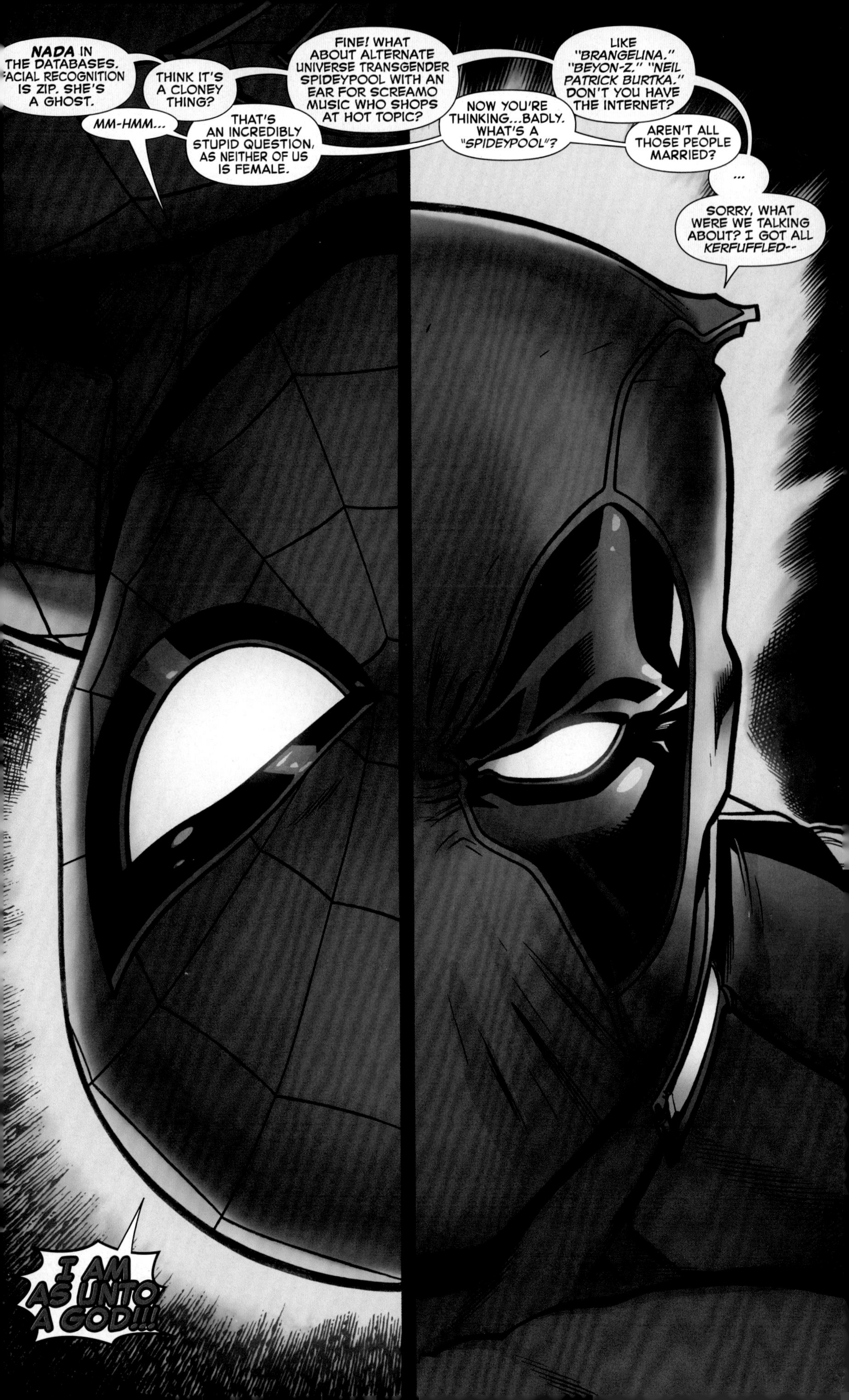
NADA IN THE DATABASES. FACIAL RECOGNITION IS ZIP. SHE'S A GHOST.
MM-HMM...
THINK IT'S A CLONEY THING?
THAT'S AN INCREDIBLY STUPID QUESTION, AS NEITHER OF US IS FEMALE.
FINE! WHAT ABOUT ALTERNATE UNIVERSE TRANSGENDER SPIDEYPOOL WITH AN EAR FOR SCREAMO MUSIC WHO SHOPS AT HOT TOPIC?
NOW YOU'RE THINKING...BADLY. WHAT'S A "SPIDEYPOOL"?
LIKE "BRANGELINA." "BEYON-Z." "NEIL PATRICK BURTKA." DON'T YOU HAVE THE INTERNET?
AREN'T ALL THOSE PEOPLE MARRIED?
...
SORRY, WHAT WERE WE TALKING ABOUT? I GOT ALL KERFUFFLED--
I AM AS UNTO A GOD!!!

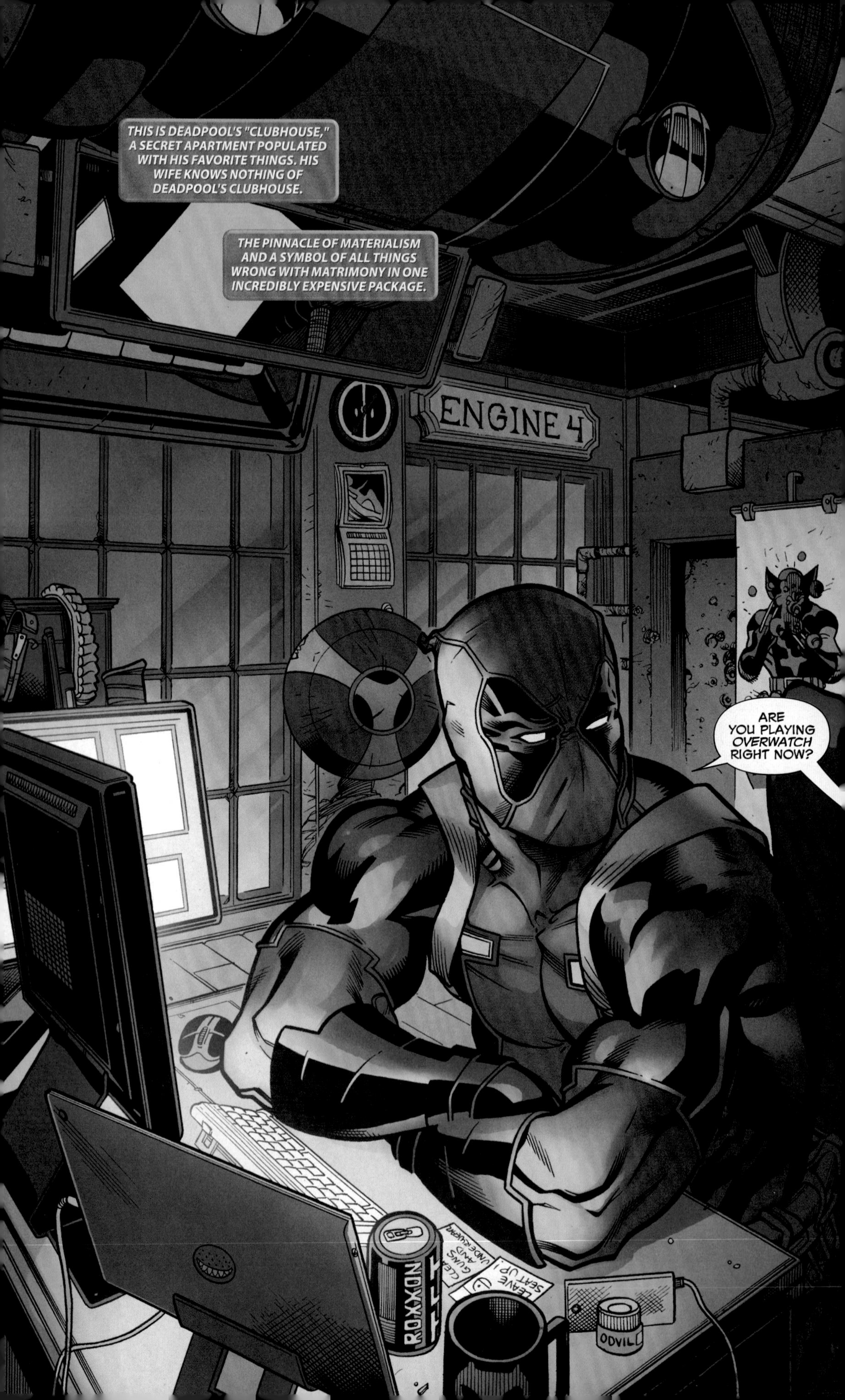
THIS IS DEADPOOL'S "CLUBHOUSE," A SECRET APARTMENT POPULATED WITH HIS FAVORITE THINGS. HIS WIFE KNOWS NOTHING OF DEADPOOL'S CLUBHOUSE.
THE PINNACLE OF MATERIALISM AND A SYMBOL OF ALL THINGS WRONG WITH MATRIMONY IN ONE INCREDIBLY EXPENSIVE PACKAGE.
ENGINE 4
ARE YOU PLAYING *OVERWATCH* RIGHT NOW?
ROXXON
LEAVE SEAT UP!
ODVIL

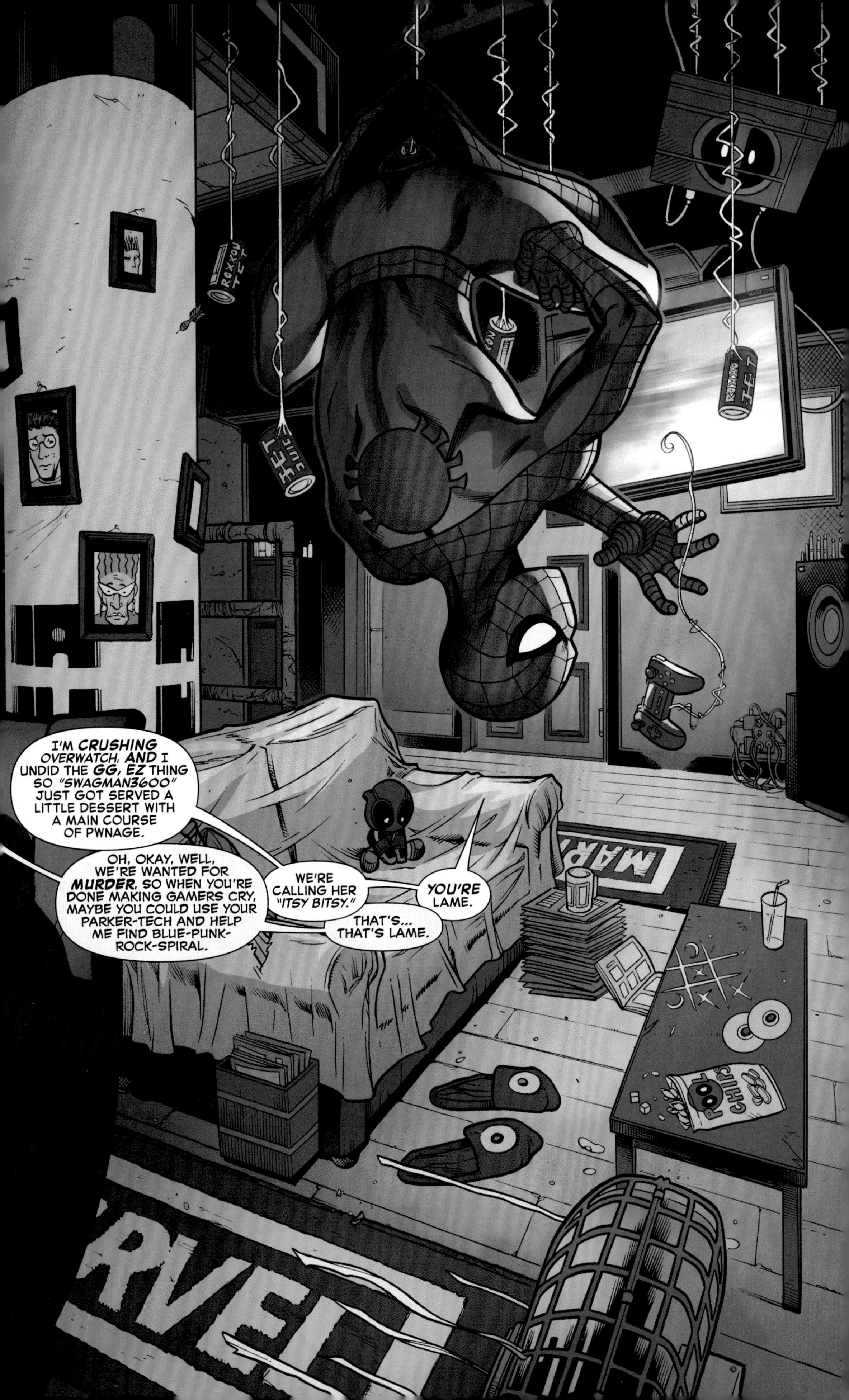
I'M **CRUSHING** *OVERWATCH*, **AND** I UNDID THE **GG, EZ** THING SO *"SWAGMAN3600"* JUST GOT SERVED A LITTLE DESSERT WITH A MAIN COURSE OF PWNAGE.
WE'RE CALLING HER *"ITSY BITSY."*
YOU'RE LAME.
OH, OKAY, WELL, WE'RE WANTED FOR ***MURDER***, SO WHEN YOU'RE DONE MAKING GAMERS CRY, MAYBE YOU COULD USE YOUR PARKER-TECH AND HELP ME FIND BLUE-PUNK-ROCK-SPIRAL.
THAT'S... THAT'S LAME.

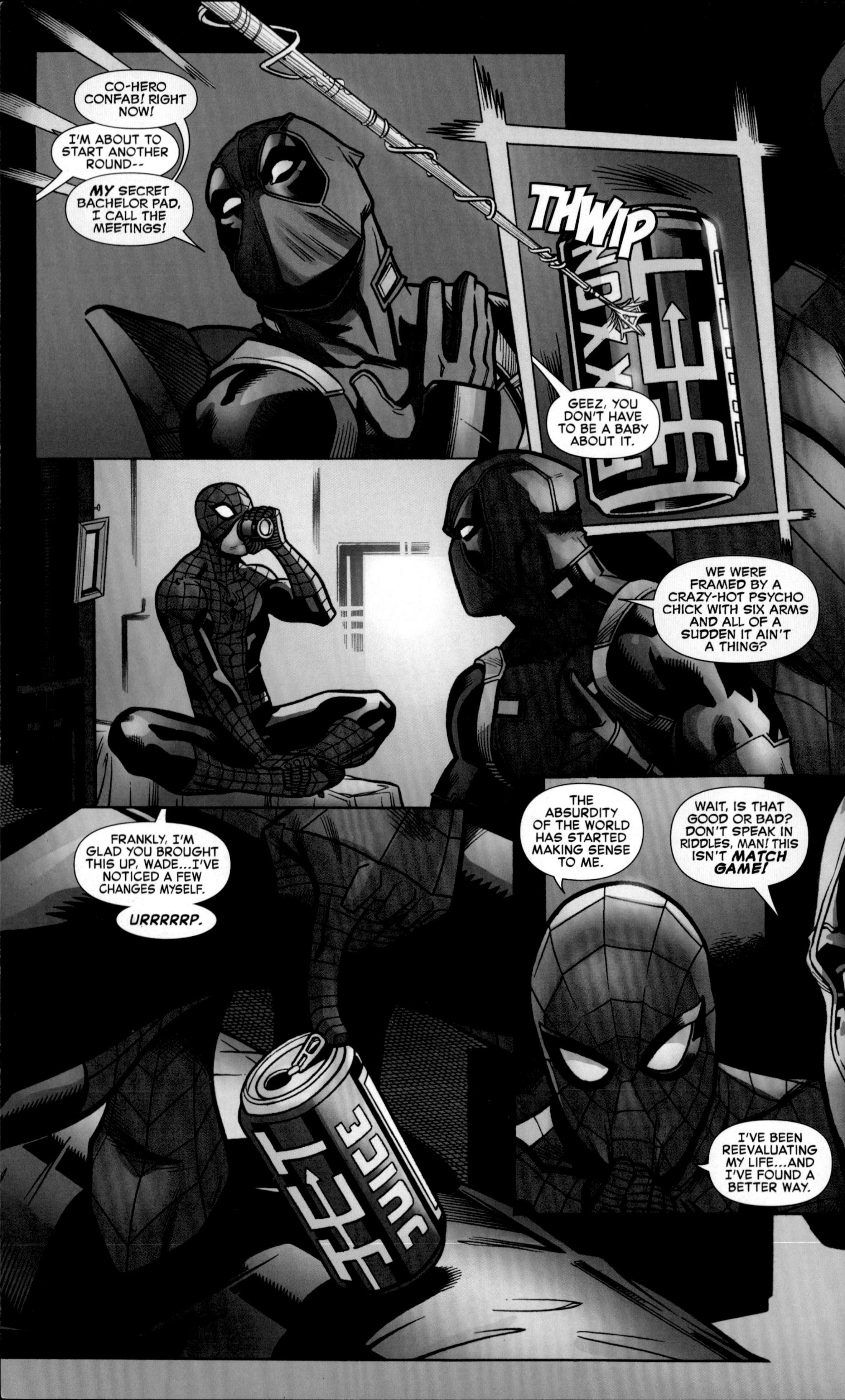

CO-HERO CONFAB! RIGHT NOW!
I'M ABOUT TO START ANOTHER ROUND--
MY SECRET BACHELOR PAD, I CALL THE MEETINGS!
THWIP
GEEZ, YOU DON'T HAVE TO BE A BABY ABOUT IT.
WE WERE FRAMED BY A CRAZY-HOT PSYCHO CHICK WITH SIX ARMS AND ALL OF A SUDDEN IT AIN'T A THING?
FRANKLY, I'M GLAD YOU BROUGHT THIS UP, WADE...I'VE NOTICED A FEW CHANGES MYSELF.
URRRRRP.
THE ABSURDITY OF THE WORLD HAS STARTED MAKING SENSE TO ME.
WAIT, IS THAT GOOD OR BAD? DON'T SPEAK IN RIDDLES, MAN! THIS ISN'T MATCH GAME!
I'VE BEEN REEVALUATING MY LIFE...AND I'VE FOUND A BETTER WAY.

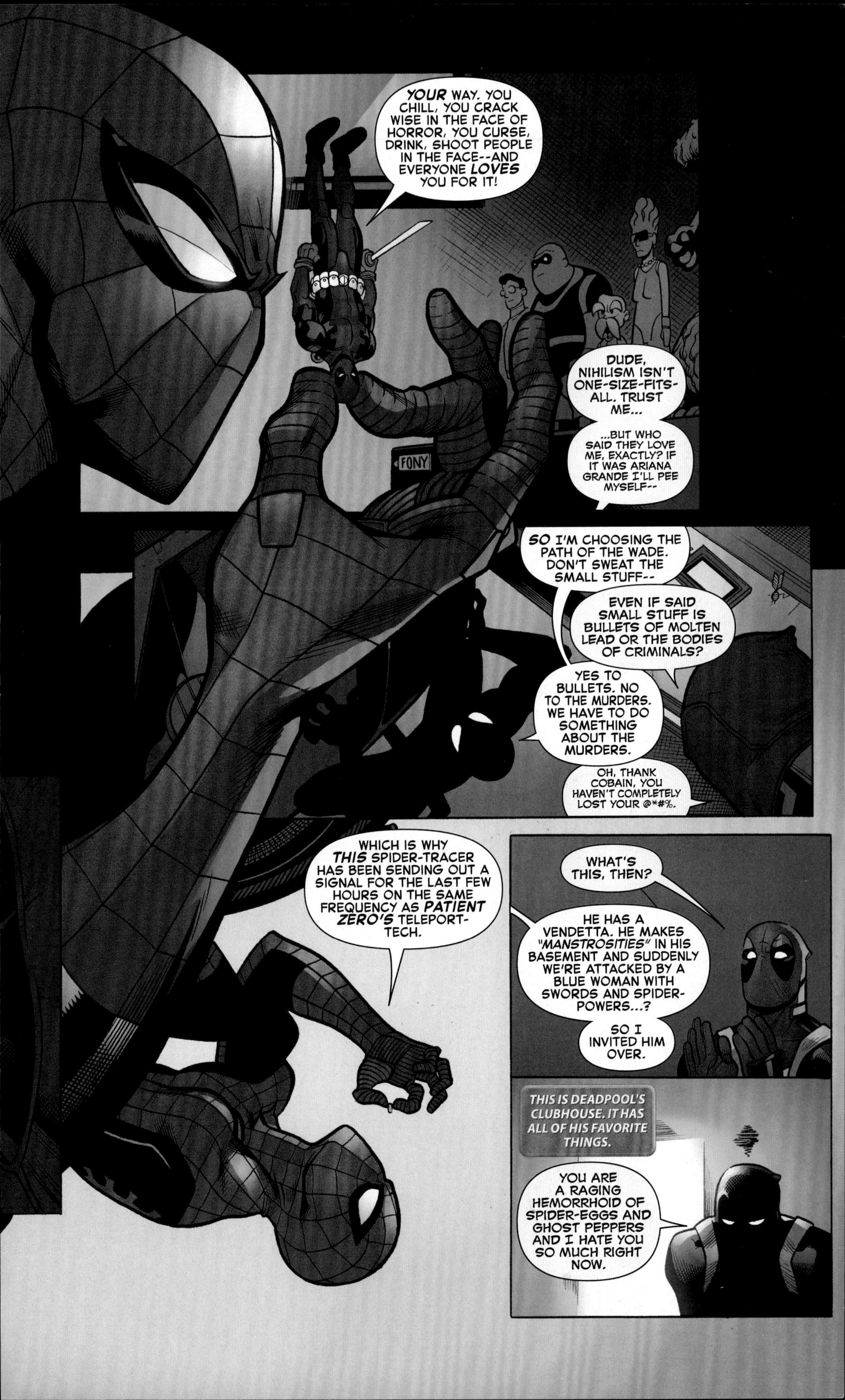
YOUR WAY. YOU CHILL, YOU CRACK WISE IN THE FACE OF HORROR, YOU CURSE, DRINK, SHOOT PEOPLE IN THE FACE--AND EVERYONE LOVES YOU FOR IT!
DUDE, NIHILISM ISN'T ONE-SIZE-FITS-ALL. TRUST ME...
...BUT WHO SAID THEY LOVE ME, EXACTLY? IF IT WAS ARIANA GRANDE I'LL PEE MYSELF--
FONY
SO I'M CHOOSING THE PATH OF THE WADE. DON'T SWEAT THE SMALL STUFF--
EVEN IF SAID SMALL STUFF IS BULLETS OF MOLTEN LEAD OR THE BODIES OF CRIMINALS?
YES TO BULLETS. NO TO THE MURDERS. WE HAVE TO DO SOMETHING ABOUT THE MURDERS.
OH, THANK COBAIN, YOU HAVEN'T COMPLETELY LOST YOUR @*#%.
WHICH IS WHY THIS SPIDER-TRACER HAS BEEN SENDING OUT A SIGNAL FOR THE LAST FEW HOURS ON THE SAME FREQUENCY AS PATIENT ZERO'S TELEPORT-TECH.
WHAT'S THIS, THEN?
HE HAS A VENDETTA. HE MAKES "MANSTROSITIES" IN HIS BASEMENT AND SUDDENLY WE'RE ATTACKED BY A BLUE WOMAN WITH SWORDS AND SPIDER-POWERS...?
SO I INVITED HIM OVER.
THIS IS DEADPOOL'S CLUBHOUSE. IT HAS ALL OF HIS FAVORITE THINGS.
YOU ARE A RAGING HEMORRHOID OF SPIDER-EGGS AND GHOST PEPPERS AND I HATE YOU SO MUCH RIGHT NOW.

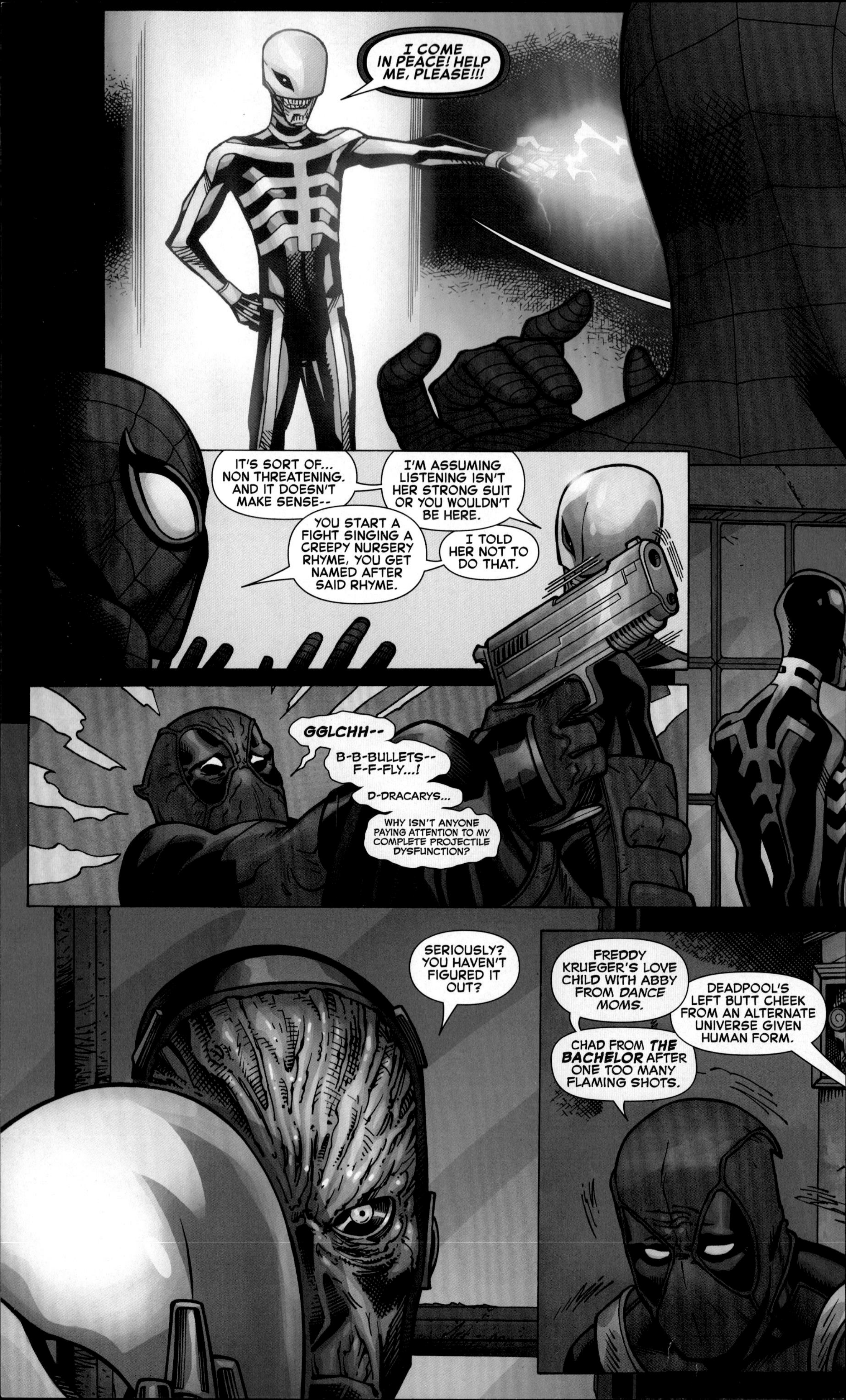
I COME IN PEACE! HELP ME, PLEASE!!!
IT'S SORT OF... NON THREATENING. AND IT DOESN'T MAKE SENSE--
I'M ASSUMING LISTENING ISN'T HER STRONG SUIT OR YOU WOULDN'T BE HERE.
YOU START A FIGHT SINGING A CREEPY NURSERY RHYME, YOU GET NAMED AFTER SAID RHYME.
I TOLD HER NOT TO DO THAT.
GGLCHH--
B-B-BULLETS-- F-F-FLY...!
D-DRACARYS...
WHY ISN'T ANYONE PAYING ATTENTION TO MY COMPLETE PROJECTILE DYSFUNCTION?
SERIOUSLY? YOU HAVEN'T FIGURED IT OUT?
FREDDY KRUEGER'S LOVE CHILD WITH ABBY FROM DANCE MOMS.
DEADPOOL'S LEFT BUTT CHEEK FROM AN ALTERNATE UNIVERSE GIVEN HUMAN FORM.
CHAD FROM THE BACHELOR AFTER ONE TOO MANY FLAMING SHOTS.

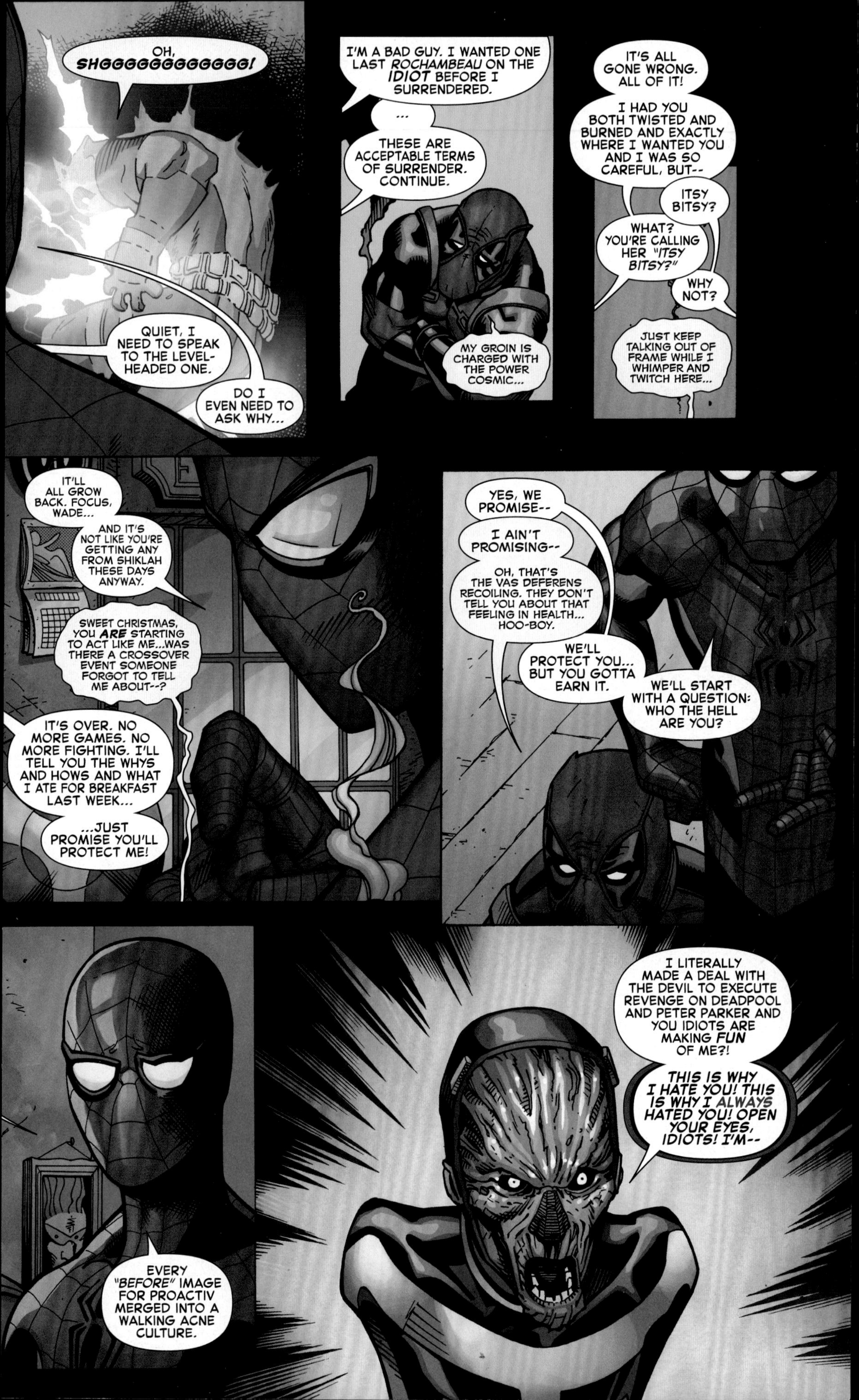
OH, SHGGGGGGGGGGGG!
QUIET, I NEED TO SPEAK TO THE LEVEL-HEADED ONE.
DO I EVEN NEED TO ASK WHY...
I'M A BAD GUY. I WANTED ONE LAST ROCHAMBEAU ON THE IDIOT BEFORE I SURRENDERED.
...
THESE ARE ACCEPTABLE TERMS OF SURRENDER. CONTINUE.
MY GROIN IS CHARGED WITH THE POWER COSMIC...
IT'S ALL GONE WRONG. ALL OF IT!
I HAD YOU BOTH TWISTED AND BURNED AND EXACTLY WHERE I WANTED YOU AND I WAS SO CAREFUL, BUT--
ITSY BITSY?
WHAT? YOU'RE CALLING HER "ITSY BITSY?"
WHY NOT?
JUST KEEP TALKING OUT OF FRAME WHILE I WHIMPER AND TWITCH HERE...
IT'LL ALL GROW BACK. FOCUS, WADE...
AND IT'S NOT LIKE YOU'RE GETTING ANY FROM SHIKLAH THESE DAYS ANYWAY.
SWEET CHRISTMAS, YOU ARE STARTING TO ACT LIKE ME...WAS THERE A CROSSOVER EVENT SOMEONE FORGOT TO TELL ME ABOUT--?
IT'S OVER. NO MORE GAMES. NO MORE FIGHTING. I'LL TELL YOU THE WHYS AND HOWS AND WHAT I ATE FOR BREAKFAST LAST WEEK...
...JUST PROMISE YOU'LL PROTECT ME!
YES, WE PROMISE--
I AIN'T PROMISING--
OH, THAT'S THE VAS DEFERENS RECOILING. THEY DON'T TELL YOU ABOUT THAT FEELING IN HEALTH... HOO-BOY.
WE'LL PROTECT YOU... BUT YOU GOTTA EARN IT.
WE'LL START WITH A QUESTION: WHO THE HELL ARE YOU?
EVERY "BEFORE" IMAGE FOR PROACTIV MERGED INTO A WALKING ACNE CULTURE.
I LITERALLY MADE A DEAL WITH THE DEVIL TO EXECUTE REVENGE ON DEADPOOL AND PETER PARKER AND YOU IDIOTS ARE MAKING FUN OF ME?!
THIS IS WHY I HATE YOU! THIS IS WHY I ALWAYS HATED YOU! OPEN YOUR EYES, IDIOTS! I'M--

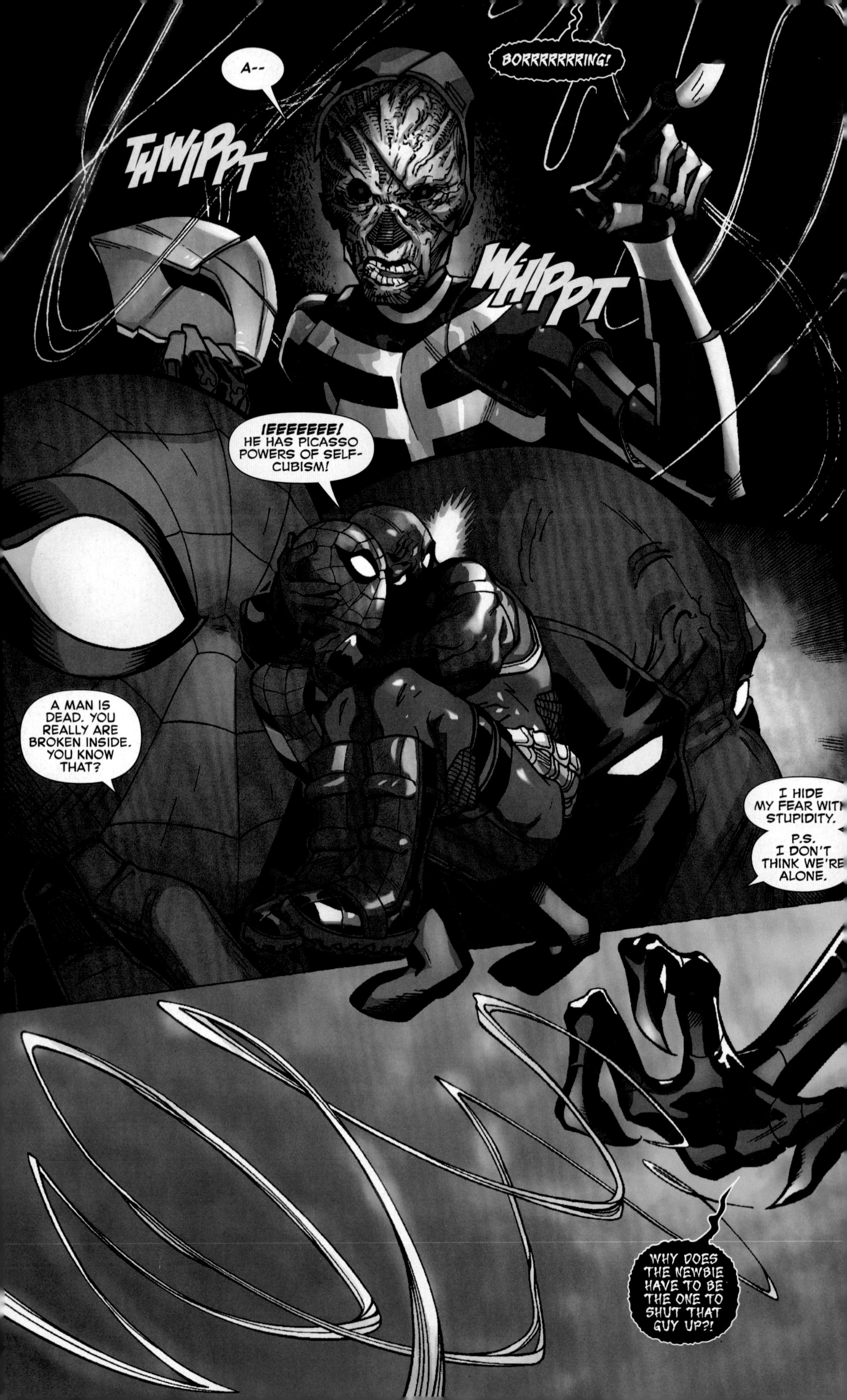
A--
BORRRRRRRING!
THWIPPT
WHIPPT
IEEEEEEE! HE HAS PICASSO POWERS OF SELF-CUBISM!
A MAN IS DEAD. YOU REALLY ARE BROKEN INSIDE. YOU KNOW THAT?
I HIDE MY FEAR WIT STUPIDITY.
P.S. I DON'T THINK WE'RE ALONE.
WHY DOES THE NEWBIE HAVE TO BE THE ONE TO SHUT THAT GUY UP?!

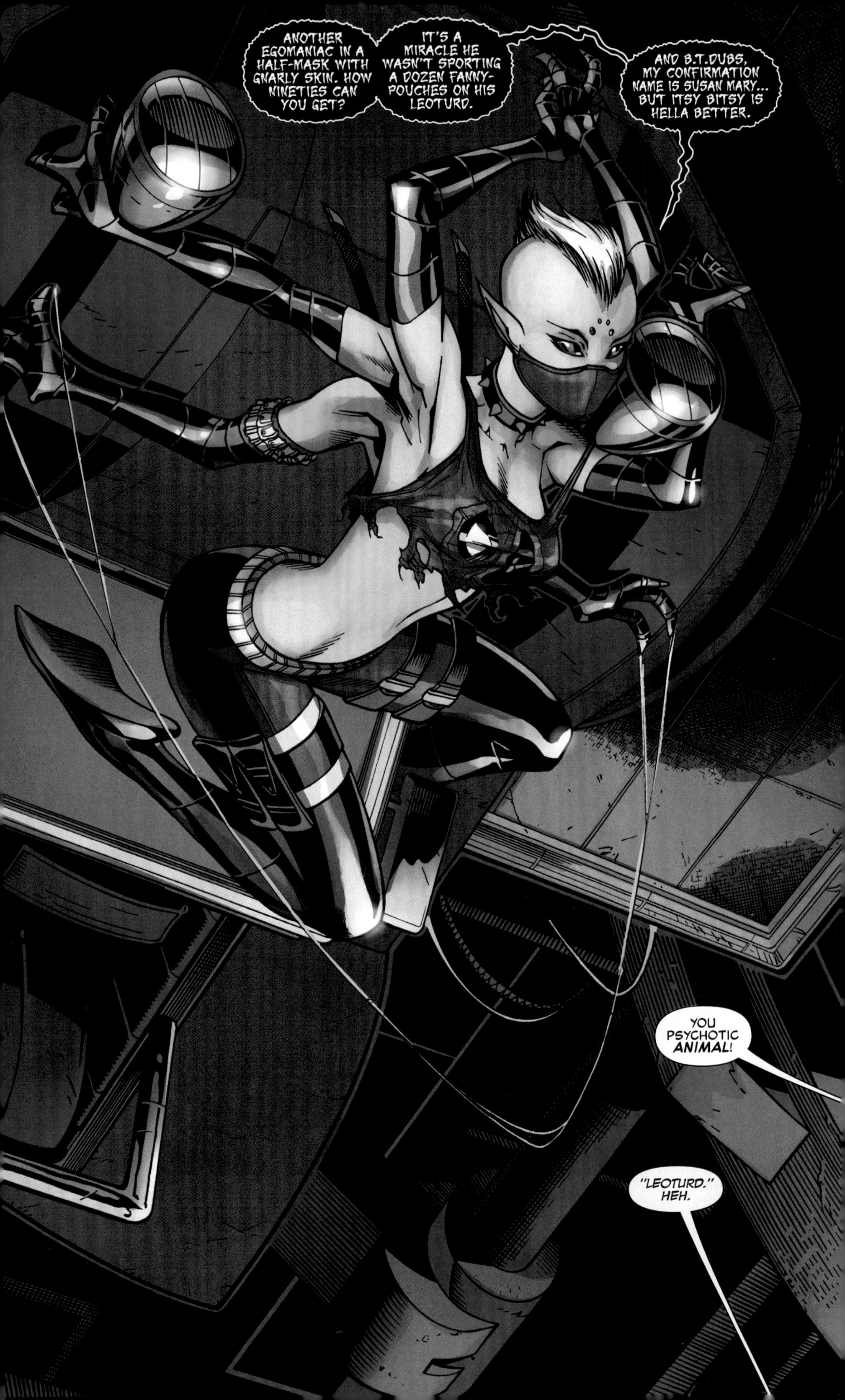
ANOTHER EGOMANIAC IN A HALF-MASK WITH GNARLY SKIN. HOW NINETIES CAN YOU GET?
IT'S A MIRACLE HE WASN'T SPORTING A DOZEN FANNY-POUCHES ON HIS LEOTURD.
AND B.T.DUBS, MY CONFIRMATION NAME IS SUSAN MARY... BUT ITSY BITSY IS HELLA BETTER.
YOU PSYCHOTIC ANIMAL!
"LEOTURD." HEH.

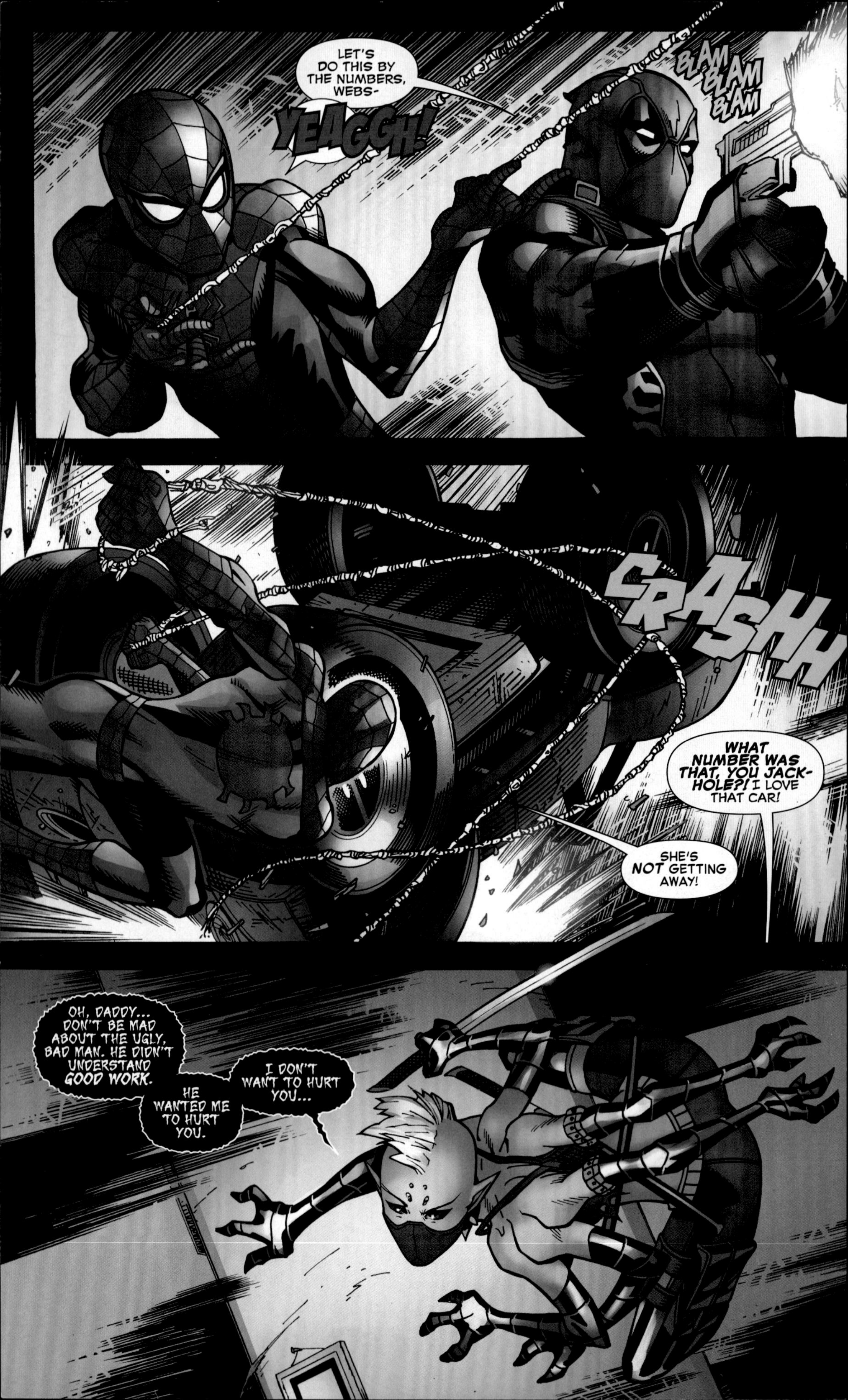
LET'S DO THIS BY THE NUMBERS, WEBS-
BLAM BLAM BLAM
YEAGGH!
CRASHH
WHAT NUMBER WAS THAT, YOU JACK-HOLE?! I LOVE THAT CAR!
SHE'S NOT GETTING AWAY!
OH, DADDY... DON'T BE MAD ABOUT THE UGLY, BAD MAN. HE DIDN'T UNDERSTAND GOOD WORK.
HE WANTED ME TO HURT YOU.
I DON'T WANT TO HURT YOU...

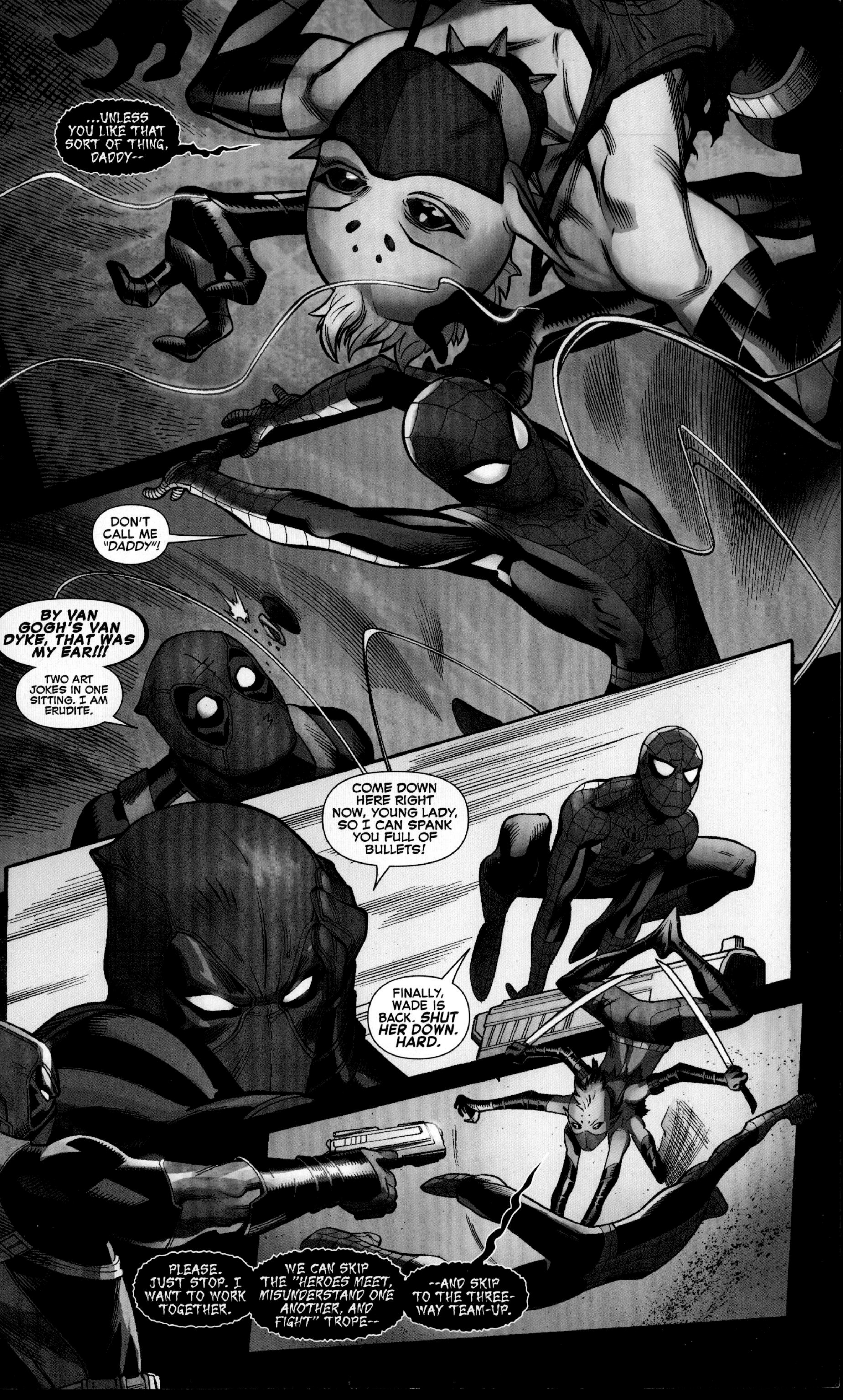
...UNLESS YOU LIKE THAT SORT OF THING, DADDY--
DON'T CALL ME "DADDY"!
BY VAN GOGH'S VAN DYKE, THAT WAS MY EAR!!!
TWO ART JOKES IN ONE SITTING. I AM ERUDITE.
COME DOWN HERE RIGHT NOW, YOUNG LADY, SO I CAN SPANK YOU FULL OF BULLETS!
FINALLY, WADE IS BACK. SHUT HER DOWN. HARD.
PLEASE. JUST STOP. I WANT TO WORK TOGETHER.
WE CAN SKIP THE "HEROES MEET, MISUNDERSTAND ONE ANOTHER, AND FIGHT" TROPE--
--AND SKIP TO THE THREE-WAY TEAM-UP.

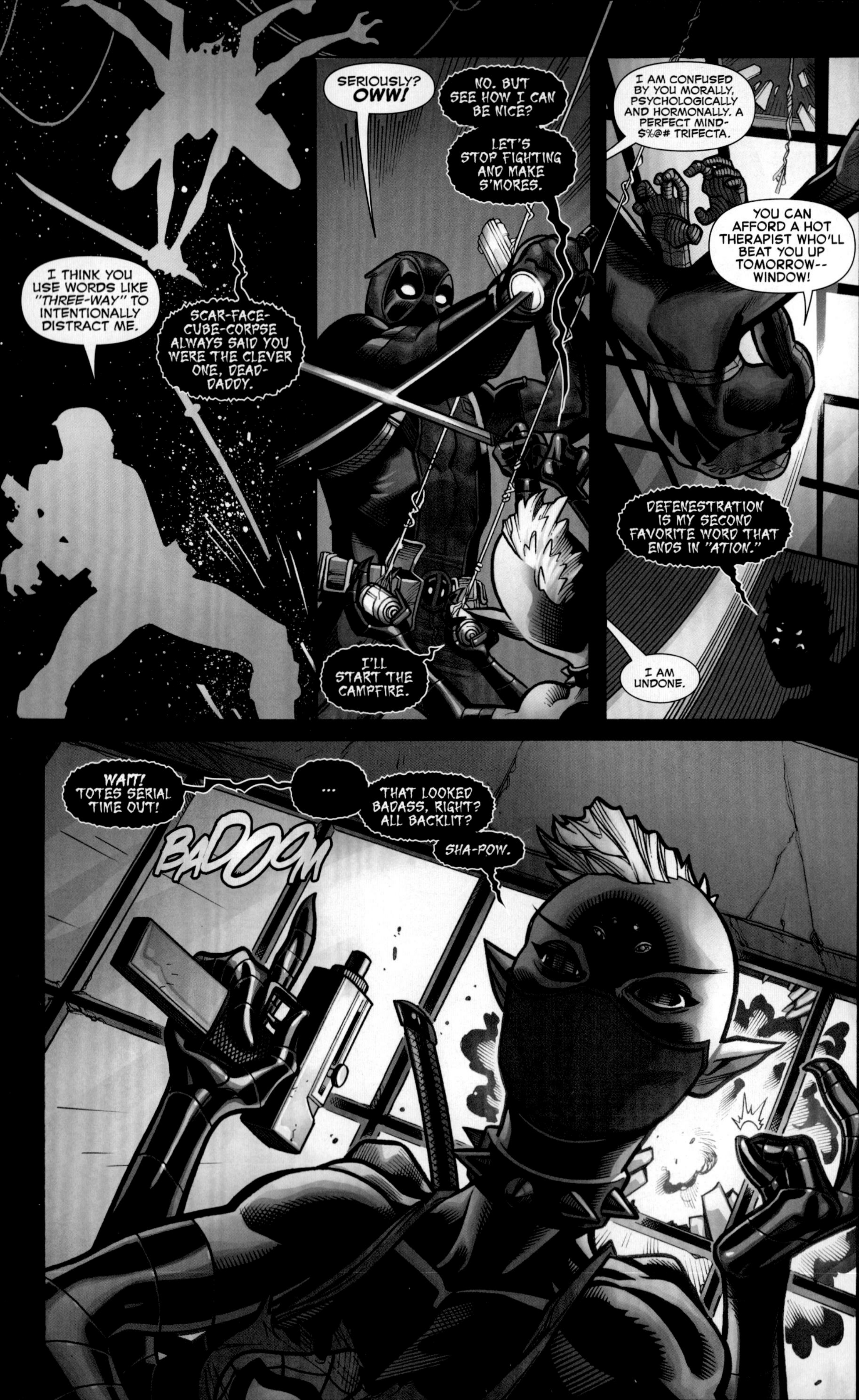
I THINK YOU USE WORDS LIKE "THREE-WAY" TO INTENTIONALLY DISTRACT ME.
SCAR-FACE-CUBE-CORPSE ALWAYS SAID YOU WERE THE CLEVER ONE, DEAD-DADDY.
SERIOUSLY? OWW!
NO. BUT SEE HOW I CAN BE NICE?
LET'S STOP FIGHTING AND MAKE S'MORES.
I'LL START THE CAMPFIRE.
I AM CONFUSED BY YOU MORALLY, PSYCHOLOGICALLY AND HORMONALLY. A PERFECT MIND-$%@# TRIFECTA.
YOU CAN AFFORD A HOT THERAPIST WHO'LL BEAT YOU UP TOMORROW-- WINDOW!
DEFENESTRATION IS MY SECOND FAVORITE WORD THAT ENDS IN "ATION."
I AM UNDONE.
WAIT! TOTES SERIAL TIME OUT!
...
THAT LOOKED BADASS, RIGHT? ALL BACKLIT?
SHA-POW.
BADOOM

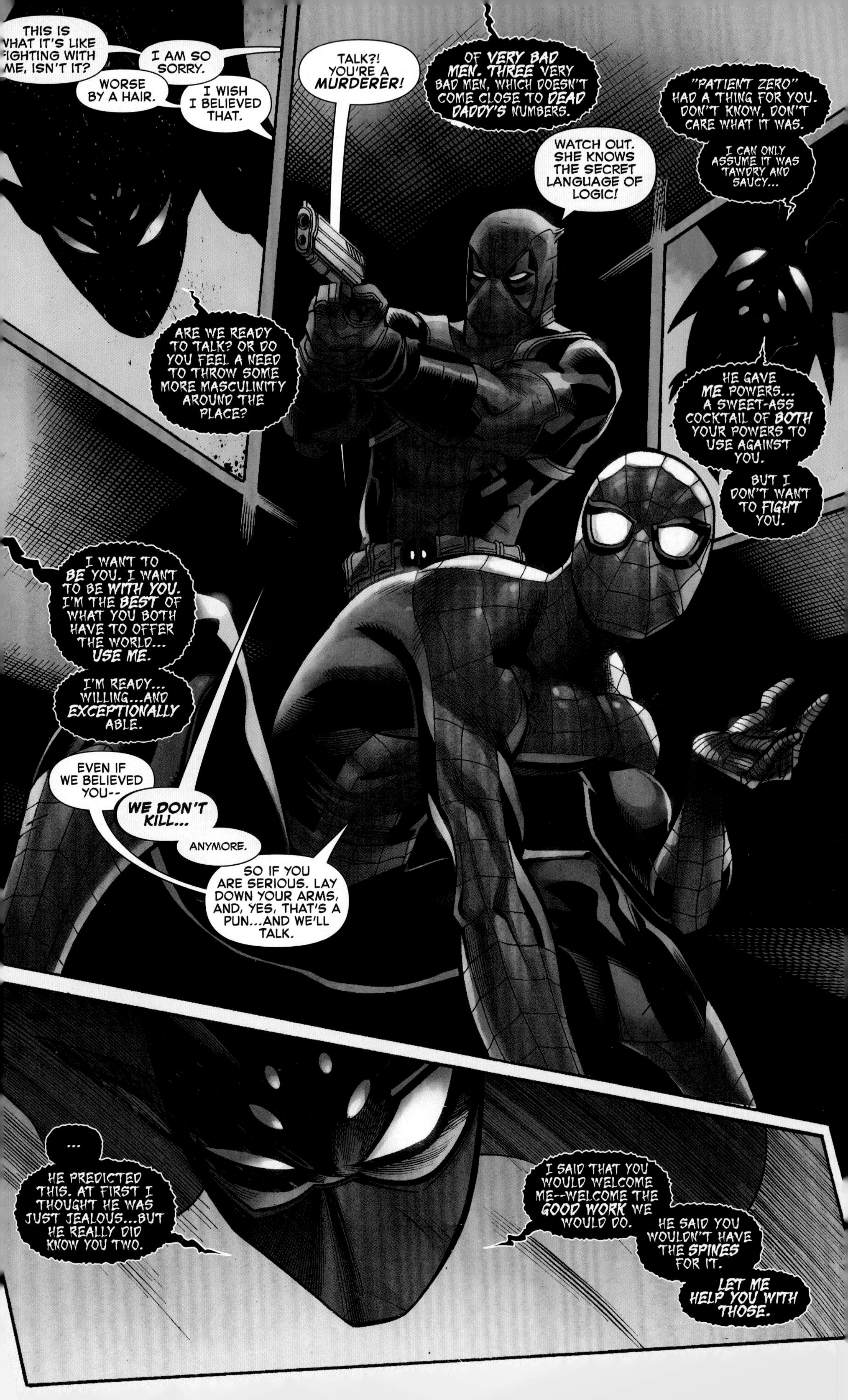

THIS IS WHAT IT'S LIKE FIGHTING WITH ME, ISN'T IT?
I AM SO SORRY.
WORSE BY A HAIR.
I WISH I BELIEVED THAT.
TALK?! YOU'RE A MURDERER!
OF VERY BAD MEN. THREE VERY BAD MEN, WHICH DOESN'T COME CLOSE TO DEAD DADDY'S NUMBERS.
WATCH OUT. SHE KNOWS THE SECRET LANGUAGE OF LOGIC!
"PATIENT ZERO" HAD A THING FOR YOU. DON'T KNOW, DON'T CARE WHAT IT WAS.
I CAN ONLY ASSUME IT WAS TAWDRY AND SAUCY...
ARE WE READY TO TALK? OR DO YOU FEEL A NEED TO THROW SOME MORE MASCULINITY AROUND THE PLACE?
HE GAVE ME POWERS... A SWEET-ASS COCKTAIL OF BOTH YOUR POWERS TO USE AGAINST YOU.
BUT I DON'T WANT TO FIGHT YOU.
I WANT TO BE YOU. I WANT TO BE WITH YOU. I'M THE BEST OF WHAT YOU BOTH HAVE TO OFFER THE WORLD... USE ME.
I'M READY... WILLING...AND EXCEPTIONALLY ABLE.
EVEN IF WE BELIEVED YOU--
WE DON'T KILL...
ANYMORE.
SO IF YOU ARE SERIOUS. LAY DOWN YOUR ARMS, AND, YES, THAT'S A PUN...AND WE'LL TALK.
...
HE PREDICTED THIS. AT FIRST I THOUGHT HE WAS JUST JEALOUS...BUT HE REALLY DID KNOW YOU TWO.
I SAID THAT YOU WOULD WELCOME ME--WELCOME THE GOOD WORK WE WOULD DO.
HE SAID YOU WOULDN'T HAVE THE SPINES FOR IT.
LET ME HELP YOU WITH THOSE.

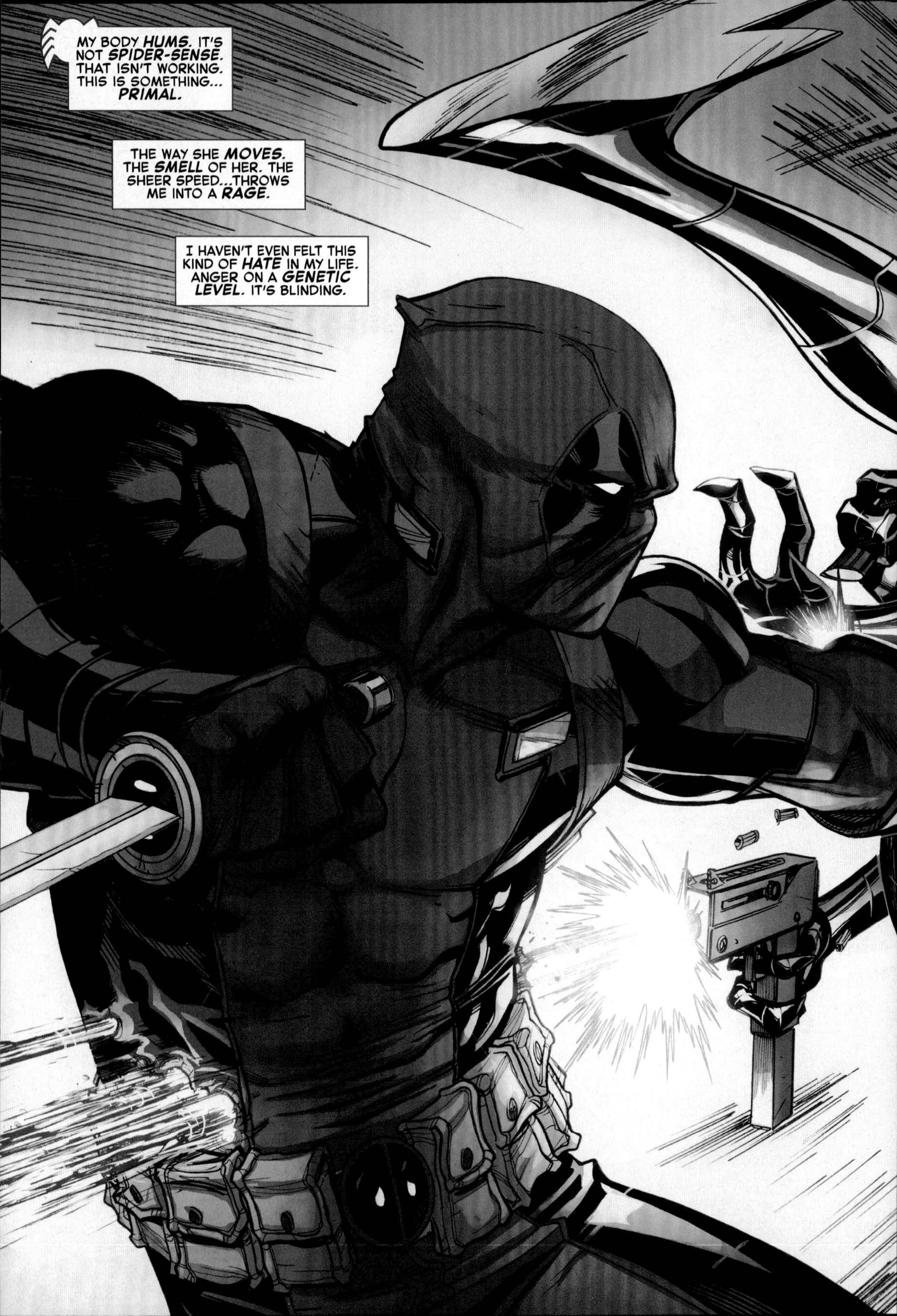
MY BODY **HUMS**. IT'S NOT **SPIDER-SENSE**. THAT ISN'T WORKING. THIS IS SOMETHING... **PRIMAL.**
THE WAY SHE **MOVES**. THE **SMELL** OF HER. THE SHEER SPEED...THROWS ME INTO A **RAGE**.
I HAVEN'T EVEN FELT THIS KIND OF **HATE** IN MY LIFE. ANGER ON A **GENETIC LEVEL**. IT'S BLINDING.

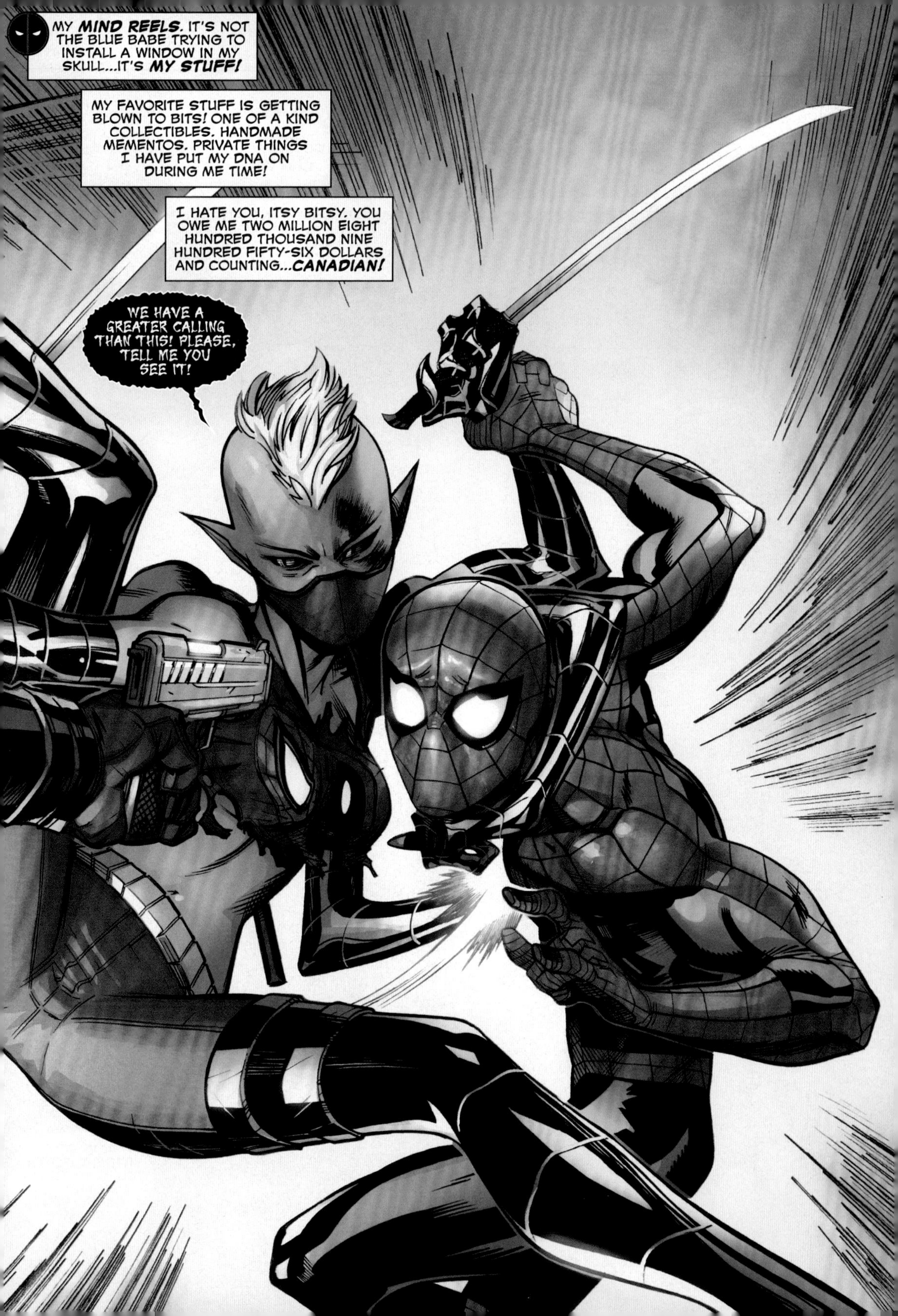
MY **MIND REELS**. IT'S NOT THE BLUE BABE TRYING TO INSTALL A WINDOW IN MY SKULL...IT'S **MY STUFF!**
MY FAVORITE STUFF IS GETTING BLOWN TO BITS! ONE OF A KIND COLLECTIBLES. HANDMADE MEMENTOS. PRIVATE THINGS I HAVE PUT MY DNA ON DURING ME TIME!
I HATE YOU, ITSY BITSY. YOU OWE ME TWO MILLION EIGHT HUNDRED THOUSAND NINE HUNDRED FIFTY-SIX DOLLARS AND COUNTING...**CANADIAN!**
WE HAVE A GREATER CALLING THAN THIS! PLEASE, TELL ME YOU SEE IT!

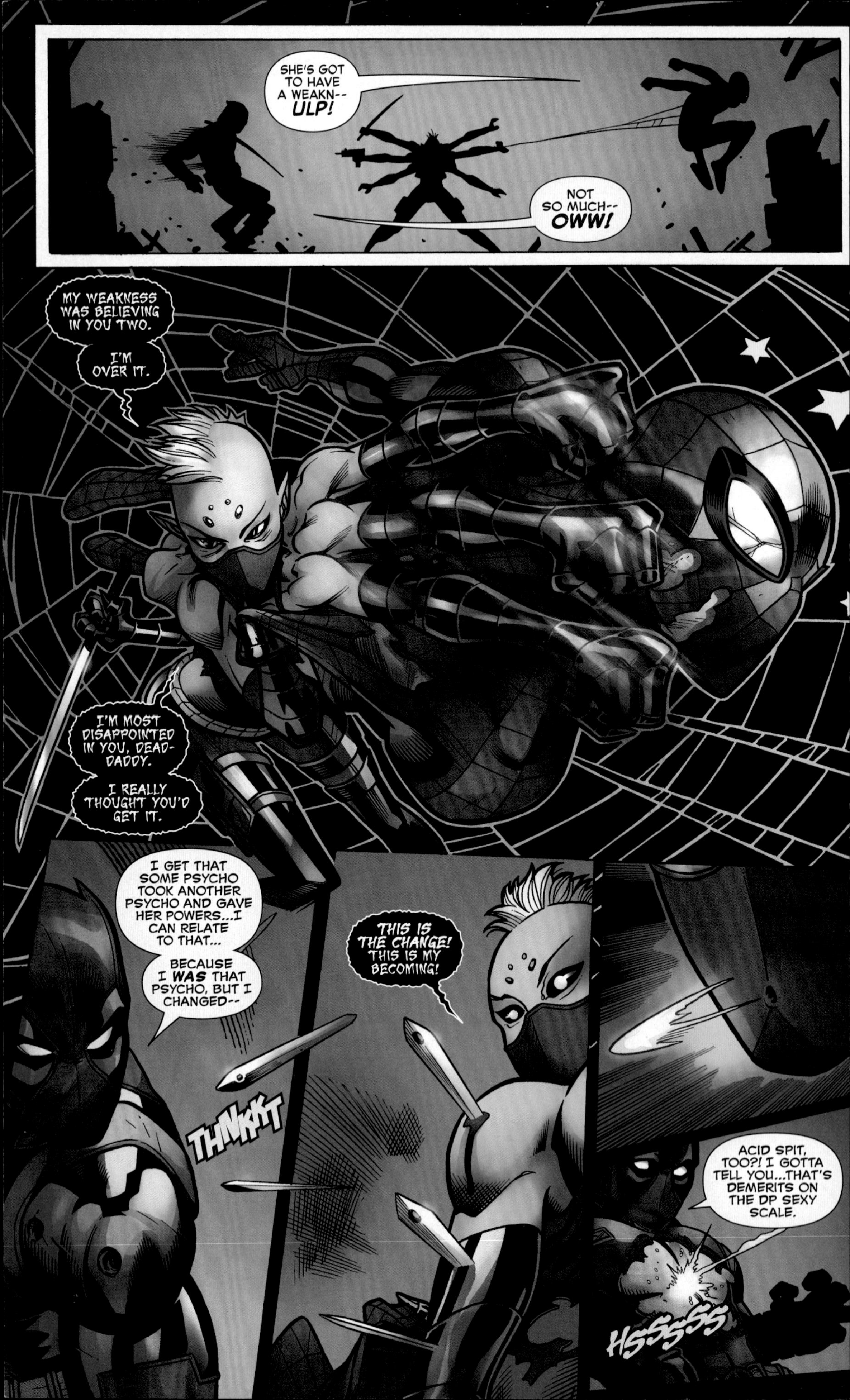

SHE'S GOT TO HAVE A WEAKN-- ULP!
NOT SO MUCH-- OWW!
MY WEAKNESS WAS BELIEVING IN YOU TWO.
I'M OVER IT.
I'M MOST DISAPPOINTED IN YOU, DEAD-DADDY.
I REALLY THOUGHT YOU'D GET IT.
I GET THAT SOME PSYCHO TOOK ANOTHER PSYCHO AND GAVE HER POWERS...I CAN RELATE TO THAT...
BECAUSE I WAS THAT PSYCHO, BUT I CHANGED--
THNKKT
THIS IS THE CHANGE! THIS IS MY BECOMING!
ACID SPIT, TOO?! I GOTTA TELL YOU...THAT'S DEMERITS ON THE DP SEXY SCALE.
HSSSSS

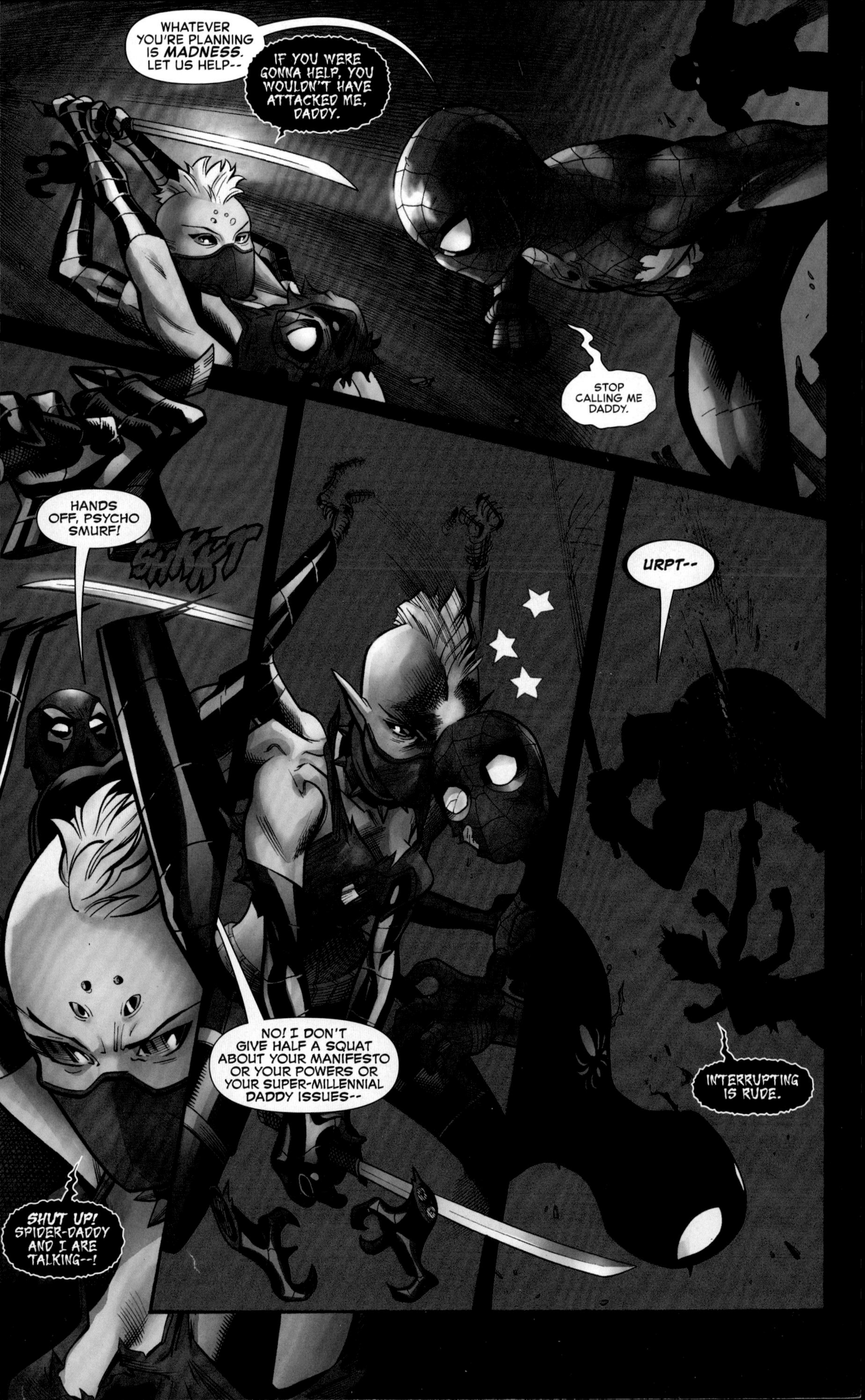
WHATEVER YOU'RE PLANNING IS MADNESS. LET US HELP--
IF YOU WERE GONNA HELP, YOU WOULDN'T HAVE ATTACKED ME, DADDY.
STOP CALLING ME DADDY.
HANDS OFF, PSYCHO SMURF!
SHKKT
NO! I DON'T GIVE HALF A SQUAT ABOUT YOUR MANIFESTO OR YOUR POWERS OR YOUR SUPER-MILLENNIAL DADDY ISSUES--
SHUT UP! SPIDER-DADDY AND I ARE TALKING--!
URPT--
INTERRUPTING IS RUDE.

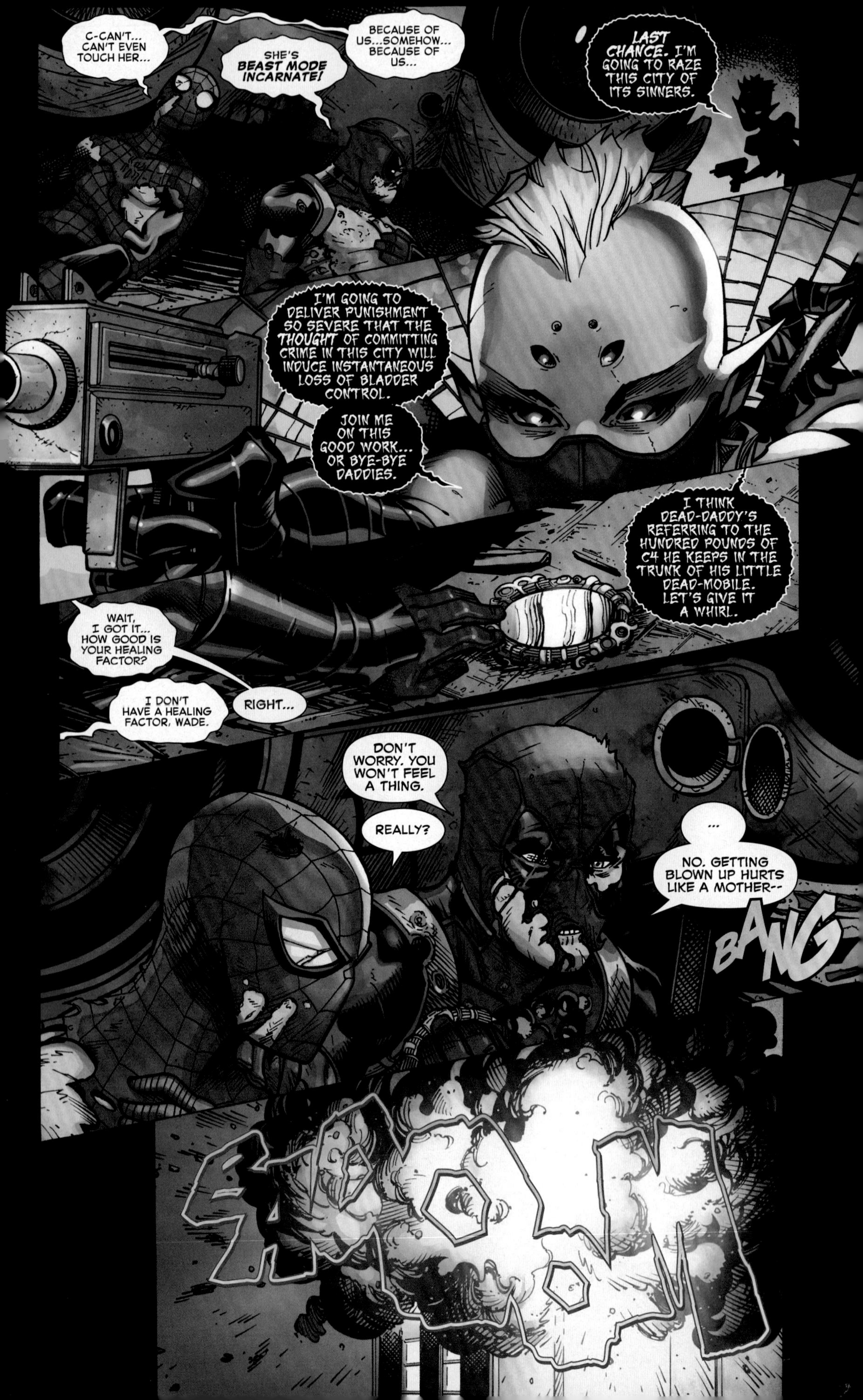
C-CAN'T... CAN'T EVEN TOUCH HER...
SHE'S BEAST MODE INCARNATE!
BECAUSE OF US...SOMEHOW... BECAUSE OF US...
LAST CHANCE. I'M GOING TO RAZE THIS CITY OF ITS SINNERS.
I'M GOING TO DELIVER PUNISHMENT SO SEVERE THAT THE THOUGHT OF COMMITTING CRIME IN THIS CITY WILL INDUCE INSTANTANEOUS LOSS OF BLADDER CONTROL.
JOIN ME ON THIS GOOD WORK... OR BYE-BYE DADDIES.
I THINK DEAD-DADDY'S REFERRING TO THE HUNDRED POUNDS OF C4 HE KEEPS IN THE TRUNK OF HIS LITTLE DEAD-MOBILE. LET'S GIVE IT A WHIRL.
WAIT, I GOT IT... HOW GOOD IS YOUR HEALING FACTOR?
I DON'T HAVE A HEALING FACTOR, WADE.
RIGHT...
DON'T WORRY. YOU WON'T FEEL A THING.
REALLY?
...
NO. GETTING BLOWN UP HURTS LIKE A MOTHER--
BANG

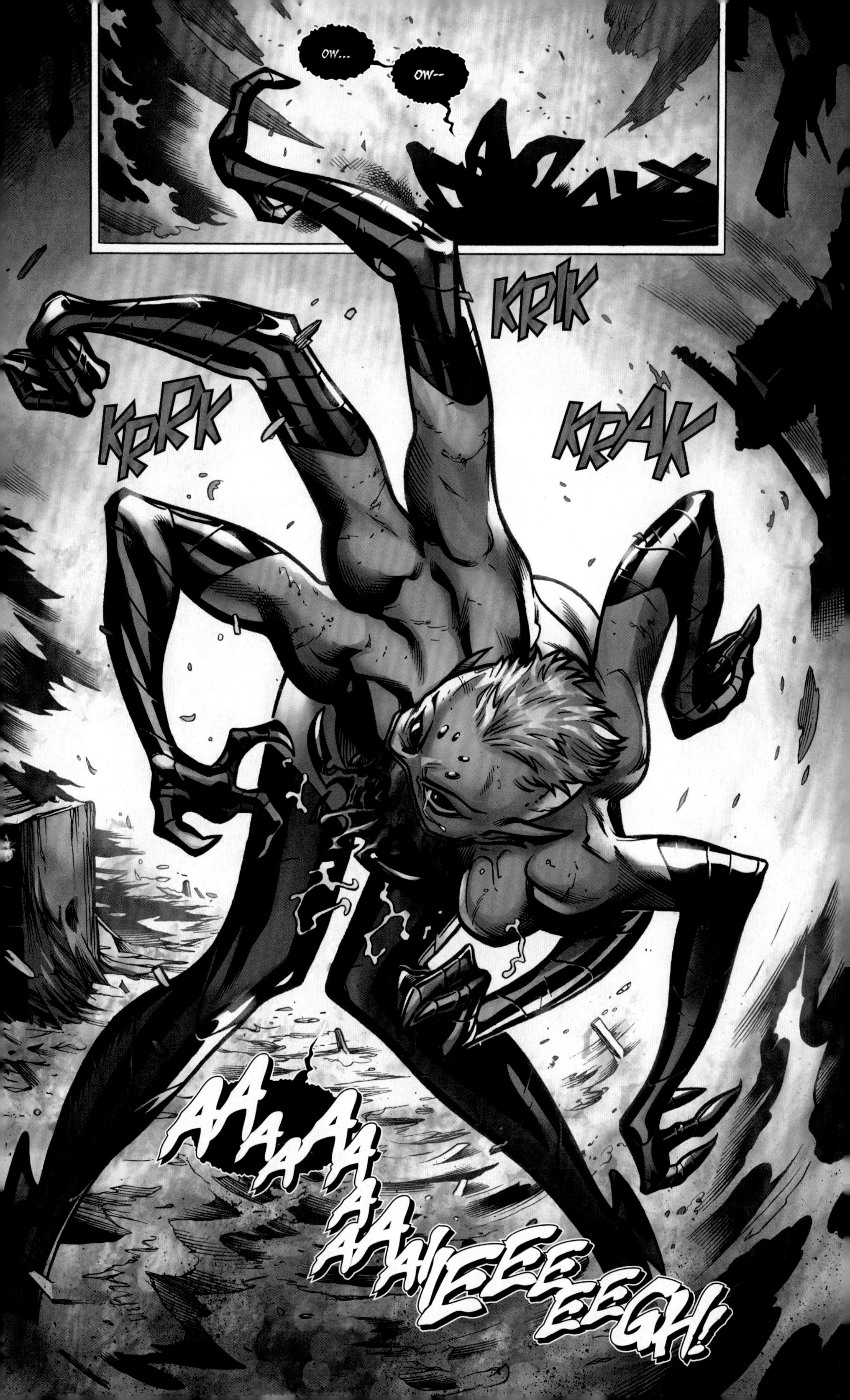
OW...
OW--
KRIK
KRRK
KRAK
AAAAAAAAAHEEEEEEGH!

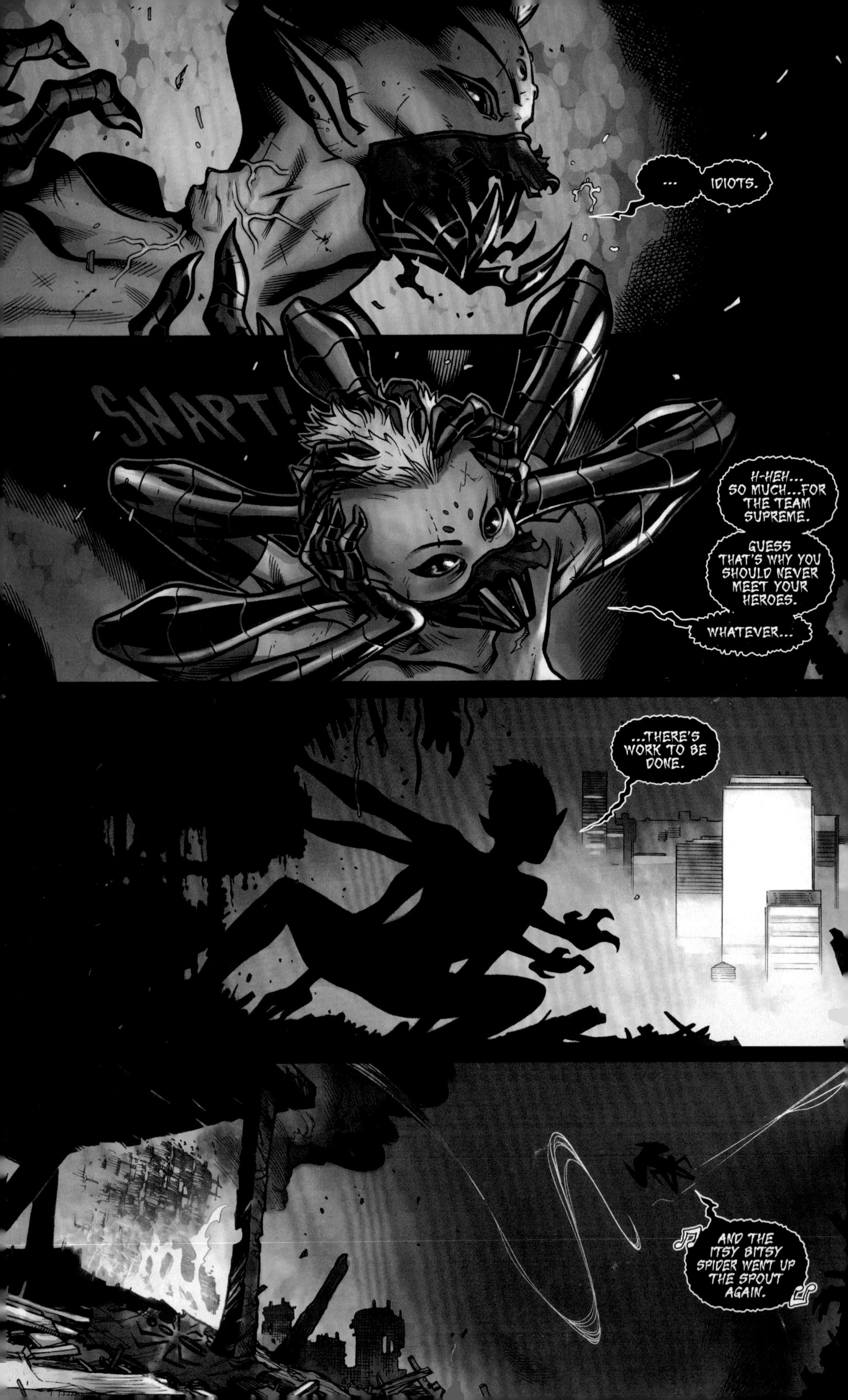
... IDIOTS.
SNAPT!
H-HEH... SO MUCH...FOR THE TEAM SUPREME.
GUESS THAT'S WHY YOU SHOULD NEVER MEET YOUR HEROES.
WHATEVER...
...THERE'S WORK TO BE DONE.
AND THE ITSY BITSY SPIDER WENT UP THE SPOUT AGAIN.

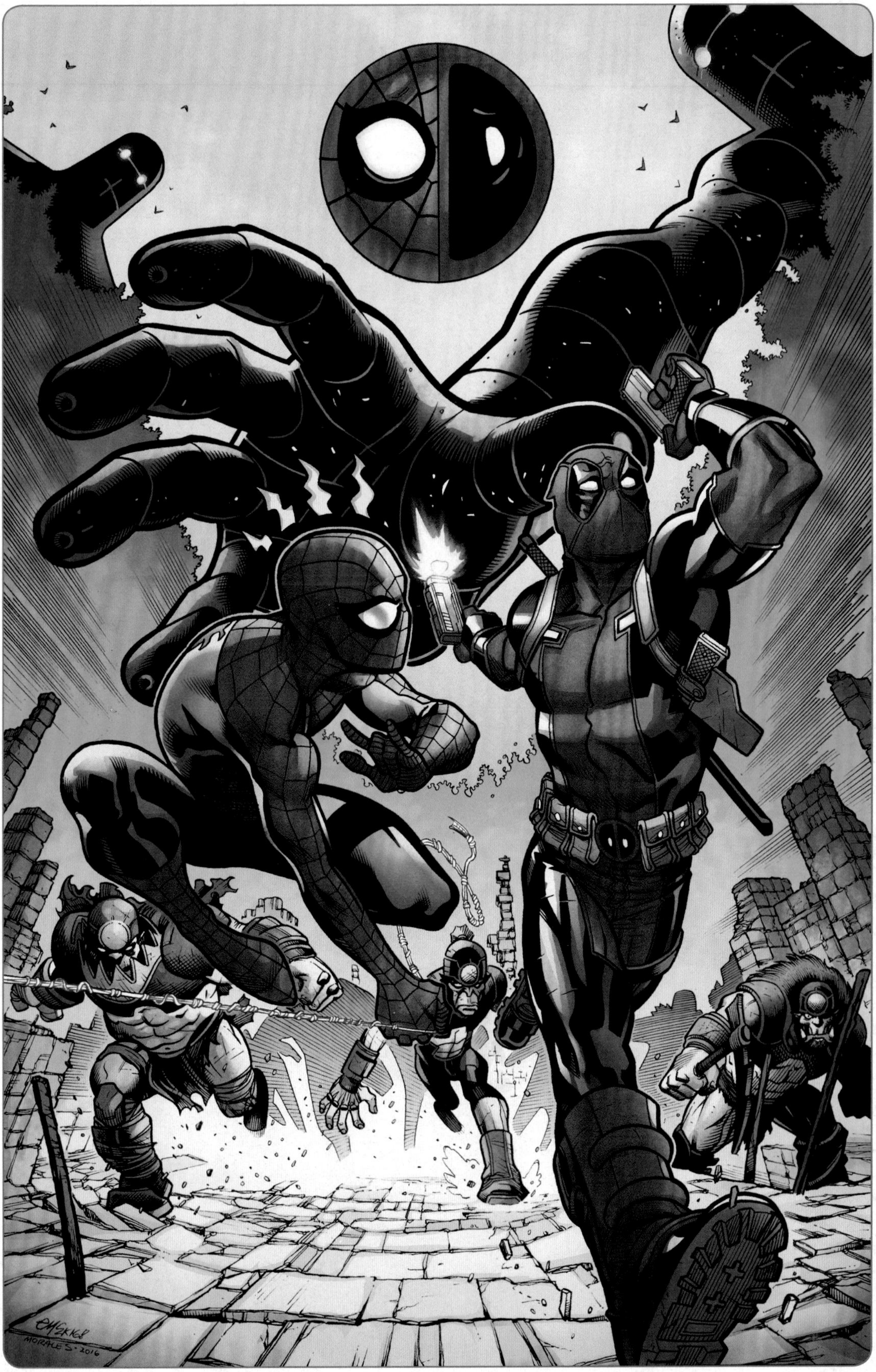
MORALES · 2016

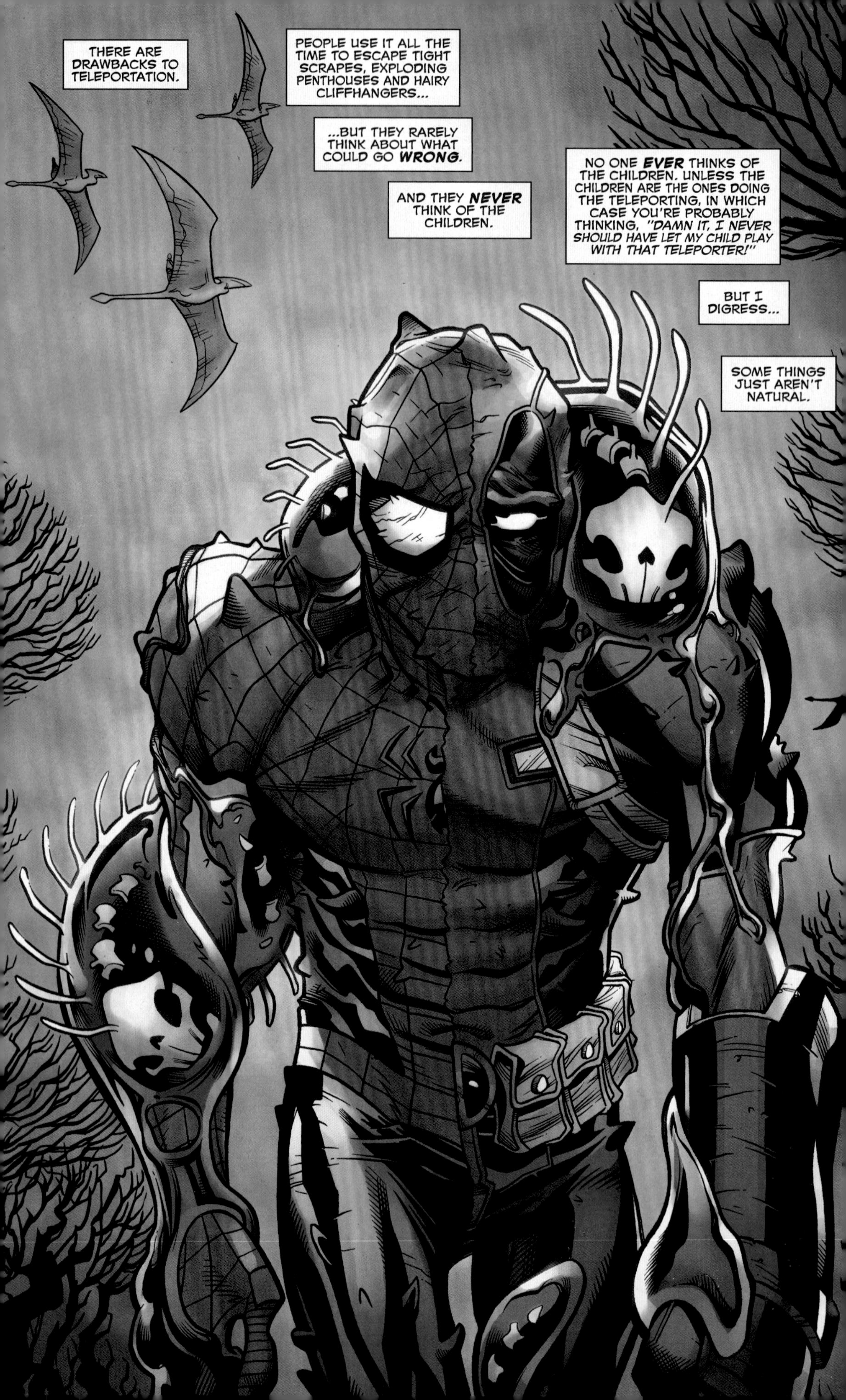
THERE ARE DRAWBACKS TO TELEPORTATION.
PEOPLE USE IT ALL THE TIME TO ESCAPE TIGHT SCRAPES, EXPLODING PENTHOUSES AND HAIRY CLIFFHANGERS...
...BUT THEY RARELY THINK ABOUT WHAT COULD GO *WRONG*.
AND THEY *NEVER* THINK OF THE CHILDREN.
NO ONE *EVER* THINKS OF THE CHILDREN. UNLESS THE CHILDREN ARE THE ONES DOING THE TELEPORTING, IN WHICH CASE YOU'RE PROBABLY THINKING, *"DAMN IT, I NEVER SHOULD HAVE LET MY CHILD PLAY WITH THAT TELEPORTER!"*
BUT I DIGRESS...
SOME THINGS JUST AREN'T NATURAL.

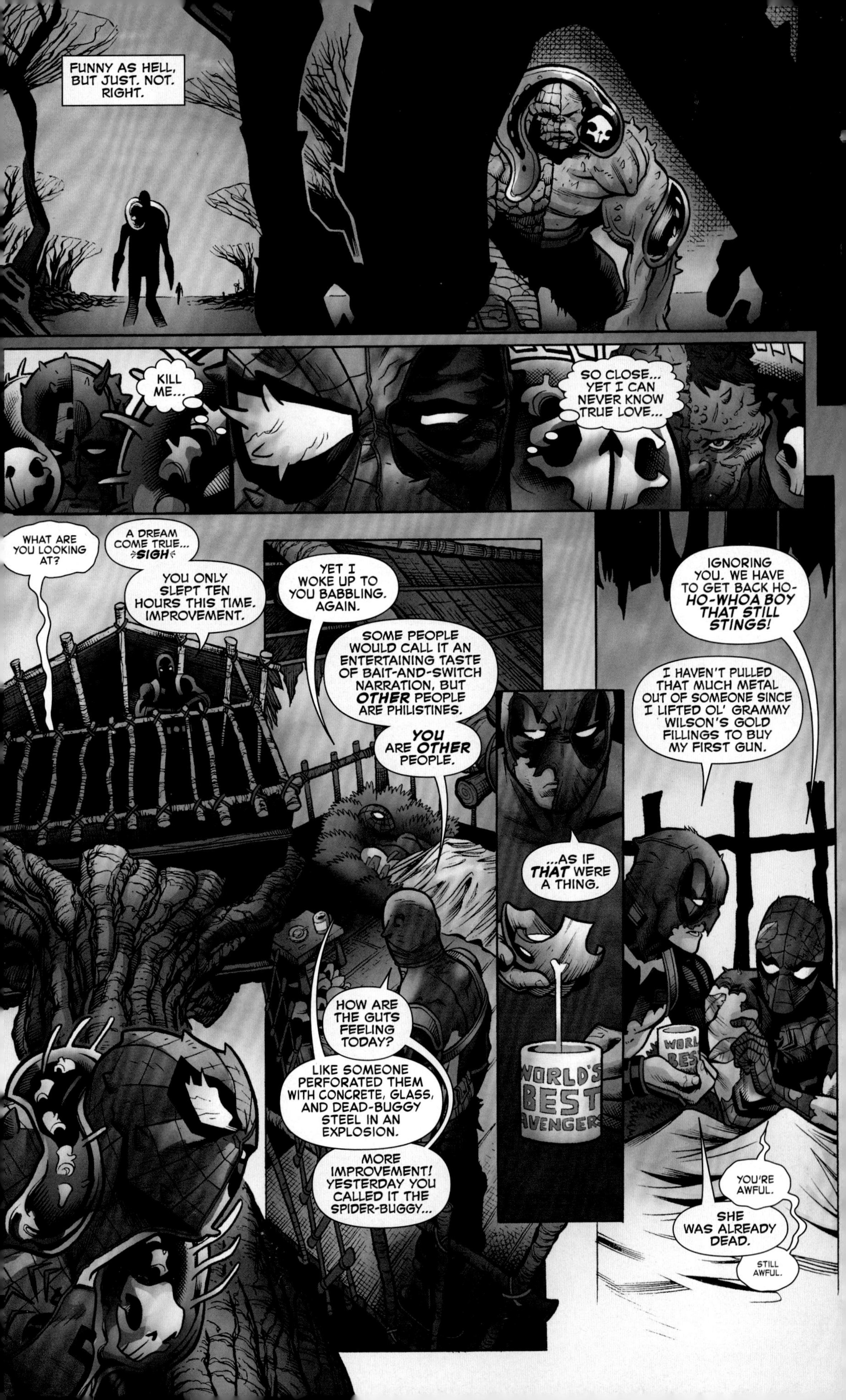
FUNNY AS HELL, BUT JUST. NOT. RIGHT.
KILL ME...
SO CLOSE... YET I CAN NEVER KNOW TRUE LOVE...
WHAT ARE YOU LOOKING AT?
A DREAM COME TRUE... *SIGH*
YOU ONLY SLEPT TEN HOURS THIS TIME. IMPROVEMENT.
YET I WOKE UP TO YOU BABBLING. AGAIN.
SOME PEOPLE WOULD CALL IT AN ENTERTAINING TASTE OF BAIT-AND-SWITCH NARRATION, BUT OTHER PEOPLE ARE PHILISTINES.
YOU ARE OTHER PEOPLE.
...AS IF THAT WERE A THING.
HOW ARE THE GUTS FEELING TODAY?
LIKE SOMEONE PERFORATED THEM WITH CONCRETE, GLASS, AND DEAD-BUGGY STEEL IN AN EXPLOSION.
MORE IMPROVEMENT! YESTERDAY YOU CALLED IT THE SPIDER-BUGGY...
WORLD'S BEST AVENGERS
IGNORING YOU. WE HAVE TO GET BACK HO-HO-WHOA BOY THAT STILL STINGS!
I HAVEN'T PULLED THAT MUCH METAL OUT OF SOMEONE SINCE I LIFTED OL' GRAMMY WILSON'S GOLD FILLINGS TO BUY MY FIRST GUN.
YOU'RE AWFUL.
SHE WAS ALREADY DEAD.
STILL AWFUL.

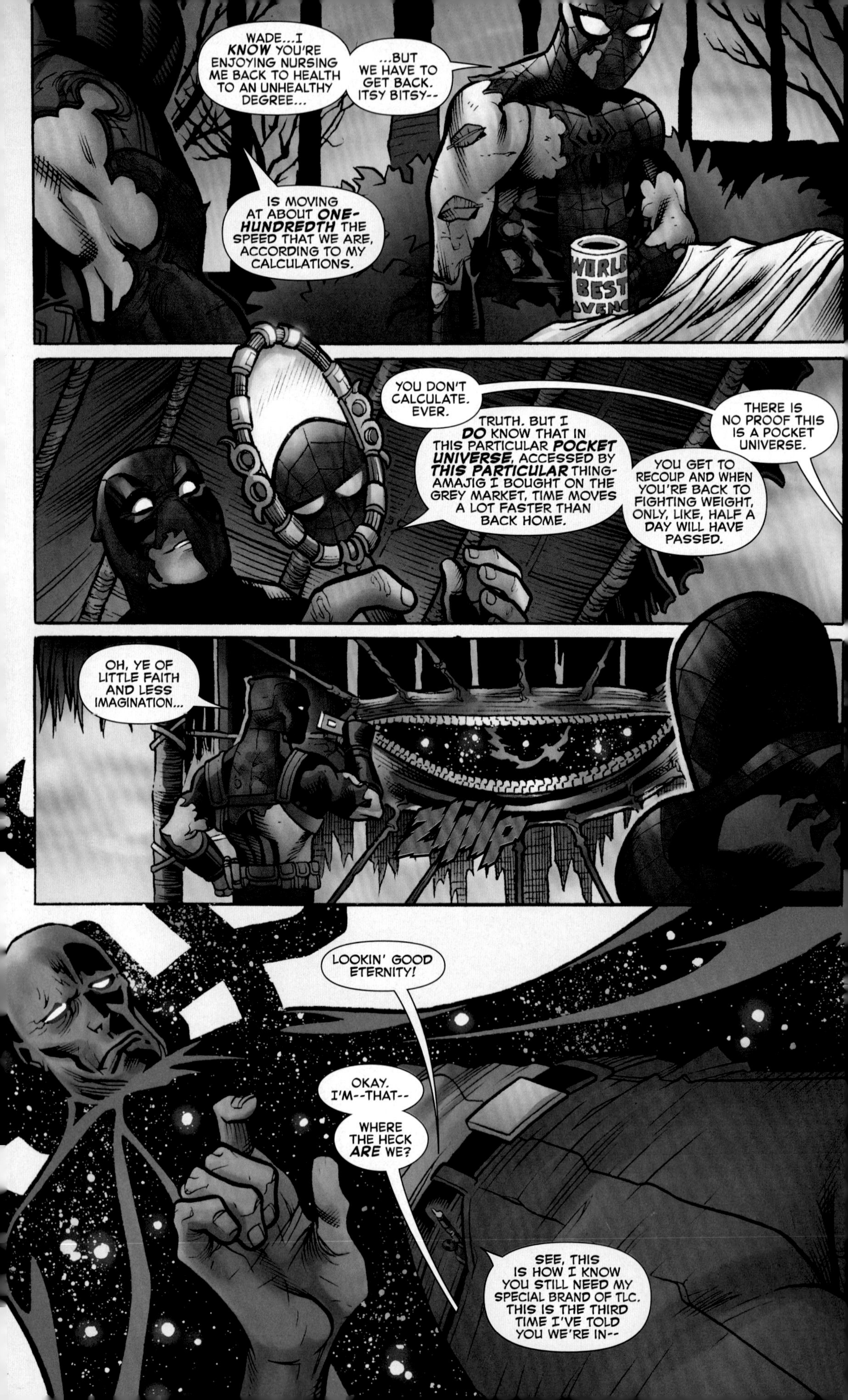
WADE...I KNOW YOU'RE ENJOYING NURSING ME BACK TO HEALTH TO AN UNHEALTHY DEGREE...
...BUT WE HAVE TO GET BACK. ITSY BITSY--
IS MOVING AT ABOUT ONE-HUNDREDTH THE SPEED THAT WE ARE, ACCORDING TO MY CALCULATIONS.
WORLD BEST AVENG
YOU DON'T CALCULATE. EVER.
TRUTH. BUT I DO KNOW THAT IN THIS PARTICULAR POCKET UNIVERSE, ACCESSED BY THIS PARTICULAR THING-AMAJIG I BOUGHT ON THE GREY MARKET, TIME MOVES A LOT FASTER THAN BACK HOME.
THERE IS NO PROOF THIS IS A POCKET UNIVERSE.
YOU GET TO RECOUP AND WHEN YOU'RE BACK TO FIGHTING WEIGHT, ONLY, LIKE, HALF A DAY WILL HAVE PASSED.
OH, YE OF LITTLE FAITH AND LESS IMAGINATION...
ZIIIP
LOOKIN' GOOD ETERNITY!
OKAY. I'M--THAT--
WHERE THE HECK ARE WE?
SEE, THIS IS HOW I KNOW YOU STILL NEED MY SPECIAL BRAND OF TLC. THIS IS THE THIRD TIME I'VE TOLD YOU WE'RE IN--

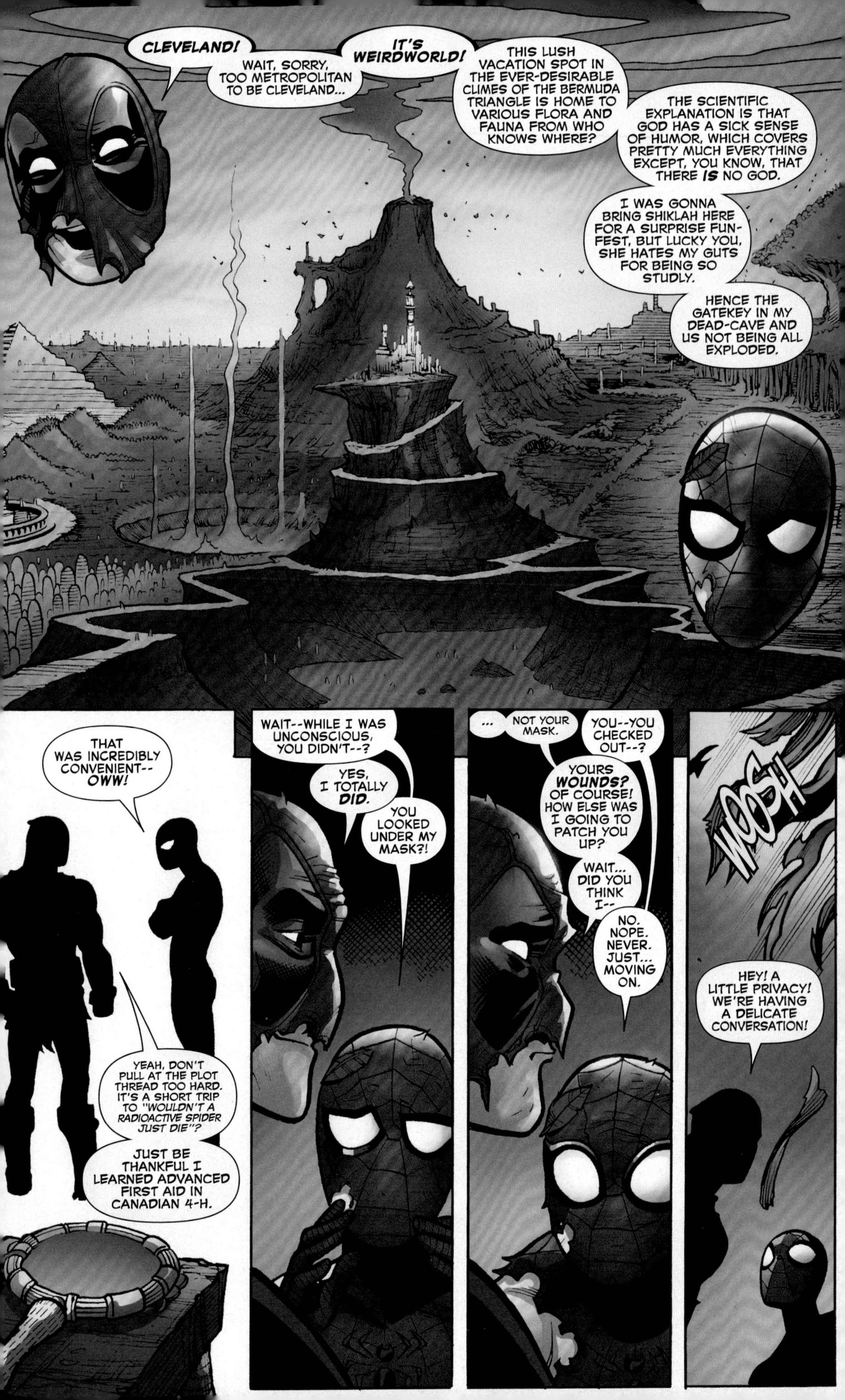
CLEVELAND!
WAIT, SORRY, TOO METROPOLITAN TO BE CLEVELAND...
IT'S WEIRDWORLD!
THIS LUSH VACATION SPOT IN THE EVER-DESIRABLE CLIMES OF THE BERMUDA TRIANGLE IS HOME TO VARIOUS FLORA AND FAUNA FROM WHO KNOWS WHERE?
THE SCIENTIFIC EXPLANATION IS THAT GOD HAS A SICK SENSE OF HUMOR, WHICH COVERS PRETTY MUCH EVERYTHING EXCEPT, YOU KNOW, THAT THERE IS NO GOD.
I WAS GONNA BRING SHIKLAH HERE FOR A SURPRISE FUN-FEST, BUT LUCKY YOU, SHE HATES MY GUTS FOR BEING SO STUDLY.
HENCE THE GATEKEY IN MY DEAD-CAVE AND US NOT BEING ALL EXPLODED.
THAT WAS INCREDIBLY CONVENIENT-- OWW!
YEAH, DON'T PULL AT THE PLOT THREAD TOO HARD. IT'S A SHORT TRIP TO "WOULDN'T A RADIOACTIVE SPIDER JUST DIE"?
JUST BE THANKFUL I LEARNED ADVANCED FIRST AID IN CANADIAN 4-H.
WAIT--WHILE I WAS UNCONSCIOUS, YOU DIDN'T--?
YES, I TOTALLY DID.
YOU LOOKED UNDER MY MASK?!
...
NOT YOUR MASK.
YOU--YOU CHECKED OUT--?
YOURS WOUNDS? OF COURSE! HOW ELSE WAS I GOING TO PATCH YOU UP?
WAIT... DID YOU THINK I--
NO. NOPE. NEVER. JUST... MOVING ON.
WOOSH
HEY! A LITTLE PRIVACY! WE'RE HAVING A DELICATE CONVERSATION!

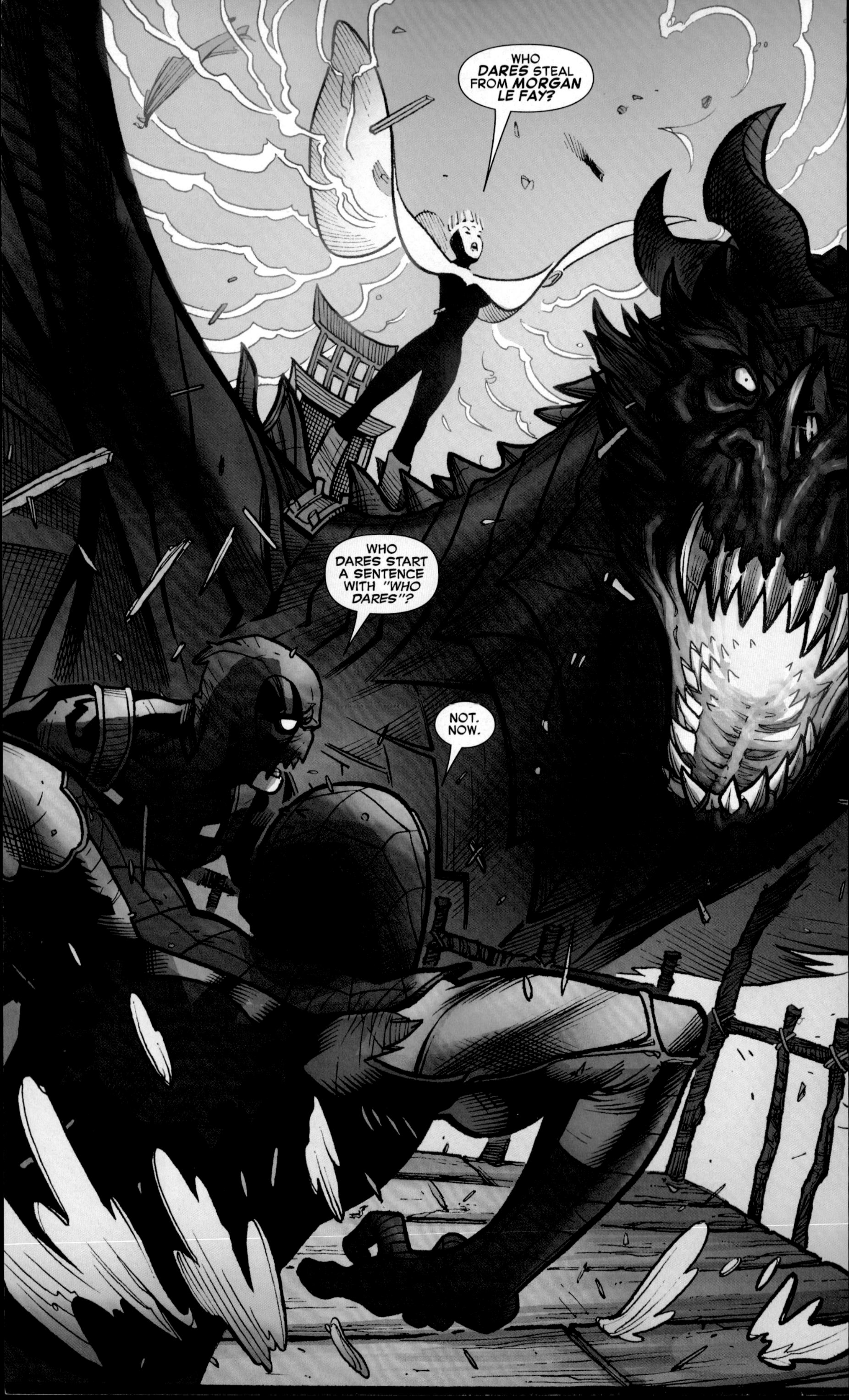
WHO DARES STEAL FROM MORGAN LE FAY?
WHO DARES START A SENTENCE WITH "WHO DARES"?
NOT. NOW.

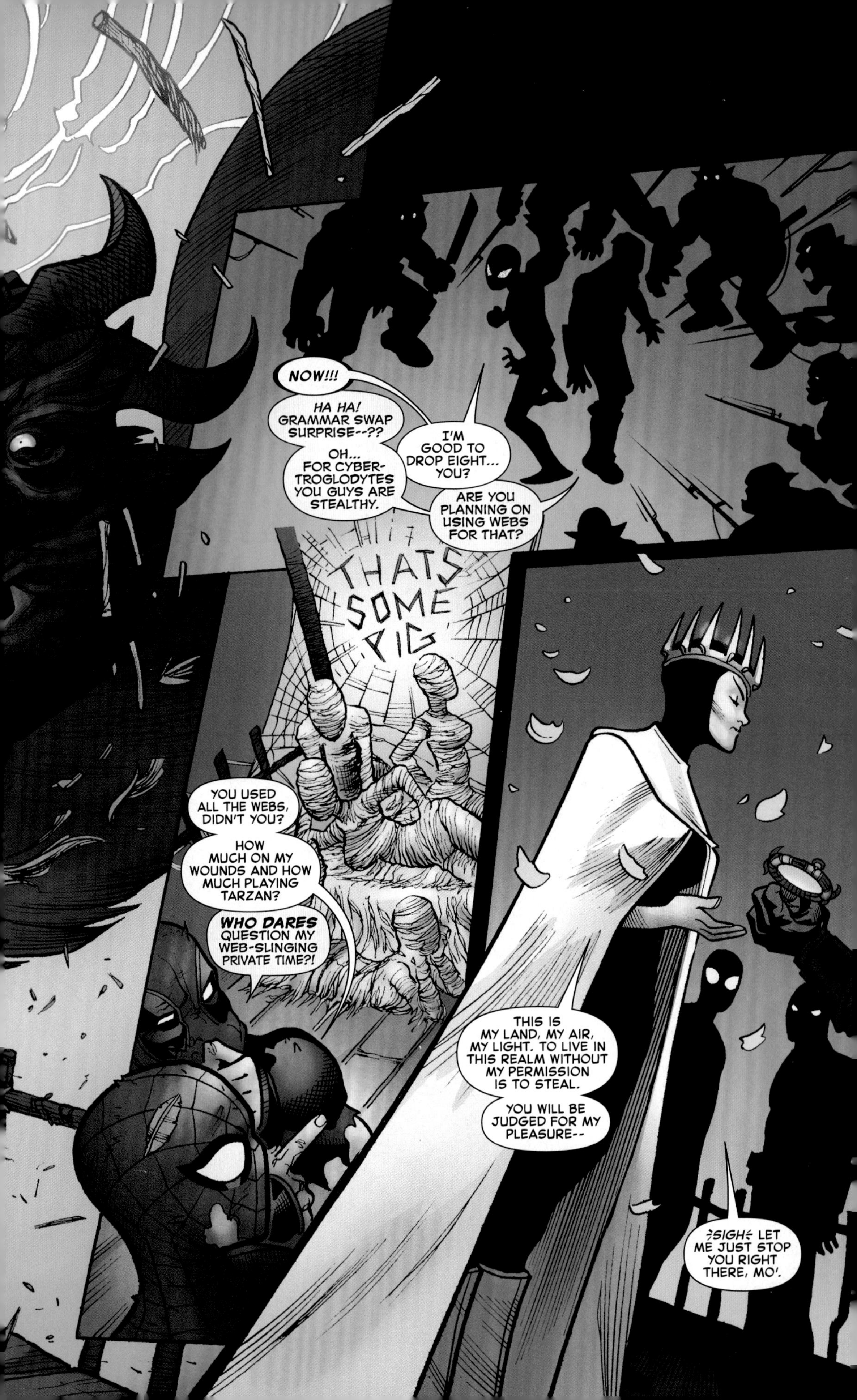
NOW!!!
HA HA! GRAMMAR SWAP SURPRISE--??
I'M GOOD TO DROP EIGHT... YOU?
OH... FOR CYBER-TROGLODYTES YOU GUYS ARE STEALTHY.
ARE YOU PLANNING ON USING WEBS FOR THAT?
THATS SOME PIG
YOU USED ALL THE WEBS, DIDN'T YOU?
HOW MUCH ON MY WOUNDS AND HOW MUCH PLAYING TARZAN?
WHO DARES QUESTION MY WEB-SLINGING PRIVATE TIME?!
THIS IS MY LAND, MY AIR, MY LIGHT. TO LIVE IN THIS REALM WITHOUT MY PERMISSION IS TO STEAL.
YOU WILL BE JUDGED FOR MY PLEASURE--
SIGH LET ME JUST STOP YOU RIGHT THERE, MO'.

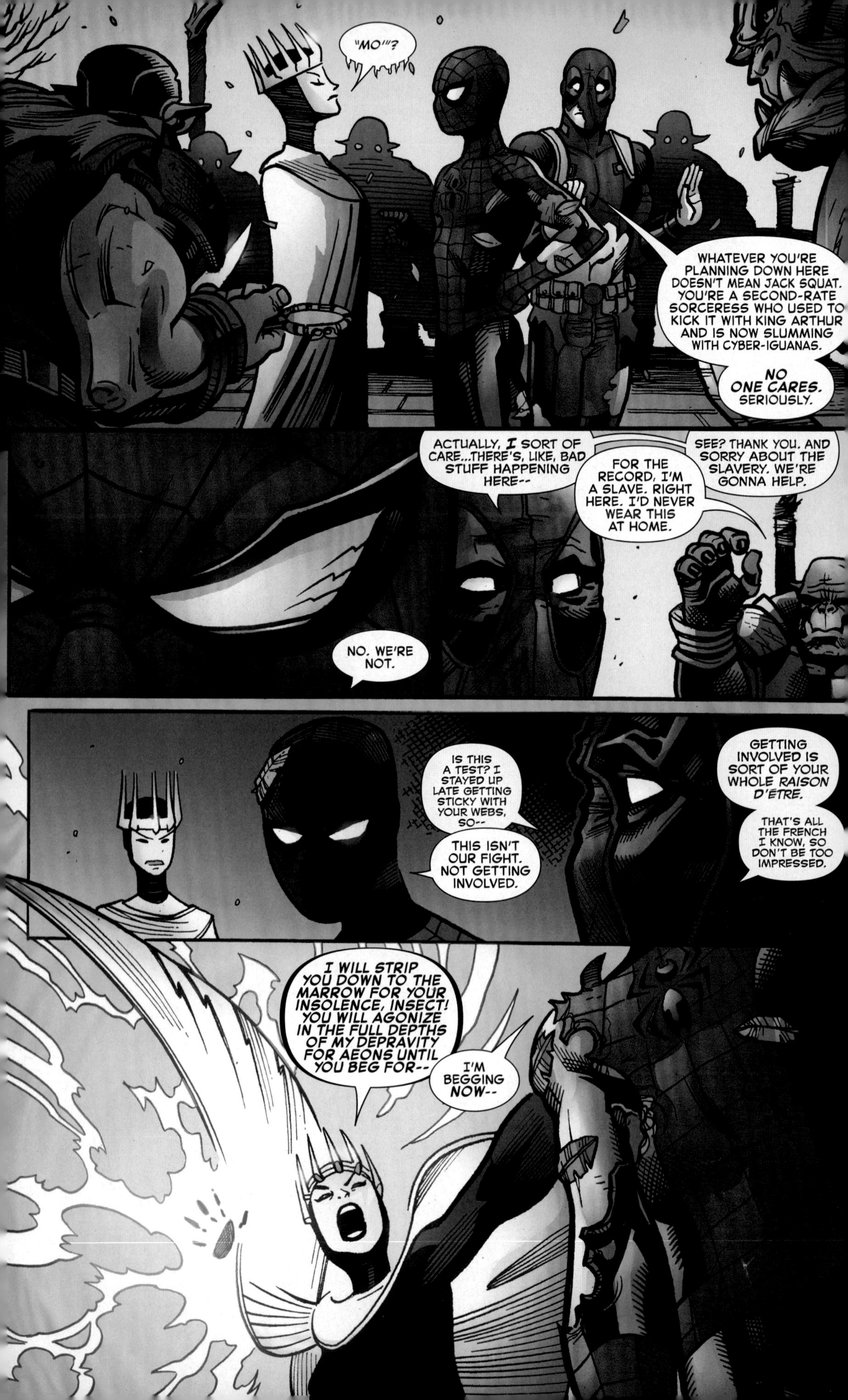
"MO'"?
WHATEVER YOU'RE PLANNING DOWN HERE DOESN'T MEAN JACK SQUAT. YOU'RE A SECOND-RATE SORCERESS WHO USED TO KICK IT WITH KING ARTHUR AND IS NOW SLUMMING WITH CYBER-IGUANAS.
NO ONE CARES. SERIOUSLY.
ACTUALLY, I SORT OF CARE...THERE'S, LIKE, BAD STUFF HAPPENING HERE--
FOR THE RECORD, I'M A SLAVE. RIGHT HERE. I'D NEVER WEAR THIS AT HOME.
SEE? THANK YOU. AND SORRY ABOUT THE SLAVERY. WE'RE GONNA HELP.
NO. WE'RE NOT.
IS THIS A TEST? I STAYED UP LATE GETTING STICKY WITH YOUR WEBS, SO--
THIS ISN'T OUR FIGHT. NOT GETTING INVOLVED.
GETTING INVOLVED IS SORT OF YOUR WHOLE RAISON D'ÊTRE.
THAT'S ALL THE FRENCH I KNOW, SO DON'T BE TOO IMPRESSED.
I WILL STRIP YOU DOWN TO THE MARROW FOR YOUR INSOLENCE, INSECT! YOU WILL AGONIZE IN THE FULL DEPTHS OF MY DEPRAVITY FOR AEONS UNTIL YOU BEG FOR--
I'M BEGGING NOW--

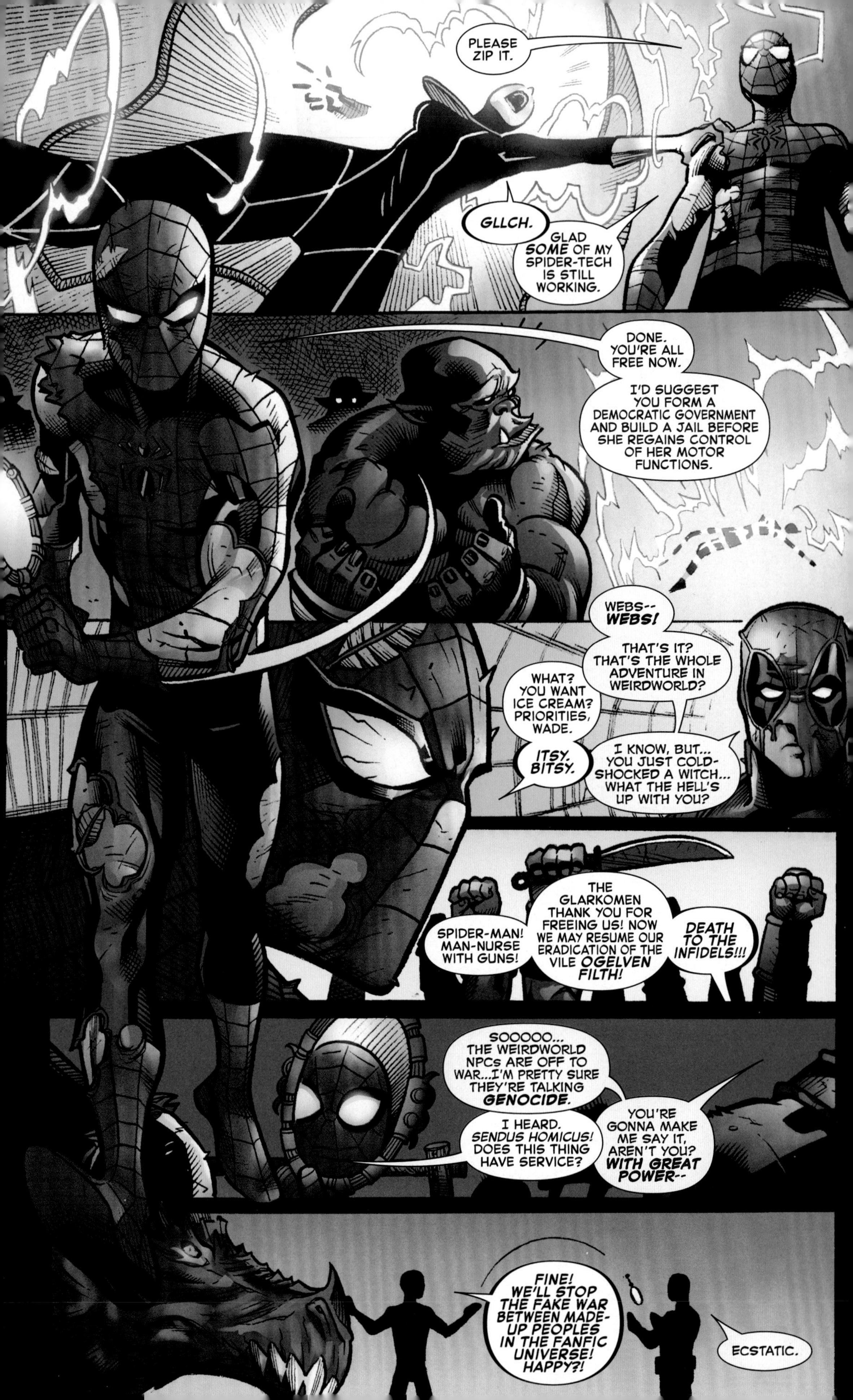
PLEASE ZIP IT.
GLLCH.
GLAD SOME OF MY SPIDER-TECH IS STILL WORKING.
DONE. YOU'RE ALL FREE NOW.
I'D SUGGEST YOU FORM A DEMOCRATIC GOVERNMENT AND BUILD A JAIL BEFORE SHE REGAINS CONTROL OF HER MOTOR FUNCTIONS.
WEBS-- WEBS!
THAT'S IT? THAT'S THE WHOLE ADVENTURE IN WEIRDWORLD?
WHAT? YOU WANT ICE CREAM? PRIORITIES, WADE.
I KNOW, BUT... YOU JUST COLD-SHOCKED A WITCH... WHAT THE HELL'S UP WITH YOU?
ITSY. BITSY.
THE GLARKOMEN THANK YOU FOR FREEING US! NOW WE MAY RESUME OUR ERADICATION OF THE VILE OGELVEN FILTH!
SPIDER-MAN! MAN-NURSE WITH GUNS!
DEATH TO THE INFIDELS!!!
SOOOOO... THE WEIRDWORLD NPCs ARE OFF TO WAR...I'M PRETTY SURE THEY'RE TALKING GENOCIDE.
I HEARD. SENDUS HOMICUS! DOES THIS THING HAVE SERVICE?
YOU'RE GONNA MAKE ME SAY IT, AREN'T YOU? WITH GREAT POWER--
FINE! WE'LL STOP THE FAKE WAR BETWEEN MADE-UP PEOPLES IN THE FANFIC UNIVERSE! HAPPY?!
ECSTATIC.

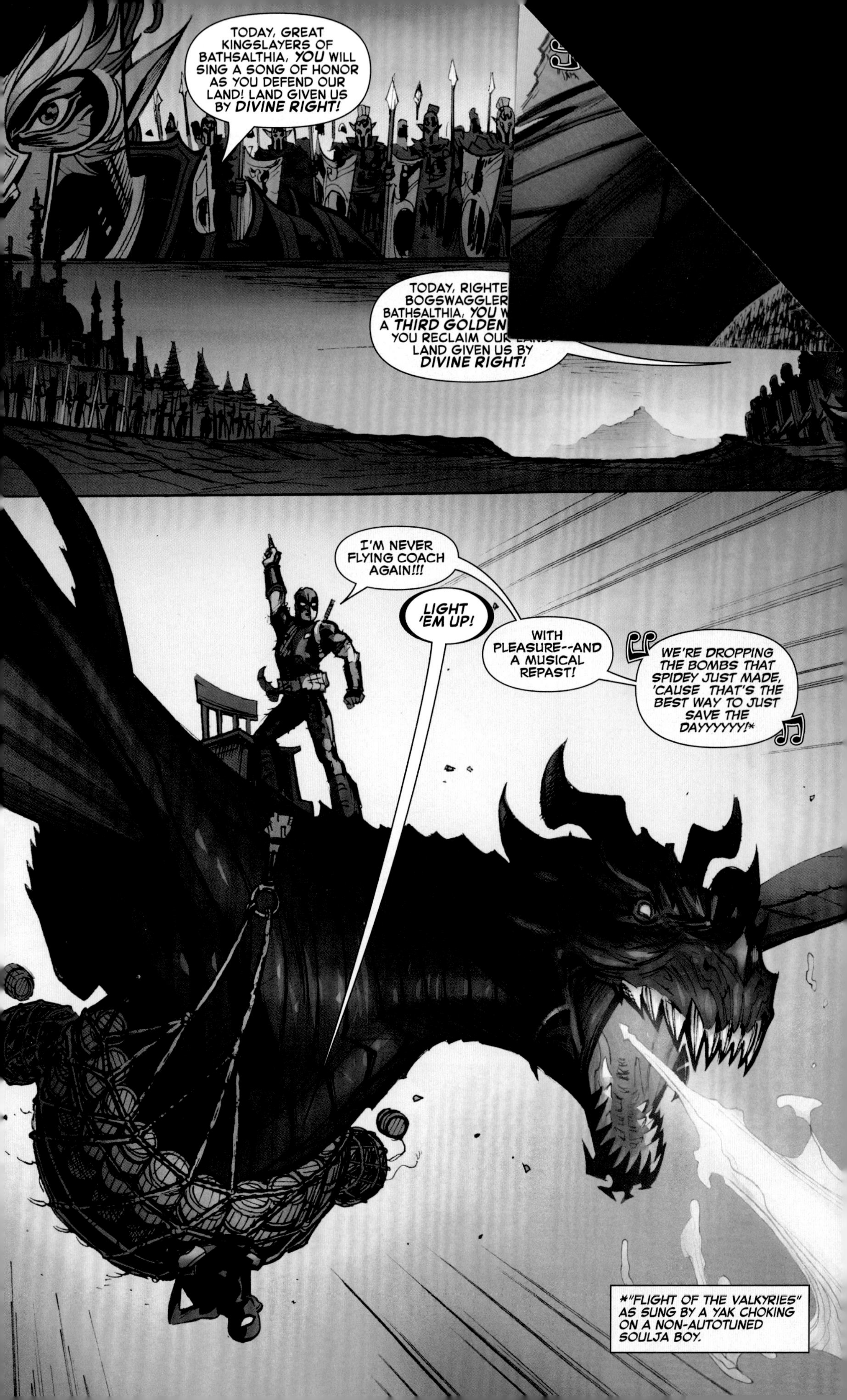
TODAY, GREAT KINGSLAYERS OF BATHSALTHIA, YOU WILL SING A SONG OF HONOR AS YOU DEFEND OUR LAND! LAND GIVEN US BY DIVINE RIGHT!
TODAY, RIGHTE BOGSWAGGLER BATHSALTHIA, YOU W A THIRD GOLDEN YOU RECLAIM OUR LAND GIVEN US BY DIVINE RIGHT!
I'M NEVER FLYING COACH AGAIN!!!
LIGHT 'EM UP!
WITH PLEASURE--AND A MUSICAL REPAST!
WE'RE DROPPING THE BOMBS THAT SPIDEY JUST MADE, 'CAUSE THAT'S THE BEST WAY TO JUST SAVE THE DAYYYYYYY!*
*"FLIGHT OF THE VALKYRIES" AS SUNG BY A YAK CHOKING ON A NON-AUTOTUNED SOULJA BOY.

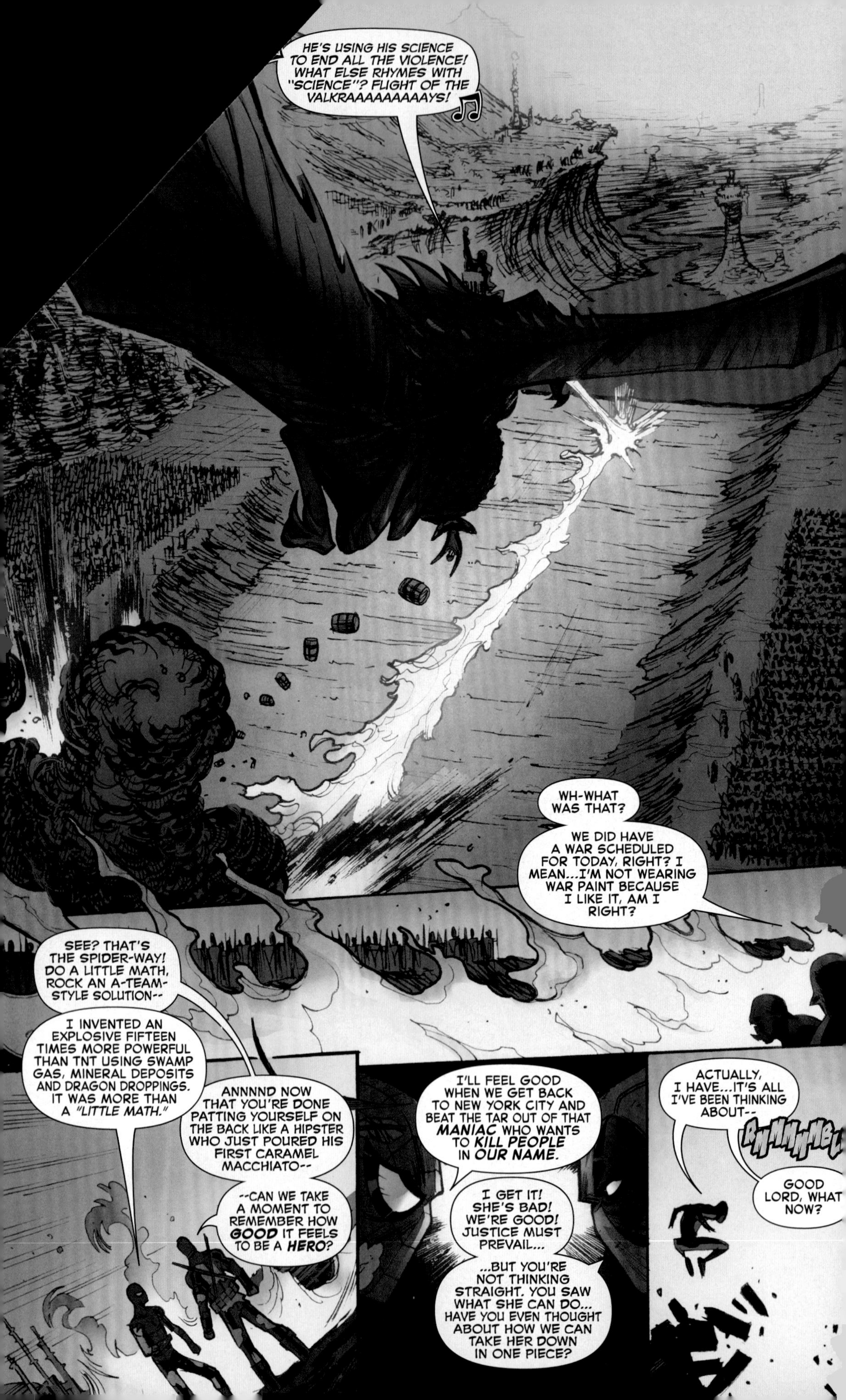
HE'S USING HIS SCIENCE TO END ALL THE VIOLENCE! WHAT ELSE RHYMES WITH "SCIENCE"? FLIGHT OF THE VALKRAAAAAAAAAAYS!
WH-WHAT WAS THAT?
WE DID HAVE A WAR SCHEDULED FOR TODAY, RIGHT? I MEAN...I'M NOT WEARING WAR PAINT BECAUSE I LIKE IT, AM I RIGHT?
SEE? THAT'S THE SPIDER-WAY! DO A LITTLE MATH, ROCK AN A-TEAM-STYLE SOLUTION--
I INVENTED AN EXPLOSIVE FIFTEEN TIMES MORE POWERFUL THAN TNT USING SWAMP GAS, MINERAL DEPOSITS AND DRAGON DROPPINGS. IT WAS MORE THAN A "LITTLE MATH."
ANNNND NOW THAT YOU'RE DONE PATTING YOURSELF ON THE BACK LIKE A HIPSTER WHO JUST POURED HIS FIRST CARAMEL MACCHIATO--
--CAN WE TAKE A MOMENT TO REMEMBER HOW GOOD IT FEELS TO BE A HERO?
I'LL FEEL GOOD WHEN WE GET BACK TO NEW YORK CITY AND BEAT THE TAR OUT OF THAT MANIAC WHO WANTS TO KILL PEOPLE IN OUR NAME.
I GET IT! SHE'S BAD! WE'RE GOOD! JUSTICE MUST PREVAIL...
...BUT YOU'RE NOT THINKING STRAIGHT. YOU SAW WHAT SHE CAN DO... HAVE YOU EVEN THOUGHT ABOUT HOW WE CAN TAKE HER DOWN IN ONE PIECE?
ACTUALLY, I HAVE...IT'S ALL I'VE BEEN THINKING ABOUT--
RMMMMBL
GOOD LORD, WHAT NOW?

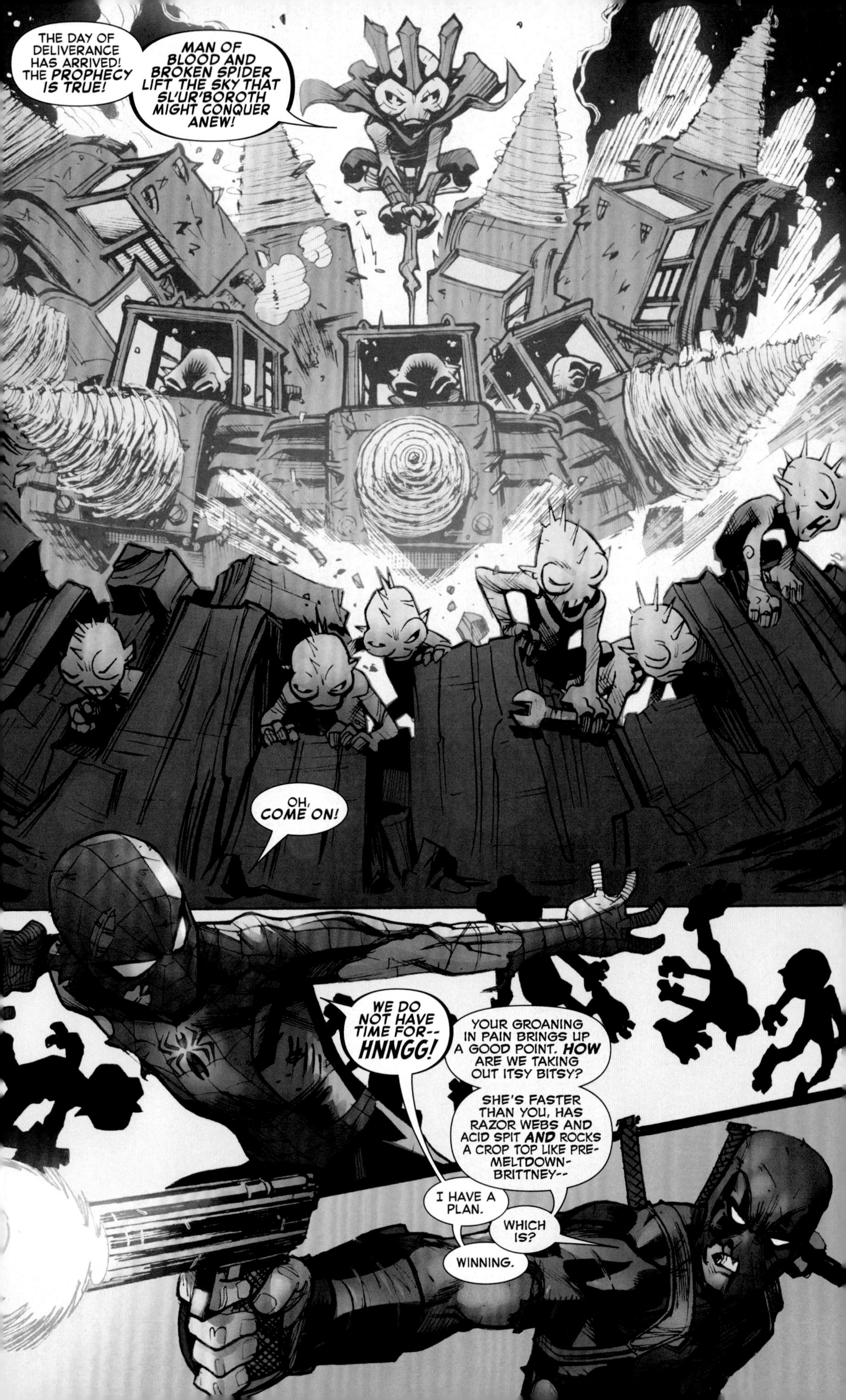
THE DAY OF DELIVERANCE HAS ARRIVED! THE PROPHECY IS TRUE!
MAN OF BLOOD AND BROKEN SPIDER LIFT THE SKY THAT SL'UR'BOROTH MIGHT CONQUER ANEW!
OH, COME ON!
WE DO NOT HAVE TIME FOR-- HNNGG!
YOUR GROANING IN PAIN BRINGS UP A GOOD POINT. HOW ARE WE TAKING OUT ITSY BITSY?
SHE'S FASTER THAN YOU, HAS RAZOR WEBS AND ACID SPIT AND ROCKS A CROP TOP LIKE PRE-MELTDOWN-BRITTNEY--
I HAVE A PLAN.
WHICH IS?
WINNING.

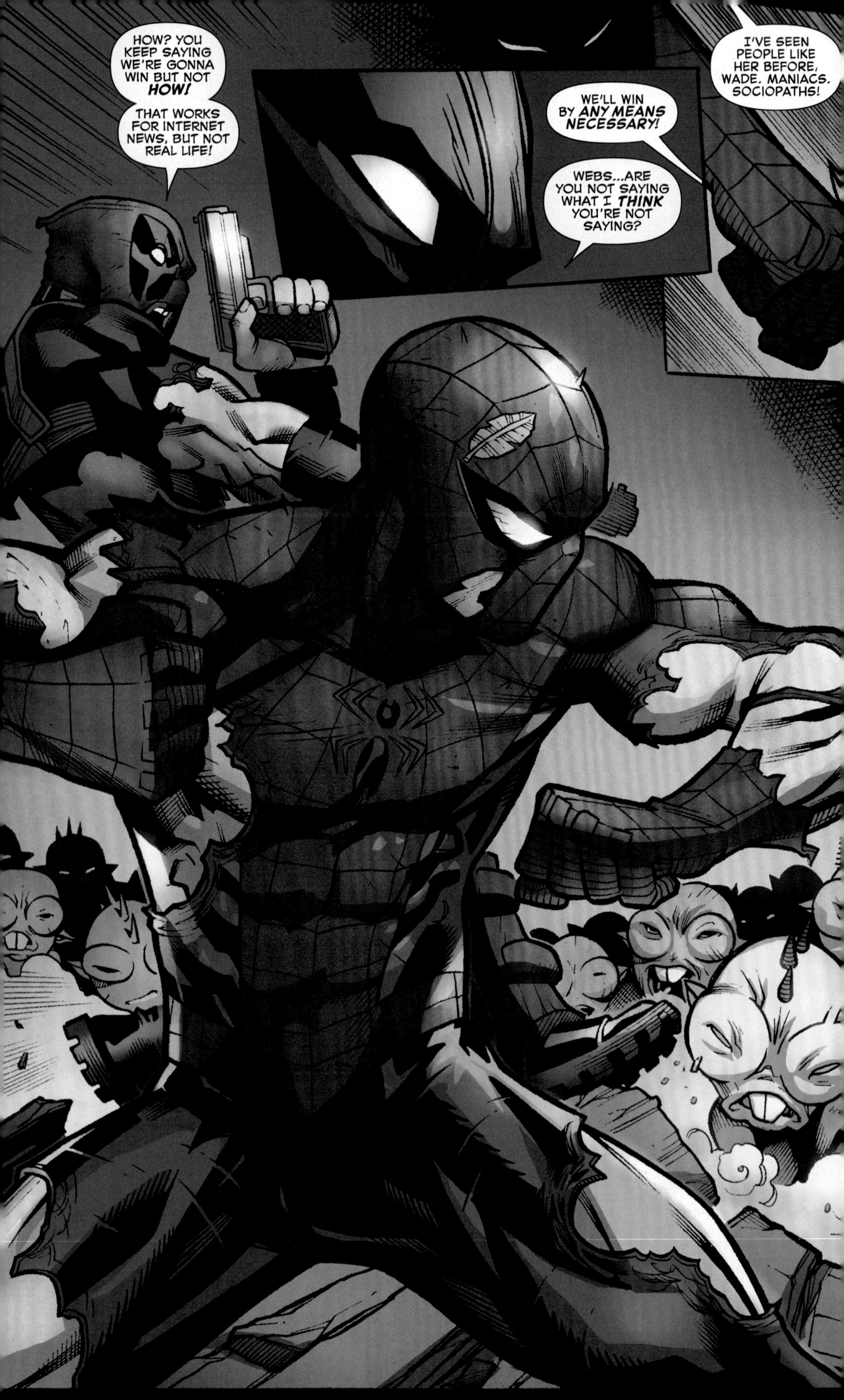

HOW? YOU KEEP SAYING WE'RE GONNA WIN BUT NOT HOW!
THAT WORKS FOR INTERNET NEWS, BUT NOT REAL LIFE!
WE'LL WIN BY ANY MEANS NECESSARY!
WEBS...ARE YOU NOT SAYING WHAT I THINK YOU'RE NOT SAYING?
I'VE SEEN PEOPLE LIKE HER BEFORE, WADE. MANIACS. SOCIOPATHS!

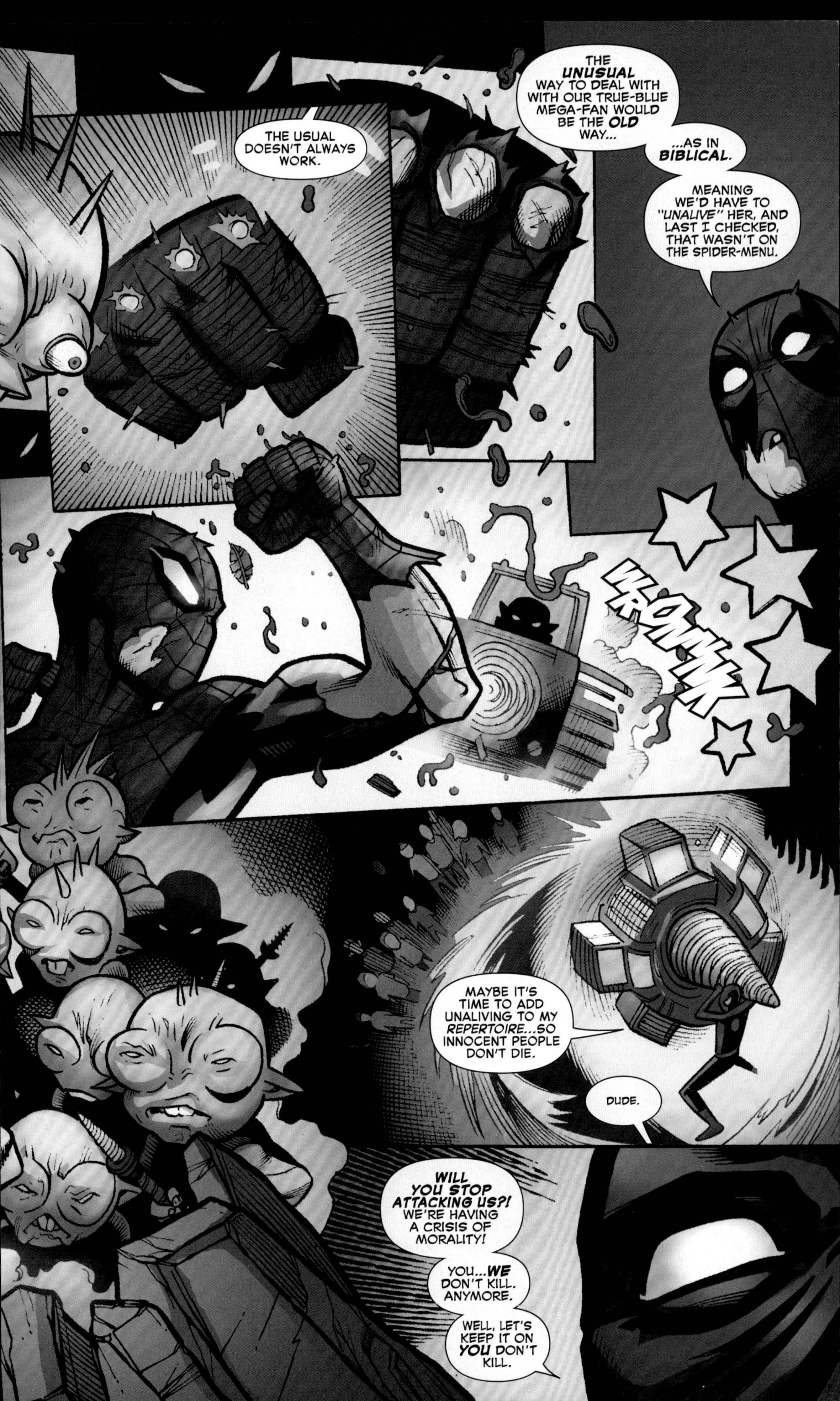
THE USUAL DOESN'T ALWAYS WORK.
THE UNUSUAL WAY TO DEAL WITH WITH OUR TRUE-BLUE MEGA-FAN WOULD BE THE OLD WAY...
...AS IN BIBLICAL.
MEANING WE'D HAVE TO "UNALIVE" HER, AND LAST I CHECKED, THAT WASN'T ON THE SPIDER-MENU.
WRONNK
MAYBE IT'S TIME TO ADD UNALIVING TO MY REPERTOIRE...SO INNOCENT PEOPLE DON'T DIE.
DUDE.
WILL YOU STOP ATTACKING US?! WE'RE HAVING A CRISIS OF MORALITY!
YOU...WE DON'T KILL. ANYMORE.
WELL, LET'S KEEP IT ON YOU DON'T KILL.

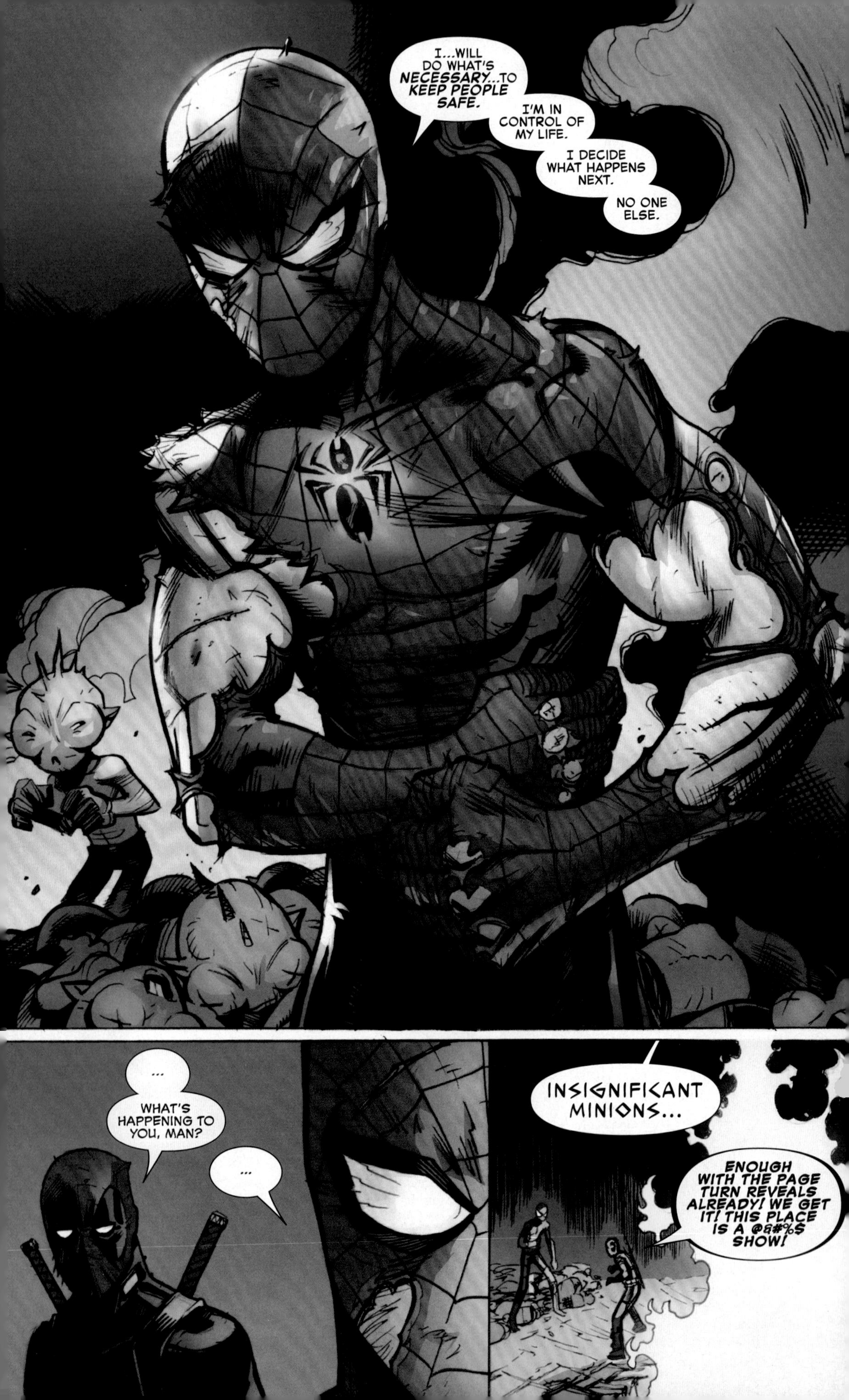

I...WILL DO WHAT'S NECESSARY...TO KEEP PEOPLE SAFE.
I'M IN CONTROL OF MY LIFE.
I DECIDE WHAT HAPPENS NEXT.
NO ONE ELSE.
...
WHAT'S HAPPENING TO YOU, MAN?
...
INSIGNIFICANT MINIONS...
ENOUGH WITH THE PAGE TURN REVEALS ALREADY! WE GET IT! THIS PLACE IS A @&#%$ SHOW!

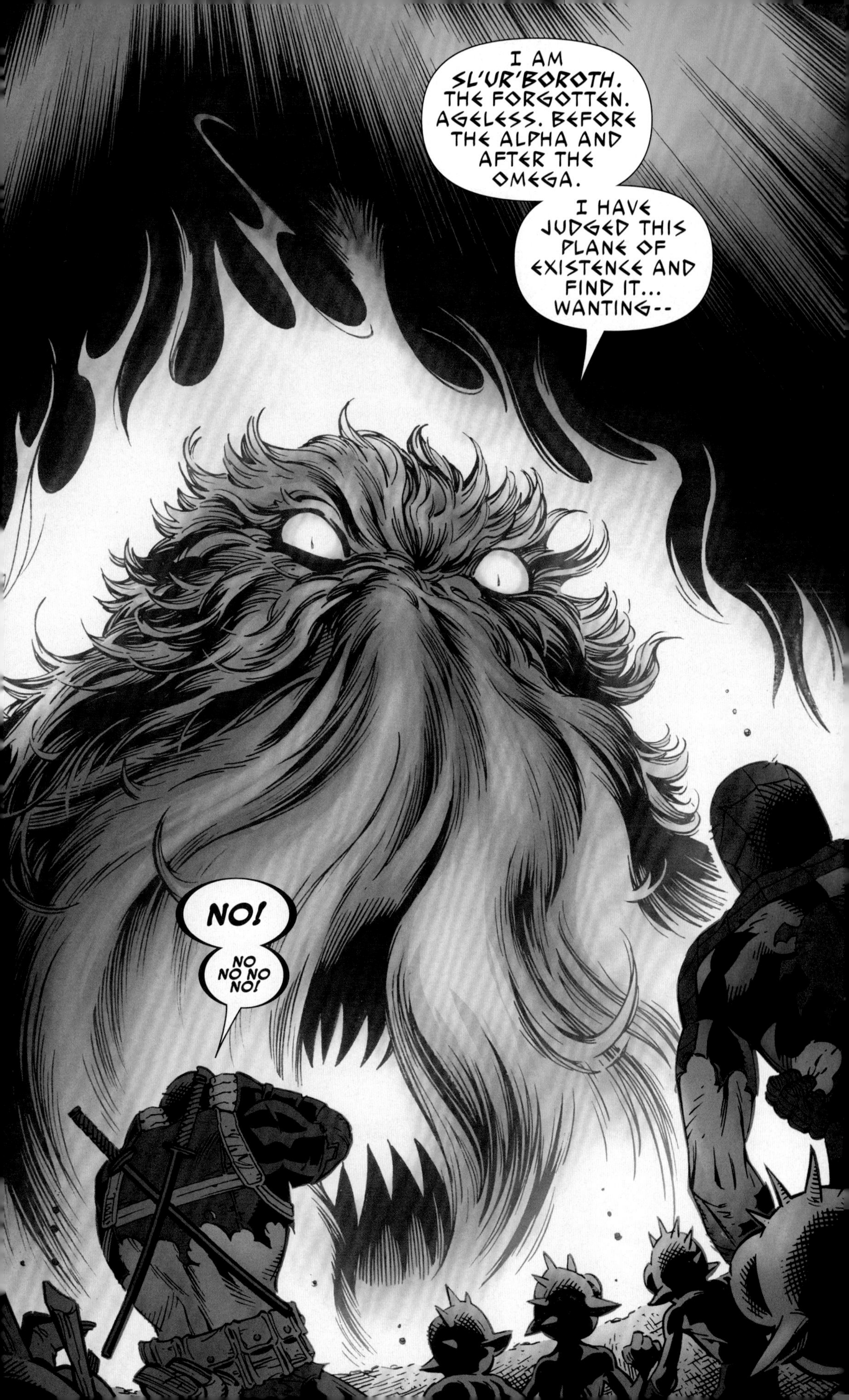
I AM SL'UR'BOROTH. THE FORGOTTEN. AGELESS. BEFORE THE ALPHA AND AFTER THE OMEGA.
I HAVE JUDGED THIS PLANE OF EXISTENCE AND FIND IT... WANTING--
NO!
NO NO NO NO!

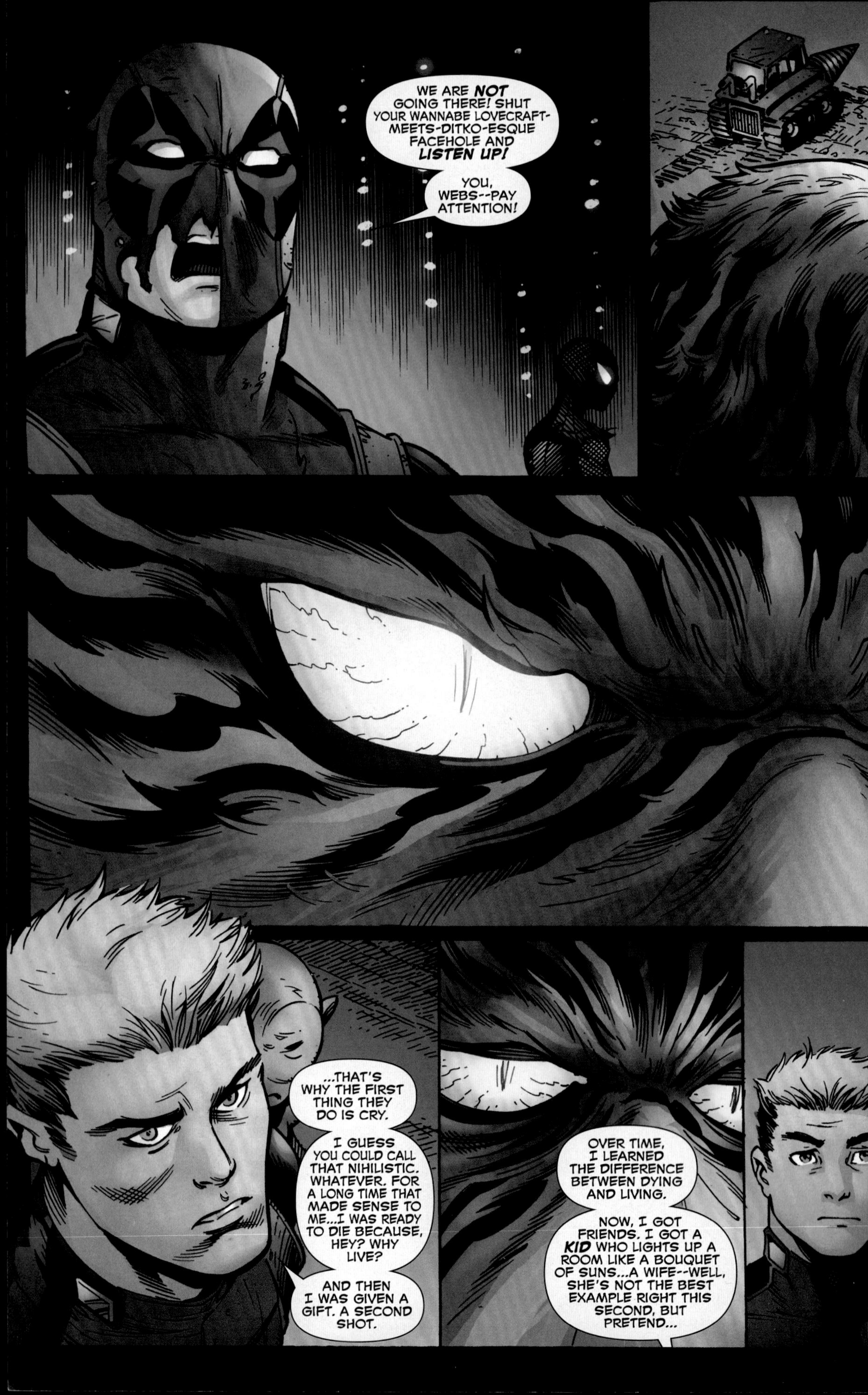

WE ARE NOT GOING THERE! SHUT YOUR WANNABE LOVECRAFT-MEETS-DITKO-ESQUE FACEHOLE AND LISTEN UP!
YOU, WEBS--PAY ATTENTION!
...THAT'S WHY THE FIRST THING THEY DO IS CRY.
I GUESS YOU COULD CALL THAT NIHILISTIC. WHATEVER. FOR A LONG TIME THAT MADE SENSE TO ME...I WAS READY TO DIE BECAUSE, HEY? WHY LIVE?
AND THEN I WAS GIVEN A GIFT. A SECOND SHOT.
OVER TIME, I LEARNED THE DIFFERENCE BETWEEN DYING AND LIVING.
NOW, I GOT FRIENDS. I GOT A KID WHO LIGHTS UP A ROOM LIKE A BOUQUET OF SUNS...A WIFE--WELL, SHE'S NOT THE BEST EXAMPLE RIGHT THIS SECOND, BUT PRETEND...

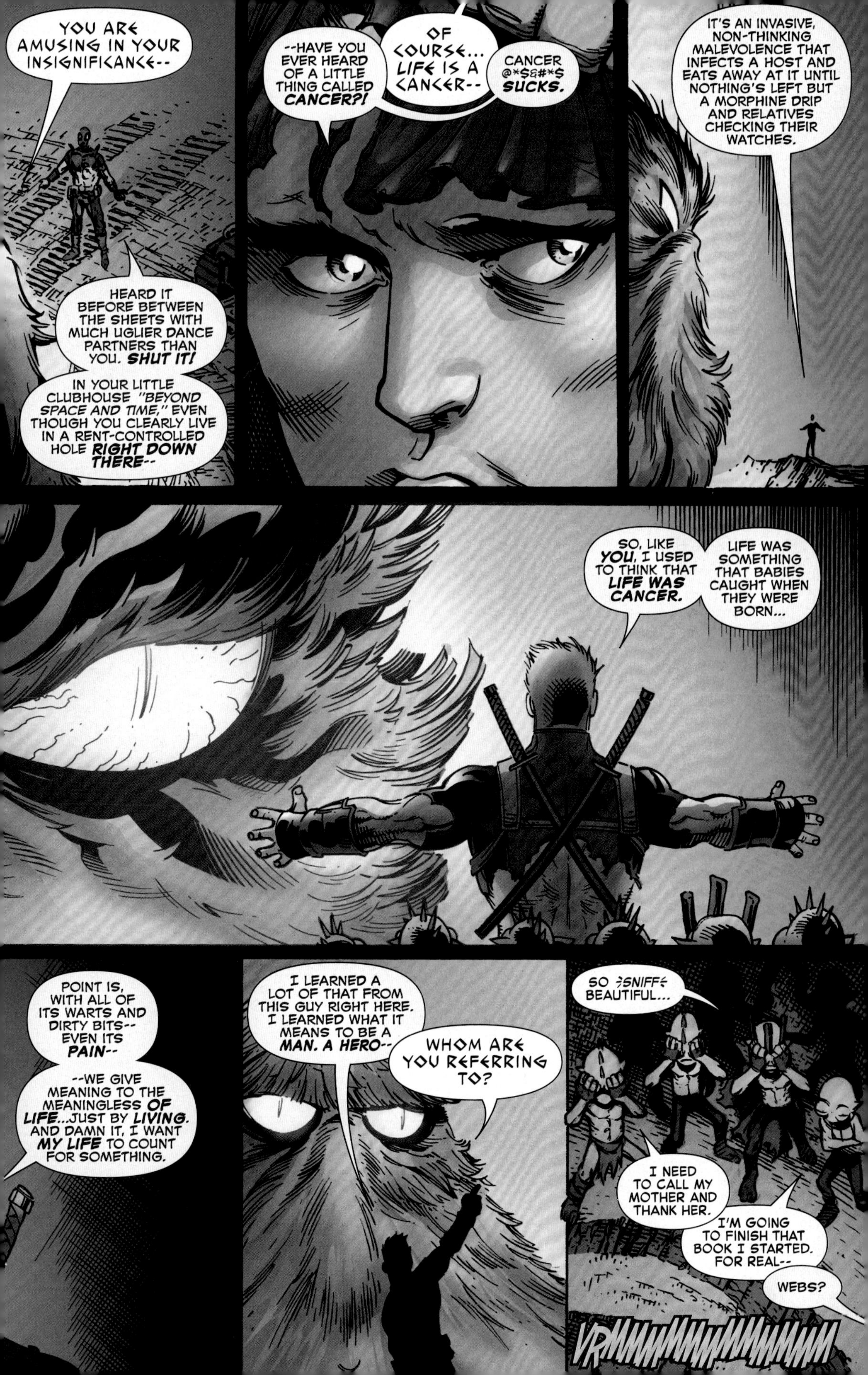
YOU ARE AMUSING IN YOUR INSIGNIFICANCE--
HEARD IT BEFORE BETWEEN THE SHEETS WITH MUCH UGLIER DANCE PARTNERS THAN YOU. SHUT IT!
IN YOUR LITTLE CLUBHOUSE "BEYOND SPACE AND TIME," EVEN THOUGH YOU CLEARLY LIVE IN A RENT-CONTROLLED HOLE RIGHT DOWN THERE--
--HAVE YOU EVER HEARD OF A LITTLE THING CALLED CANCER?!
OF COURSE... LIFE IS A CANCER--
CANCER @*$&#*$ SUCKS.
IT'S AN INVASIVE, NON-THINKING MALEVOLENCE THAT INFECTS A HOST AND EATS AWAY AT IT UNTIL NOTHING'S LEFT BUT A MORPHINE DRIP AND RELATIVES CHECKING THEIR WATCHES.
SO, LIKE YOU, I USED TO THINK THAT LIFE WAS CANCER.
LIFE WAS SOMETHING THAT BABIES CAUGHT WHEN THEY WERE BORN...
POINT IS, WITH ALL OF ITS WARTS AND DIRTY BITS-- EVEN ITS PAIN--
--WE GIVE MEANING TO THE MEANINGLESS OF LIFE...JUST BY LIVING. AND DAMN IT, I WANT MY LIFE TO COUNT FOR SOMETHING.
I LEARNED A LOT OF THAT FROM THIS GUY RIGHT HERE. I LEARNED WHAT IT MEANS TO BE A MAN. A HERO--
WHOM ARE YOU REFERRING TO?
SO ⊰SNIFF⊱ BEAUTIFUL...
I NEED TO CALL MY MOTHER AND THANK HER.
I'M GOING TO FINISH THAT BOOK I STARTED. FOR REAL--
WEBS?
VRMMMMMMMMMMMMMM

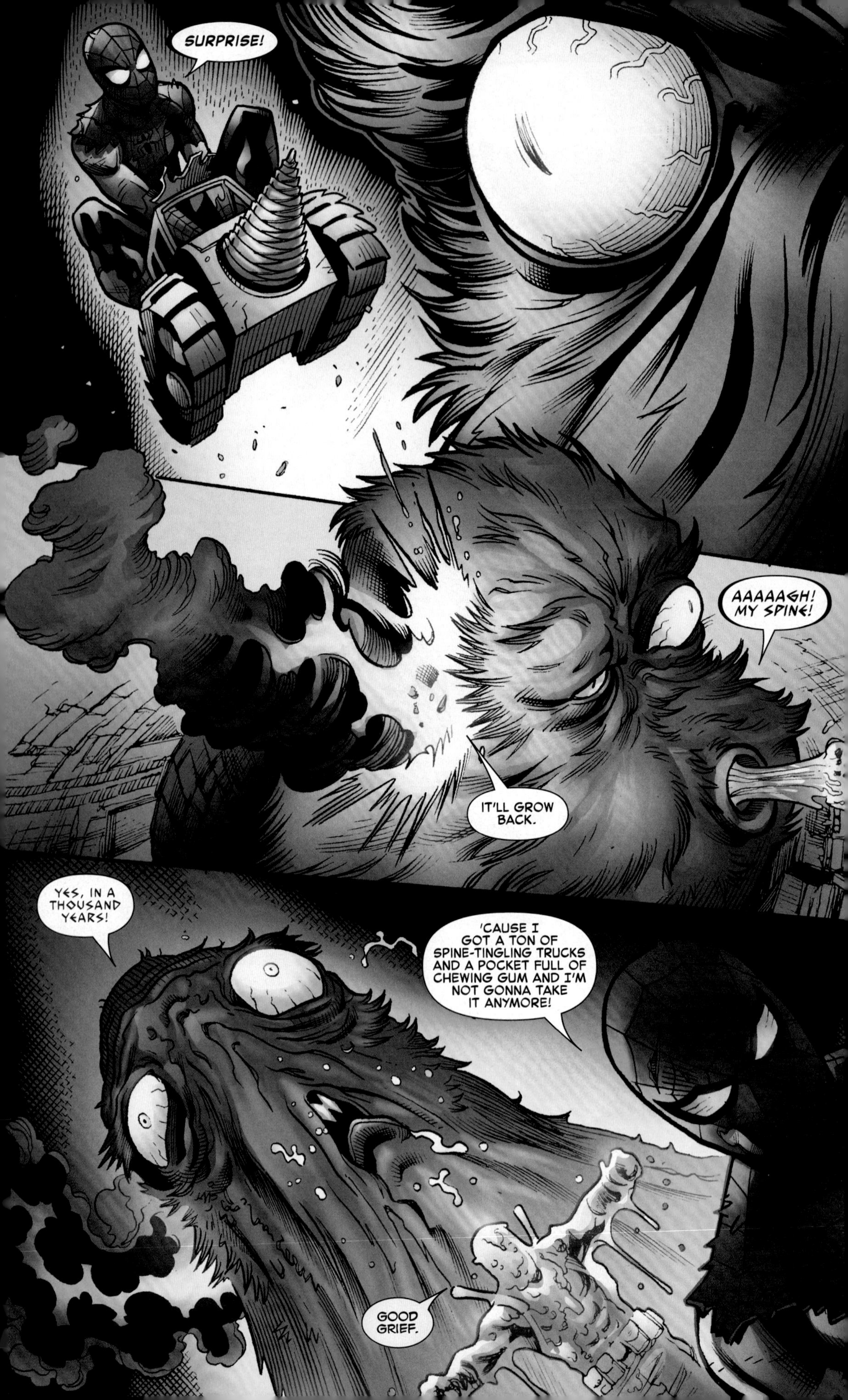
SURPRISE!
AAAAAGH! MY SPINE!
IT'LL GROW BACK.
YES, IN A THOUSAND YEARS!
'CAUSE I GOT A TON OF SPINE-TINGLING TRUCKS AND A POCKET FULL OF CHEWING GUM AND I'M NOT GONNA TAKE IT ANYMORE!
GOOD GRIEF.

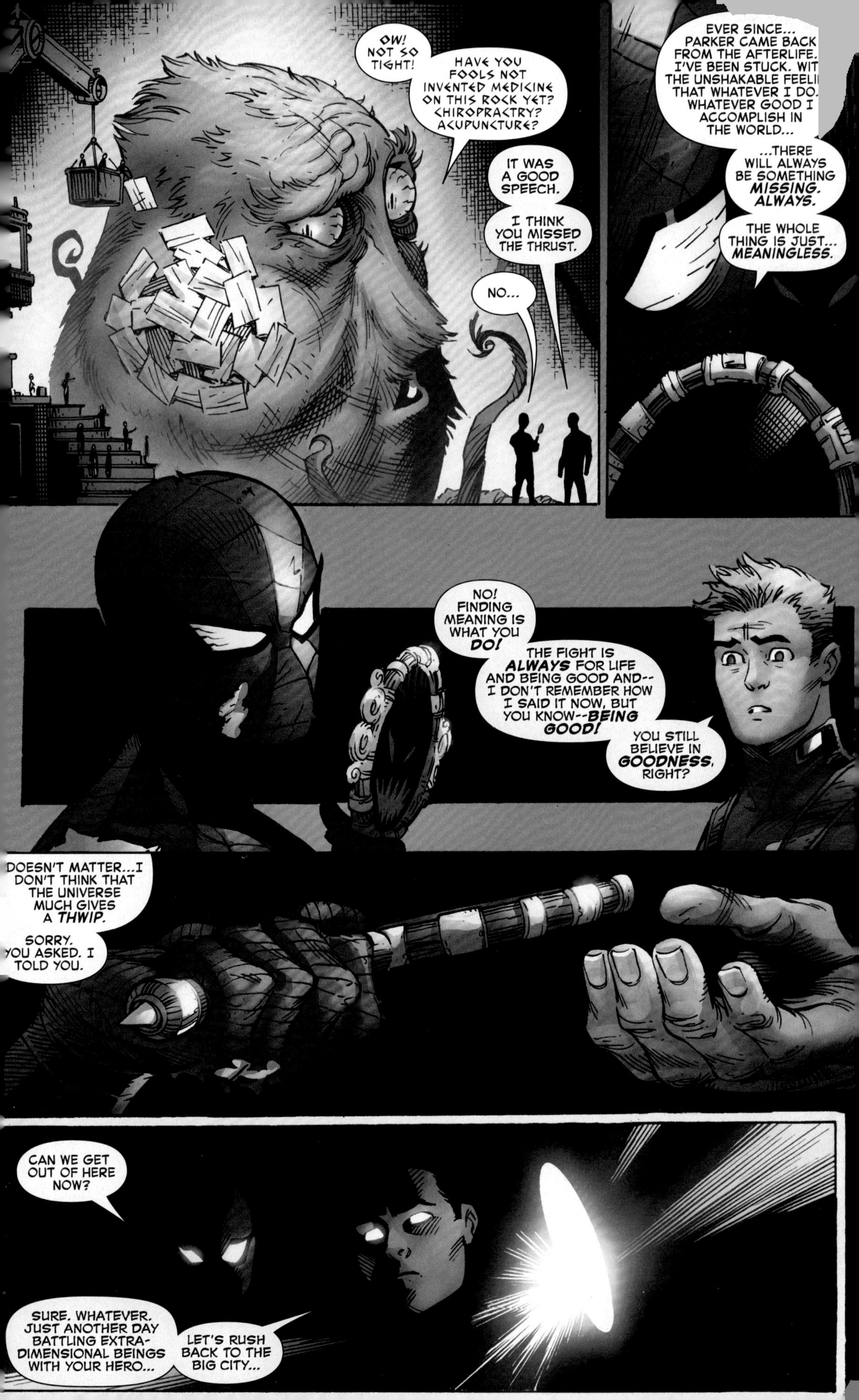
OW! NOT SO TIGHT!
HAVE YOU FOOLS NOT INVENTED MEDICINE ON THIS ROCK YET? CHIROPRACTRY? ACUPUNCTURE?
IT WAS A GOOD SPEECH.
I THINK YOU MISSED THE THRUST.
NO...
EVER SINCE... PARKER CAME BACK FROM THE AFTERLIFE. I'VE BEEN STUCK. WIT THE UNSHAKABLE FEELI THAT WHATEVER I DO. WHATEVER GOOD I ACCOMPLISH IN THE WORLD...
...THERE WILL ALWAYS BE SOMETHING MISSING. ALWAYS.
THE WHOLE THING IS JUST... MEANINGLESS.
NO! FINDING MEANING IS WHAT YOU DO!
THE FIGHT IS ALWAYS FOR LIFE AND BEING GOOD AND-- I DON'T REMEMBER HOW I SAID IT NOW, BUT YOU KNOW--BEING GOOD!
YOU STILL BELIEVE IN GOODNESS, RIGHT?
DOESN'T MATTER...I DON'T THINK THAT THE UNIVERSE MUCH GIVES A THWIP.
SORRY. YOU ASKED. I TOLD YOU.
CAN WE GET OUT OF HERE NOW?
SURE. WHATEVER. JUST ANOTHER DAY BATTLING EXTRA-DIMENSIONAL BEINGS WITH YOUR HERO...
LET'S RUSH BACK TO THE BIG CITY...

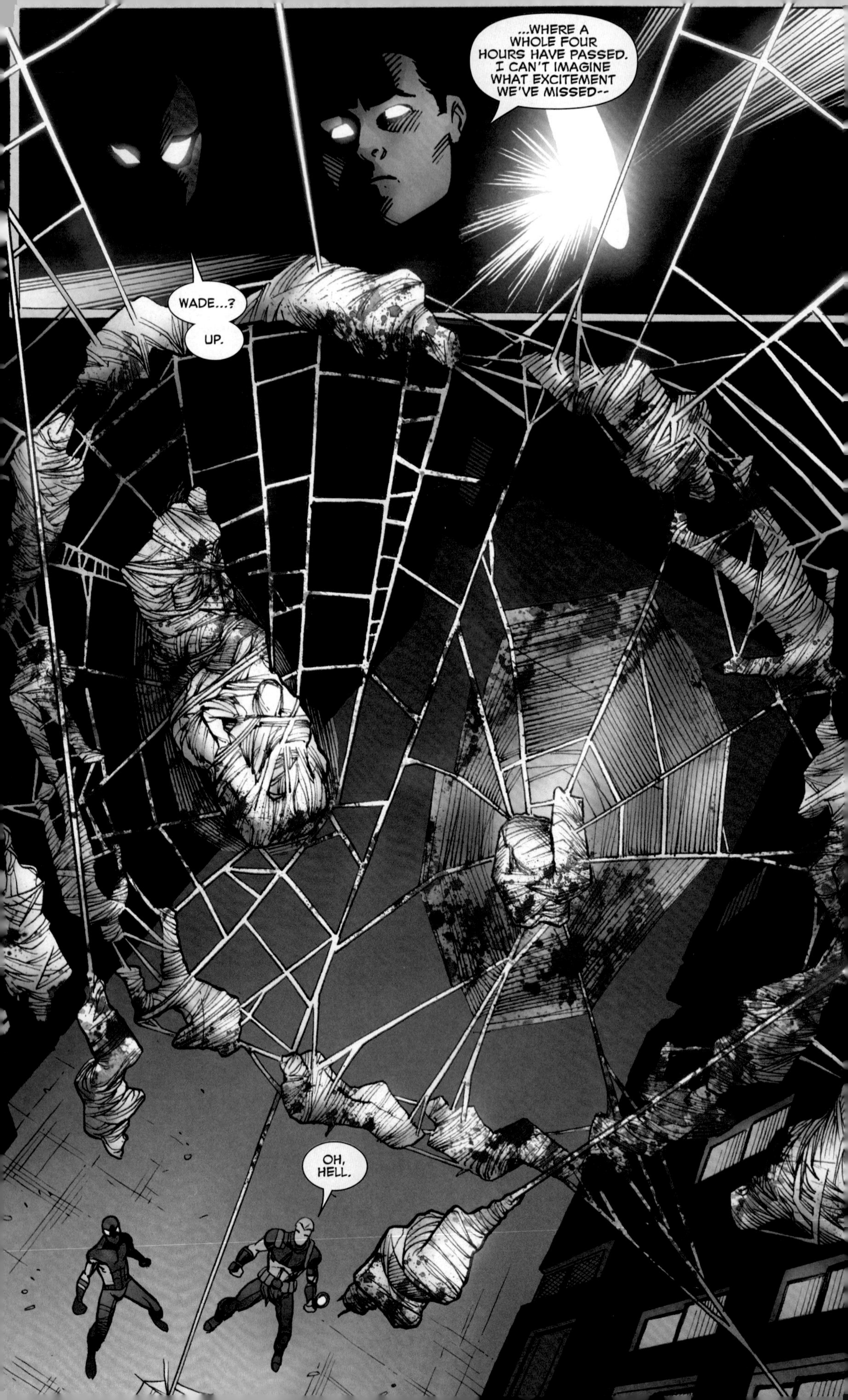
...WHERE A WHOLE FOUR HOURS HAVE PASSED. I CAN'T IMAGINE WHAT EXCITEMENT WE'VE MISSED--
WADE...?
UP.
OH, HELL.

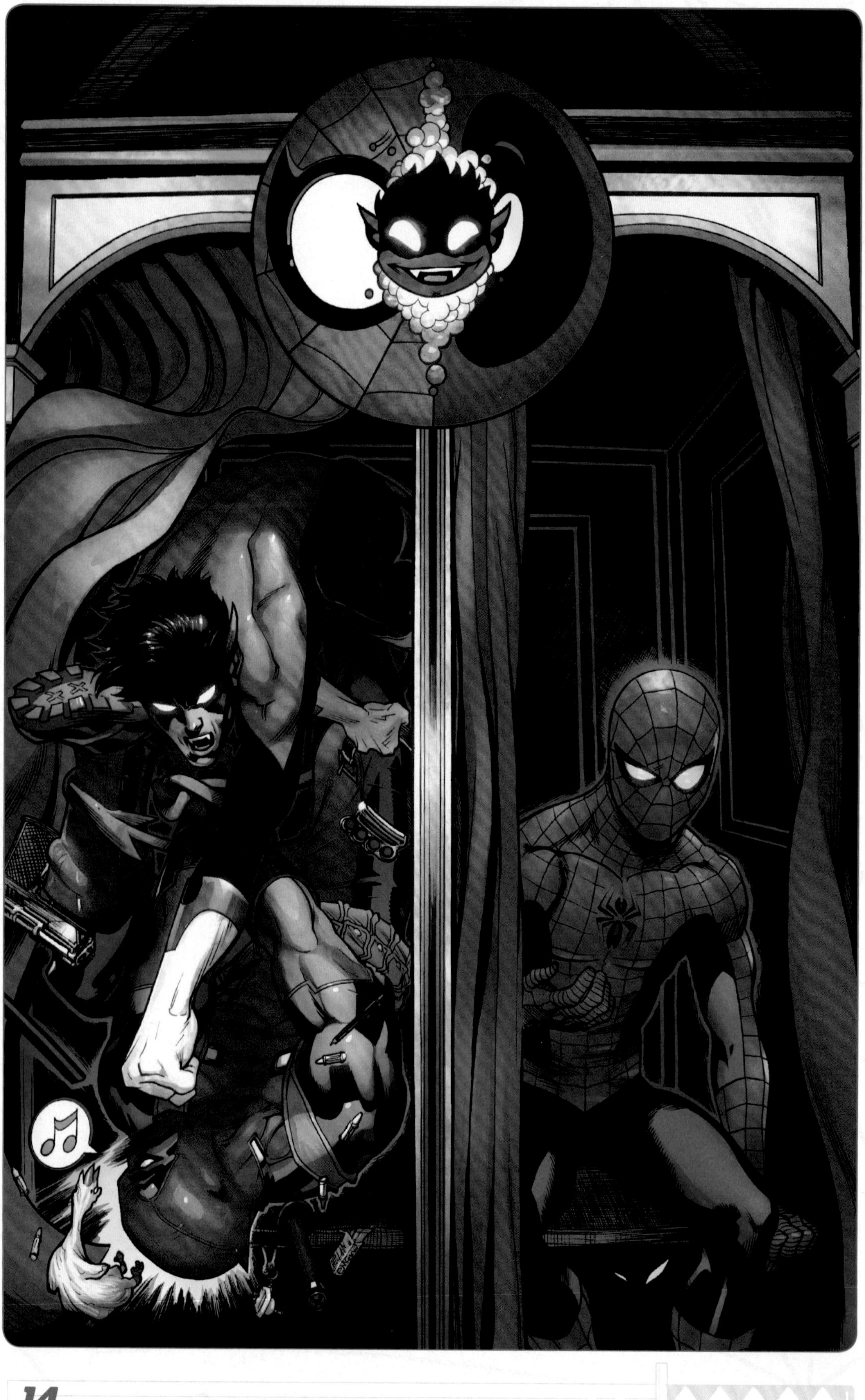

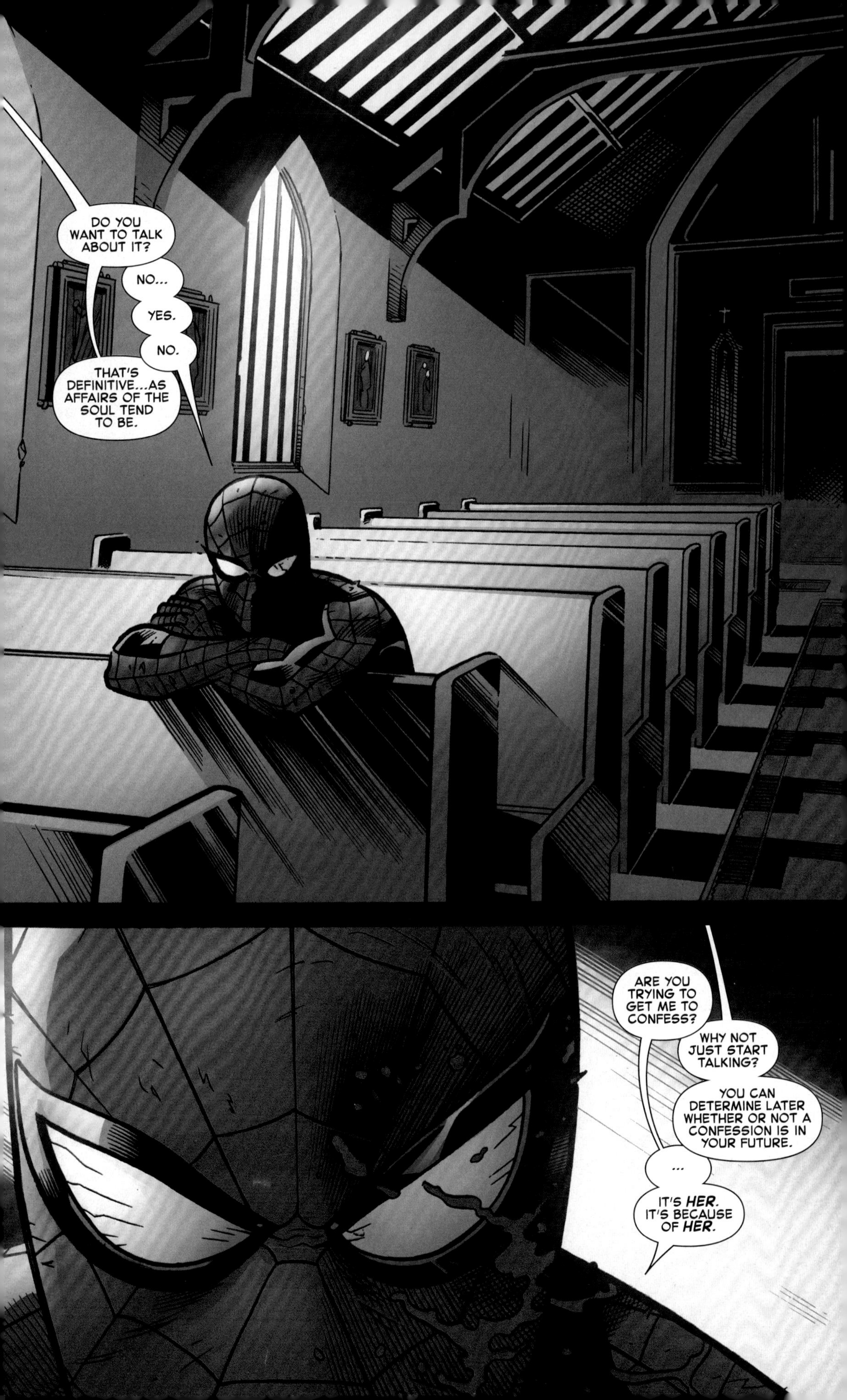
DO YOU WANT TO TALK ABOUT IT?
NO...
YES.
NO.
THAT'S DEFINITIVE...AS AFFAIRS OF THE SOUL TEND TO BE.
ARE YOU TRYING TO GET ME TO CONFESS?
WHY NOT JUST START TALKING?
YOU CAN DETERMINE LATER WHETHER OR NOT A CONFESSION IS IN YOUR FUTURE.
...
IT'S HER. IT'S BECAUSE OF HER.

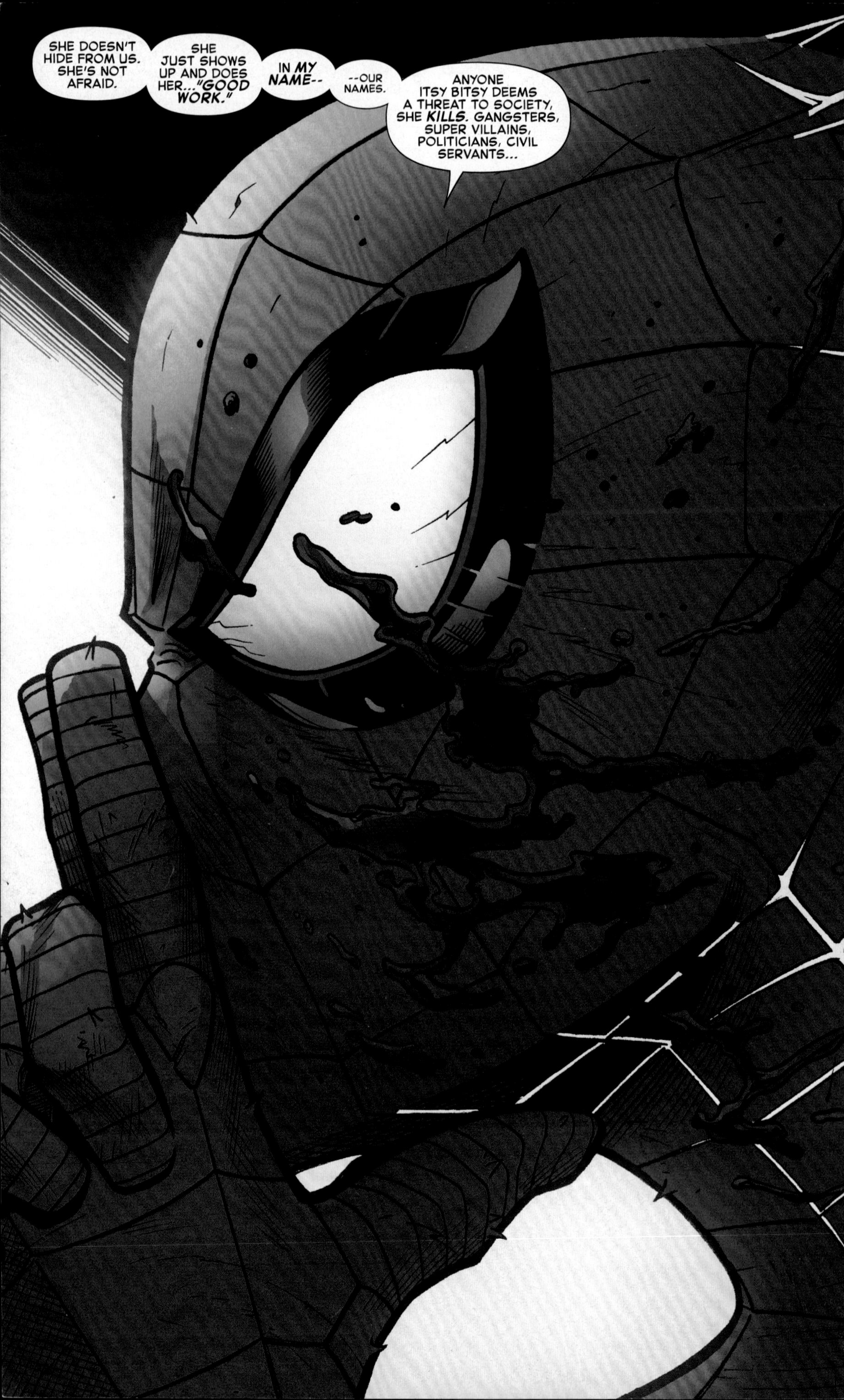
SHE DOESN'T HIDE FROM US. SHE'S NOT AFRAID.
SHE JUST SHOWS UP AND DOES HER..."GOOD WORK."
IN MY NAME--
--OUR NAMES.
ANYONE ITSY BITSY DEEMS A THREAT TO SOCIETY, SHE KILLS. GANGSTERS, SUPER VILLAINS, POLITICIANS, CIVIL SERVANTS...

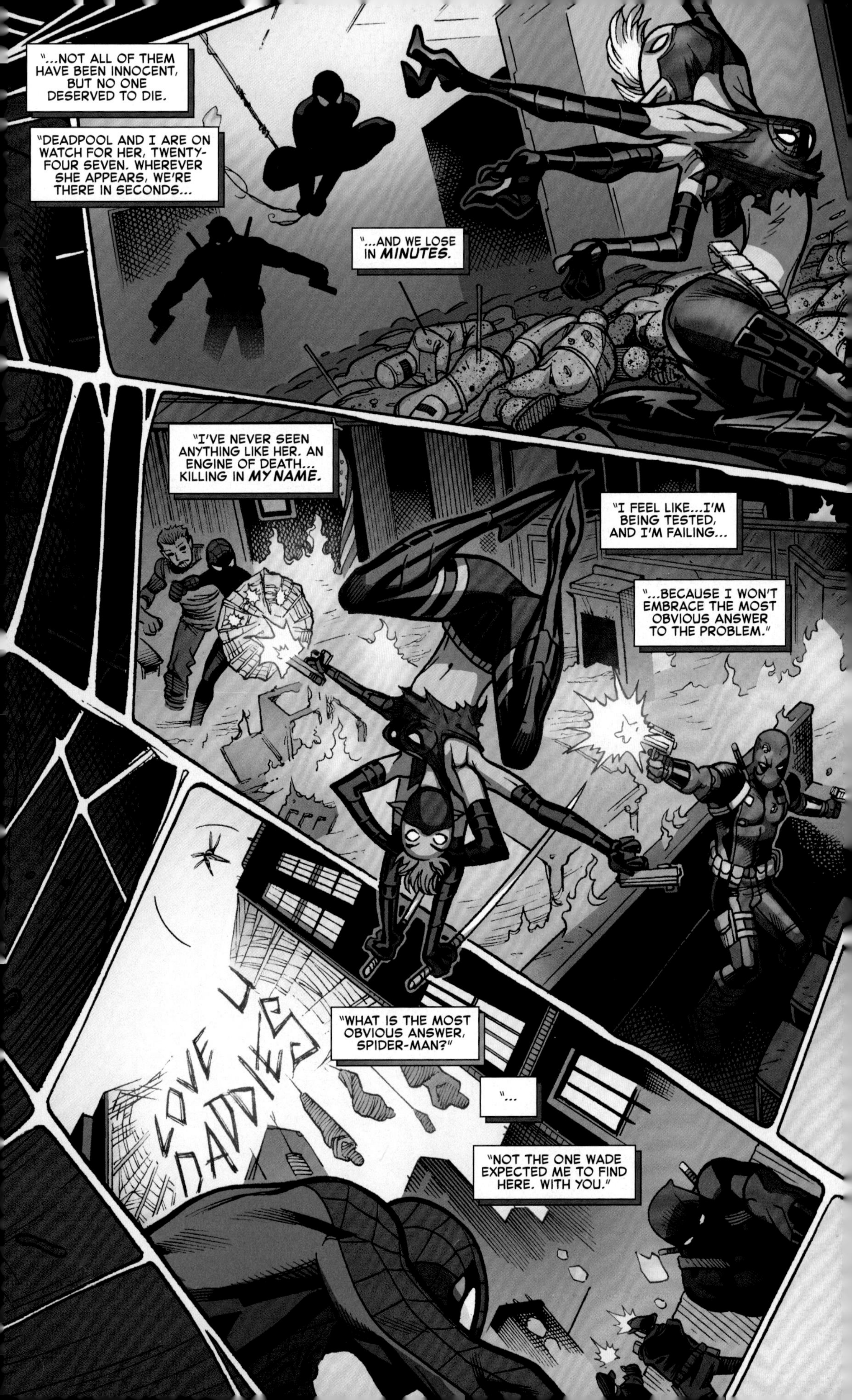
"...NOT ALL OF THEM HAVE BEEN INNOCENT, BUT NO ONE DESERVED TO DIE.
"DEADPOOL AND I ARE ON WATCH FOR HER, TWENTY-FOUR SEVEN. WHEREVER SHE APPEARS, WE'RE THERE IN SECONDS...
"...AND WE LOSE IN *MINUTES.*
"I'VE NEVER SEEN ANYTHING LIKE HER. AN ENGINE OF DEATH... KILLING IN *MY NAME.*
"I FEEL LIKE...I'M BEING TESTED, AND I'M FAILING...
"...BECAUSE I WON'T EMBRACE THE MOST OBVIOUS ANSWER TO THE PROBLEM."
LOVE U DADDIES
"WHAT IS THE MOST OBVIOUS ANSWER, SPIDER-MAN?"
"...
"NOT THE ONE WADE EXPECTED ME TO FIND HERE. WITH YOU."

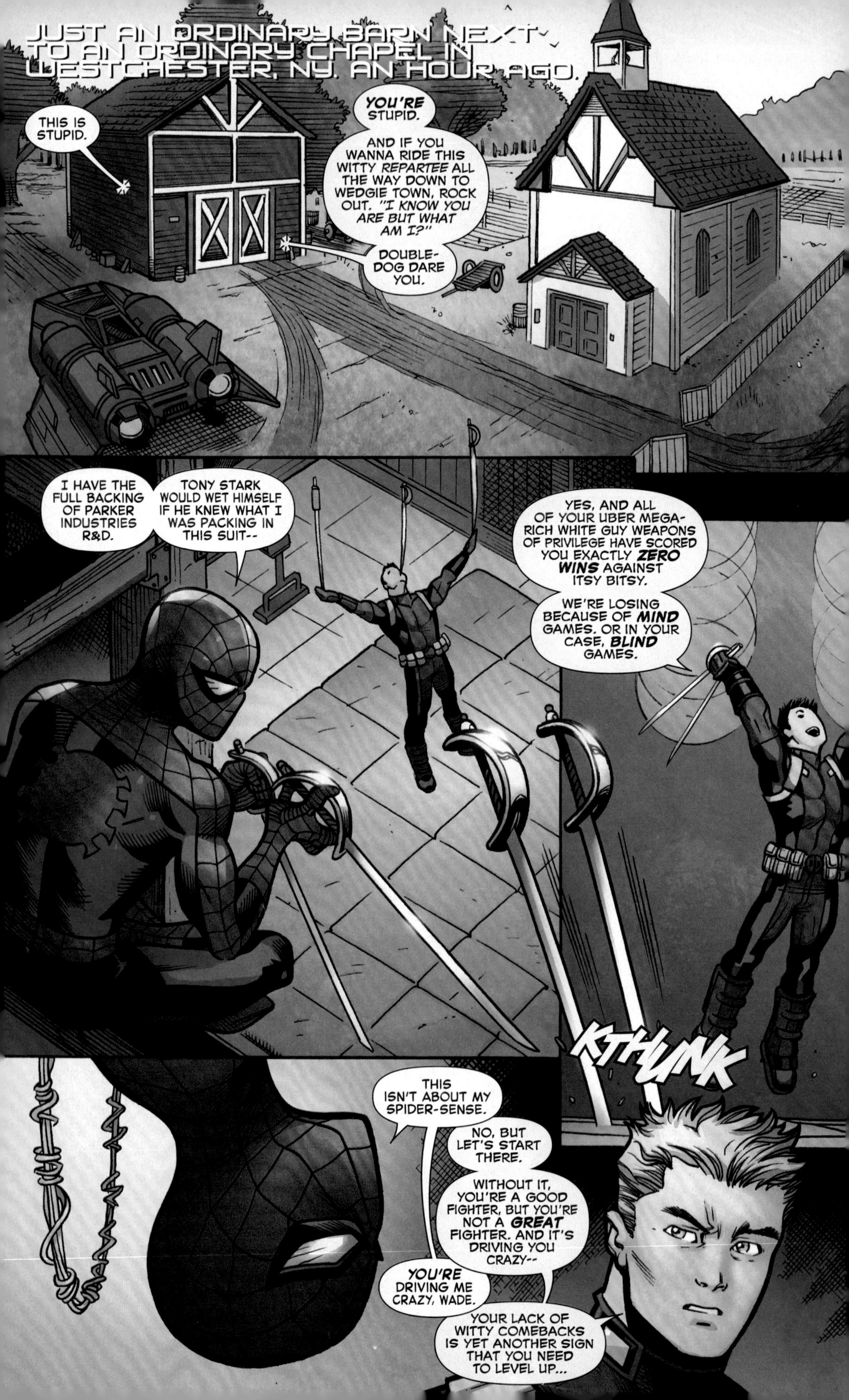
JUST AN ORDINARY BARN NEXT TO AN ORDINARY CHAPEL IN WESTCHESTER, NY. AN HOUR AGO.
THIS IS STUPID.
YOU'RE STUPID.
AND IF YOU WANNA RIDE THIS WITTY REPARTEE ALL THE WAY DOWN TO WEDGIE TOWN, ROCK OUT. "I KNOW YOU ARE BUT WHAT AM I?"
DOUBLE-DOG DARE YOU.
I HAVE THE FULL BACKING OF PARKER INDUSTRIES R&D.
TONY STARK WOULD WET HIMSELF IF HE KNEW WHAT I WAS PACKING IN THIS SUIT--
YES, AND ALL OF YOUR UBER MEGA-RICH WHITE GUY WEAPONS OF PRIVILEGE HAVE SCORED YOU EXACTLY ZERO WINS AGAINST ITSY BITSY.
WE'RE LOSING BECAUSE OF MIND GAMES. OR IN YOUR CASE, BLIND GAMES.
KTHUNK
THIS ISN'T ABOUT MY SPIDER-SENSE.
NO, BUT LET'S START THERE.
WITHOUT IT, YOU'RE A GOOD FIGHTER, BUT YOU'RE NOT A GREAT FIGHTER. AND IT'S DRIVING YOU CRAZY--
YOU'RE DRIVING ME CRAZY, WADE.
YOUR LACK OF WITTY COMEBACKS IS YET ANOTHER SIGN THAT YOU NEED TO LEVEL UP...

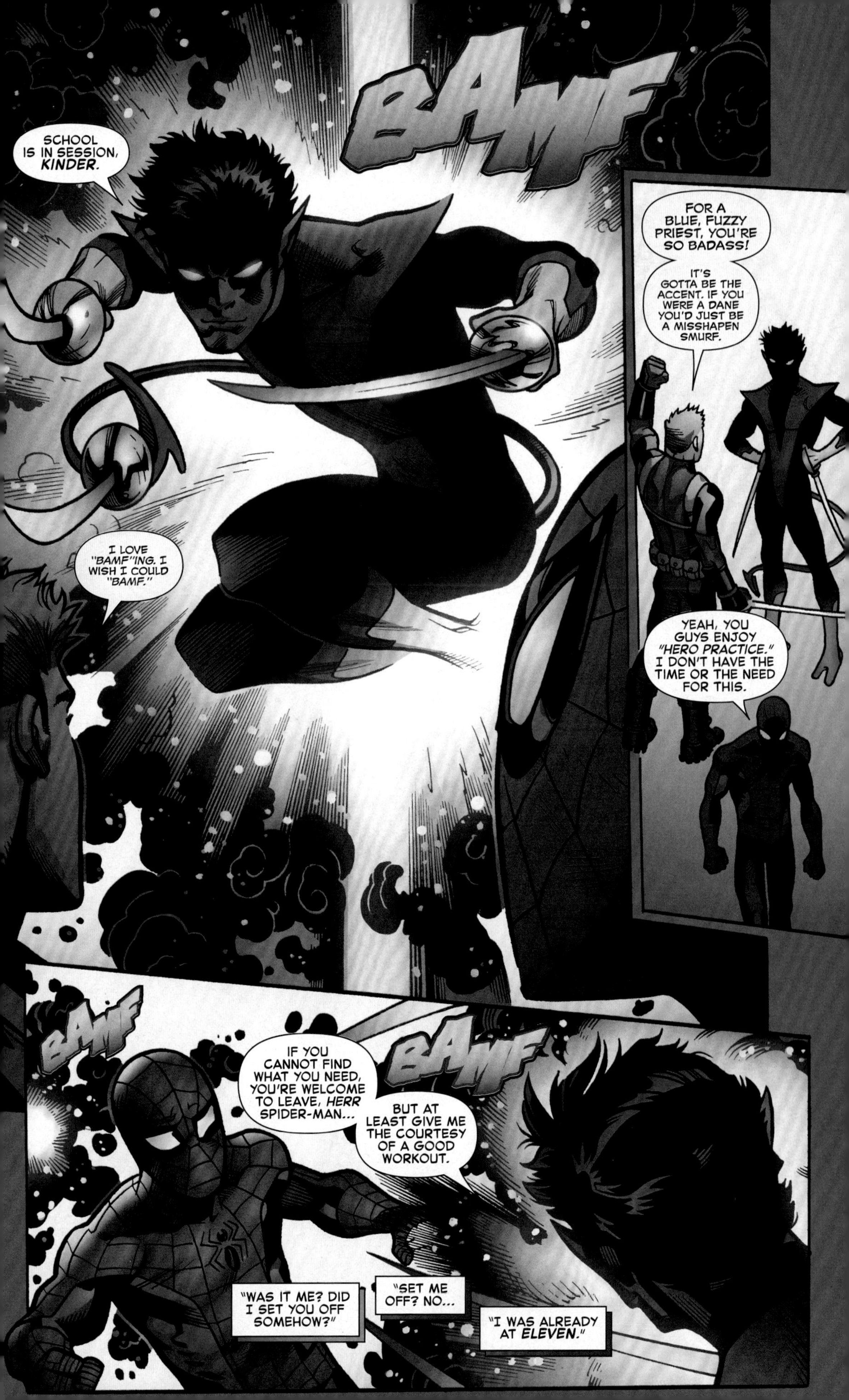
BAMF
SCHOOL IS IN SESSION, KINDER.
FOR A BLUE, FUZZY PRIEST, YOU'RE SO BADASS!
IT'S GOTTA BE THE ACCENT. IF YOU WERE A DANE YOU'D JUST BE A MISSHAPEN SMURF.
I LOVE "BAMF"ING. I WISH I COULD "BAMF."
YEAH, YOU GUYS ENJOY "HERO PRACTICE." I DON'T HAVE THE TIME OR THE NEED FOR THIS.
BAMF
BAMF
IF YOU CANNOT FIND WHAT YOU NEED, YOU'RE WELCOME TO LEAVE, HERR SPIDER-MAN...
BUT AT LEAST GIVE ME THE COURTESY OF A GOOD WORKOUT.
"WAS IT ME? DID I SET YOU OFF SOMEHOW?"
"SET ME OFF? NO...
"I WAS ALREADY AT ELEVEN."

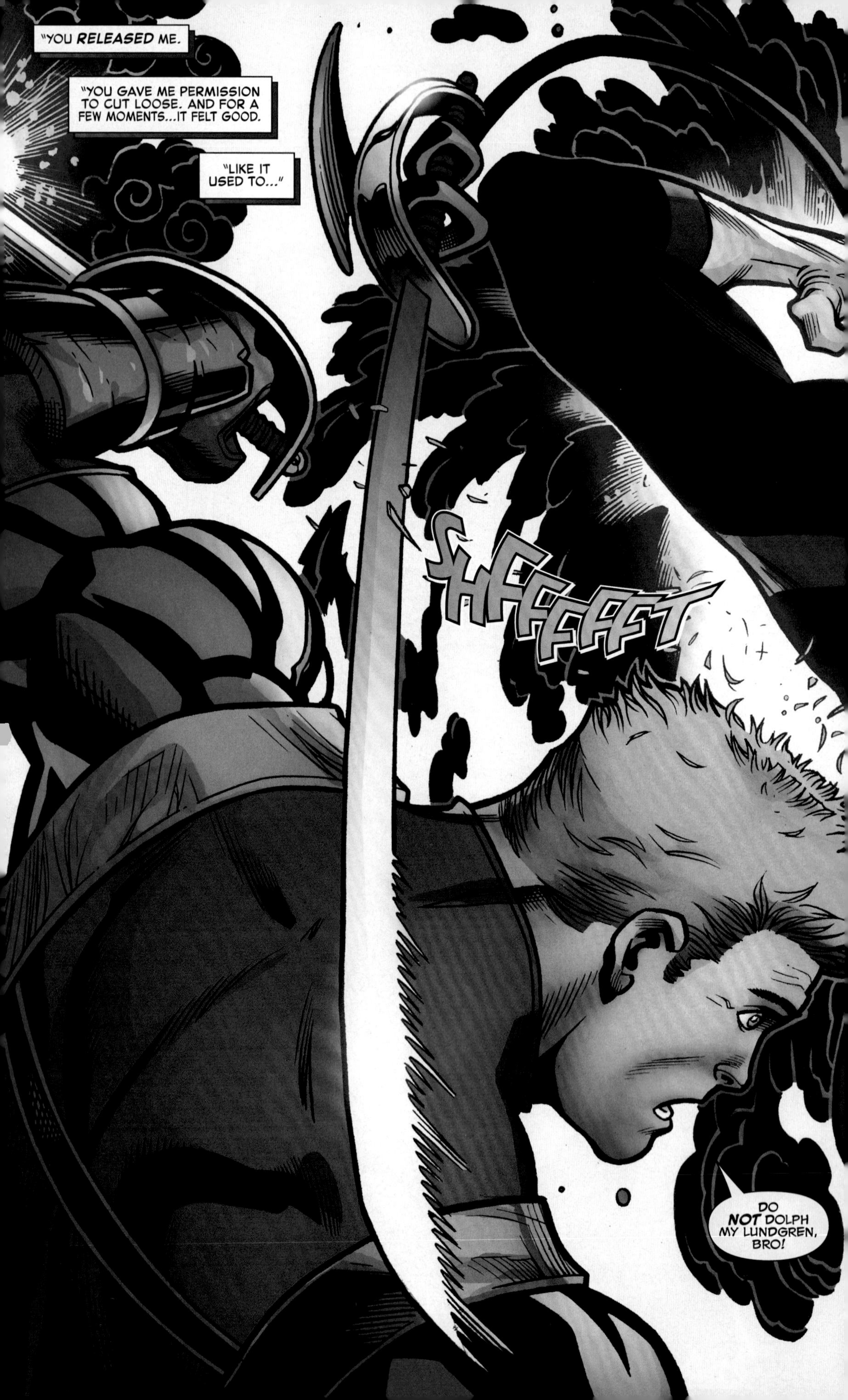
"YOU **RELEASED** ME.
"YOU GAVE ME PERMISSION TO CUT LOOSE. AND FOR A FEW MOMENTS...IT FELT GOOD.
"LIKE IT USED TO..."
SHFFFFFT
DO **NOT** DOLPH MY LUNDGREN, BRO!

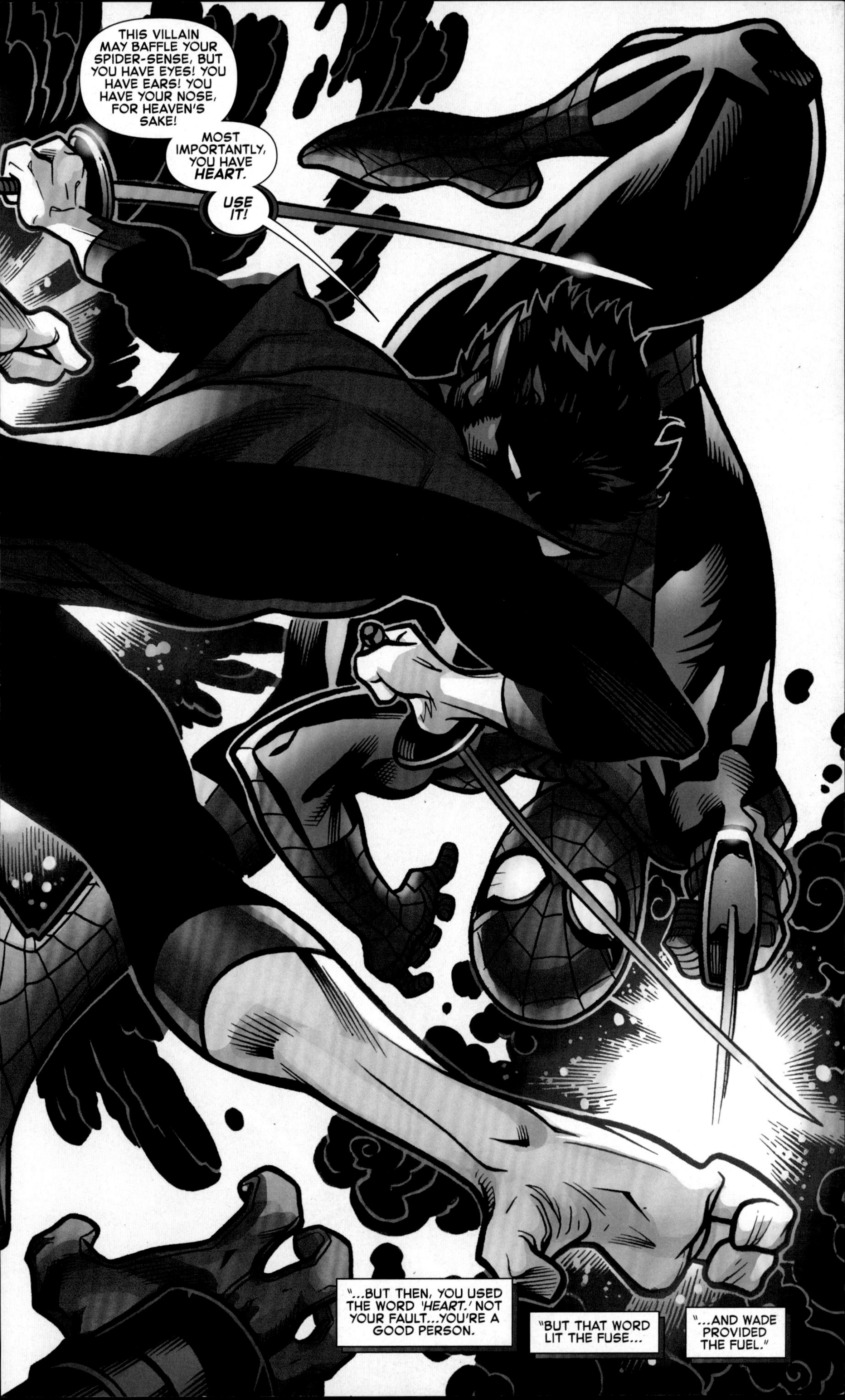
THIS VILLAIN MAY BAFFLE YOUR SPIDER-SENSE, BUT YOU HAVE EYES! YOU HAVE EARS! YOU HAVE YOUR NOSE, FOR HEAVEN'S SAKE!
MOST IMPORTANTLY, YOU HAVE *HEART.*
USE IT!
"...BUT THEN, YOU USED THE WORD *'HEART.'* NOT YOUR FAULT...YOU'RE A GOOD PERSON.
"BUT THAT WORD LIT THE FUSE...
"...AND WADE PROVIDED THE FUEL."

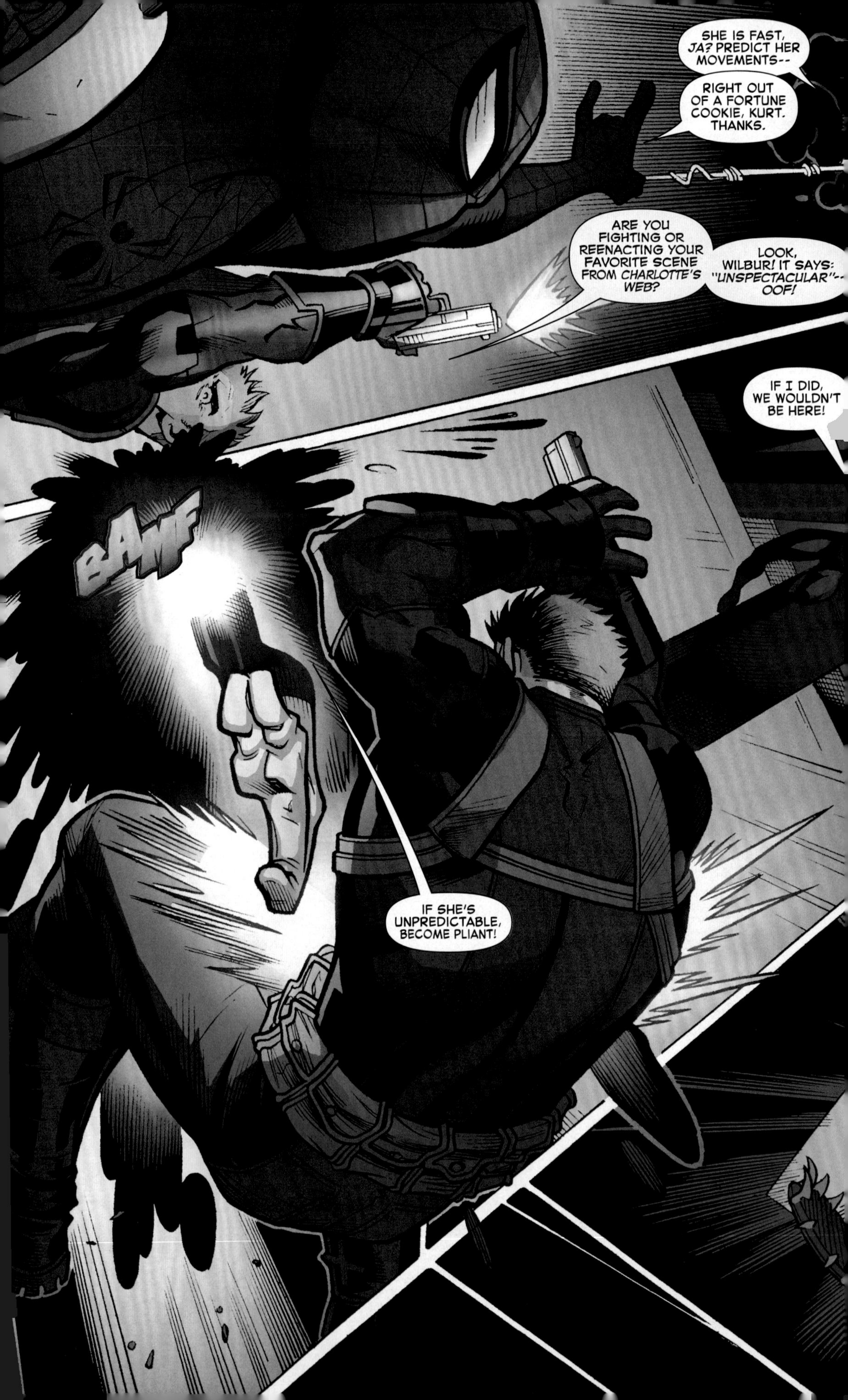
SHE IS FAST, JA? PREDICT HER MOVEMENTS--
RIGHT OUT OF A FORTUNE COOKIE, KURT. THANKS.
ARE YOU FIGHTING OR REENACTING YOUR FAVORITE SCENE FROM CHARLOTTE'S WEB?
LOOK, WILBUR! IT SAYS: "UNSPECTACULAR"-- OOF!
IF I DID, WE WOULDN'T BE HERE!
BAMF
IF SHE'S UNPREDICTABLE, BECOME PLIANT!

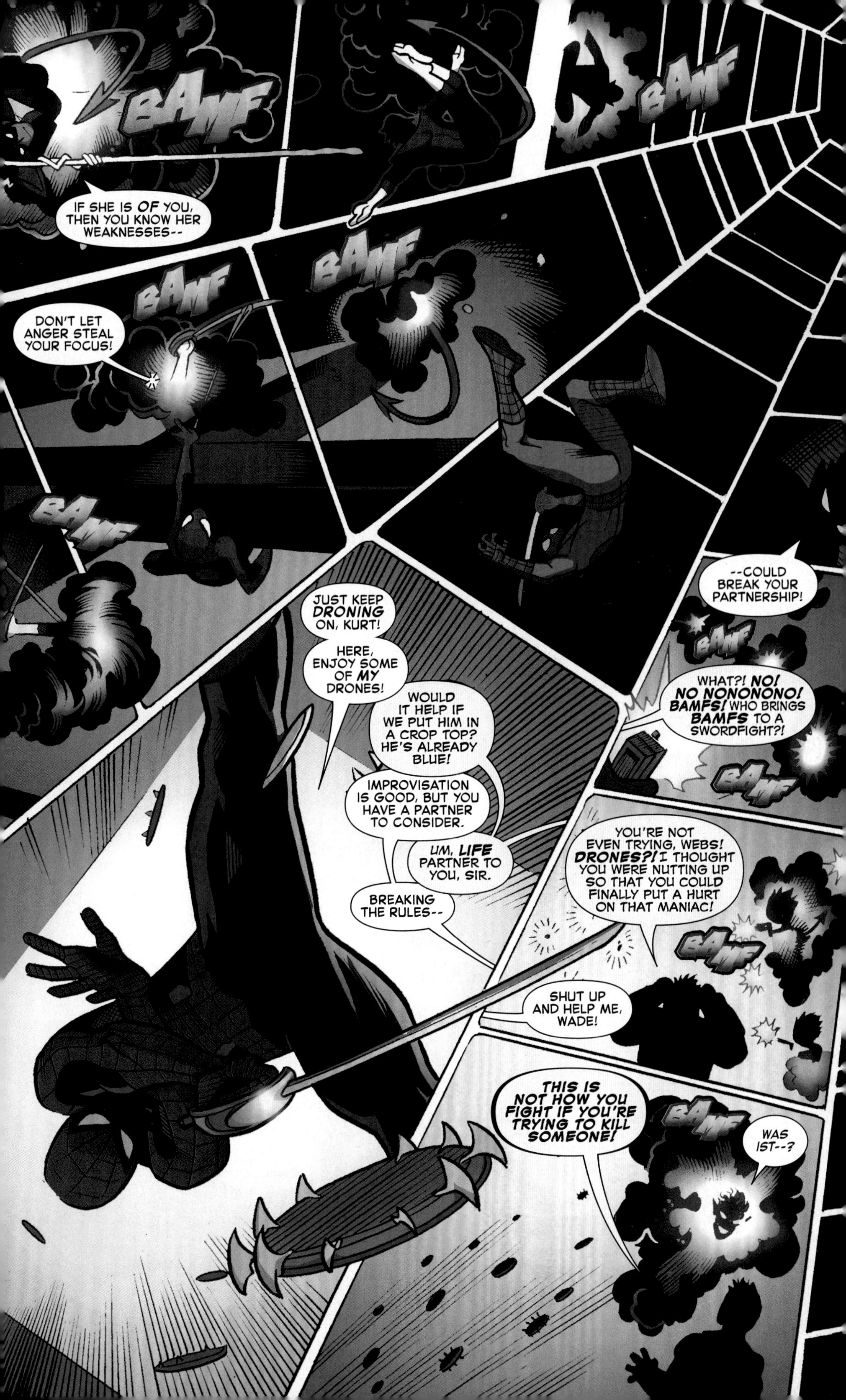
BAMF
BAMF
BAMF
IF SHE IS OF YOU, THEN YOU KNOW HER WEAKNESSES--
BAMF
DON'T LET ANGER STEAL YOUR FOCUS!
BAMF
BAMF
--COULD BREAK YOUR PARTNERSHIP!
BAMF
WHAT?! NO! NO NONONONO! BAMFS! WHO BRINGS BAMFS TO A SWORDFIGHT?!
BAMF
JUST KEEP DRONING ON, KURT!
HERE, ENJOY SOME OF MY DRONES!
WOULD IT HELP IF WE PUT HIM IN A CROP TOP? HE'S ALREADY BLUE!
IMPROVISATION IS GOOD, BUT YOU HAVE A PARTNER TO CONSIDER.
UM, LIFE PARTNER TO YOU, SIR.
BREAKING THE RULES--
YOU'RE NOT EVEN TRYING, WEBS! DRONES?! I THOUGHT YOU WERE NUTTING UP SO THAT YOU COULD FINALLY PUT A HURT ON THAT MANIAC!
BAMF
SHUT UP AND HELP ME, WADE!
THIS IS NOT HOW YOU FIGHT IF YOU'RE TRYING TO KILL SOMEONE!
BAMF
WAS IST--?

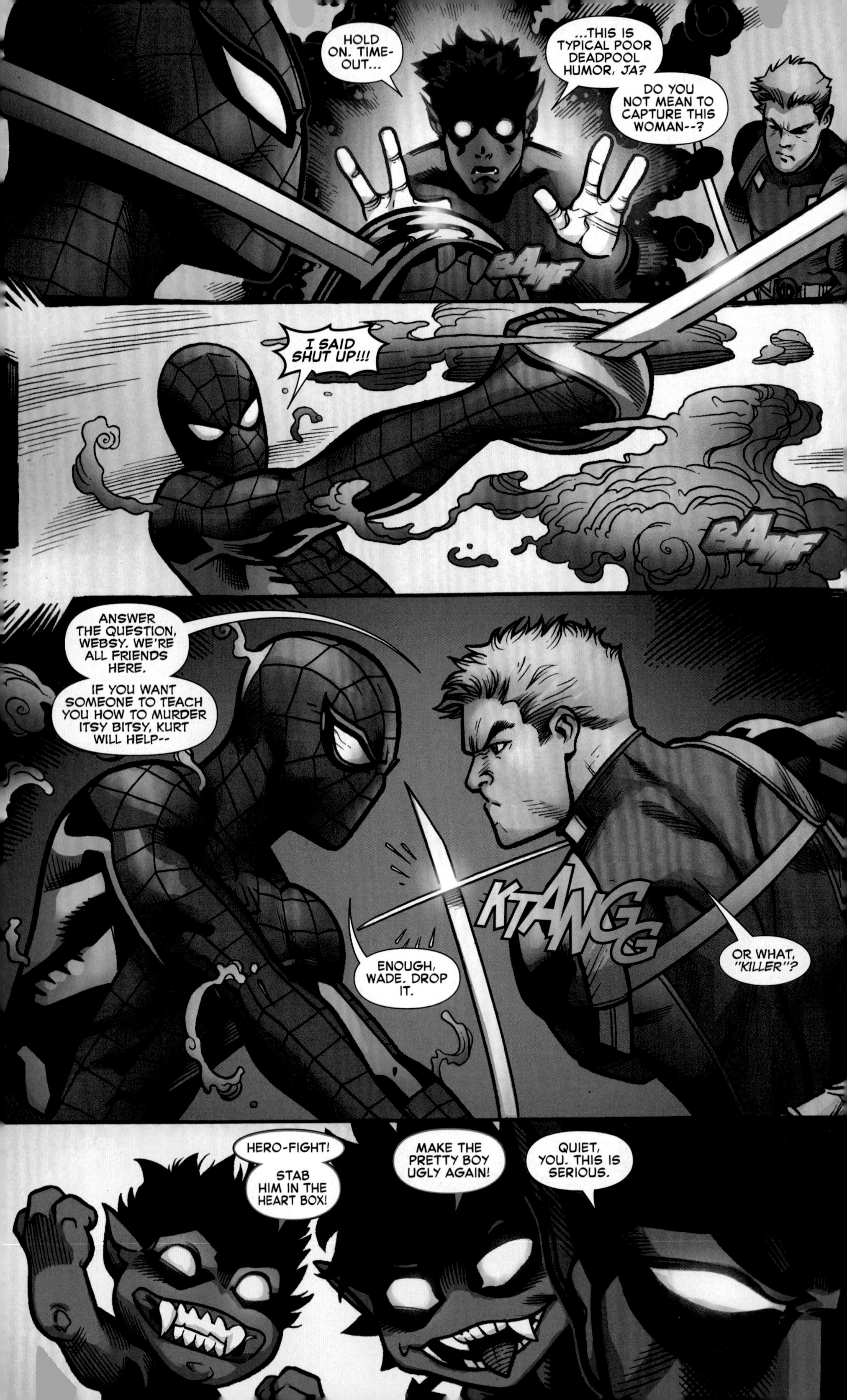
HOLD ON. TIME-OUT...
...THIS IS TYPICAL POOR DEADPOOL HUMOR, JA?
DO YOU NOT MEAN TO CAPTURE THIS WOMAN--?
BAMF
I SAID SHUT UP!!!
BAMF
ANSWER THE QUESTION, WEBSY. WE'RE ALL FRIENDS HERE.
IF YOU WANT SOMEONE TO TEACH YOU HOW TO MURDER ITSY BITSY, KURT WILL HELP--
KTANGG
ENOUGH, WADE. DROP IT.
OR WHAT, "KILLER"?
HERO-FIGHT!
STAB HIM IN THE HEART BOX!
MAKE THE PRETTY BOY UGLY AGAIN!
QUIET, YOU. THIS IS SERIOUS.

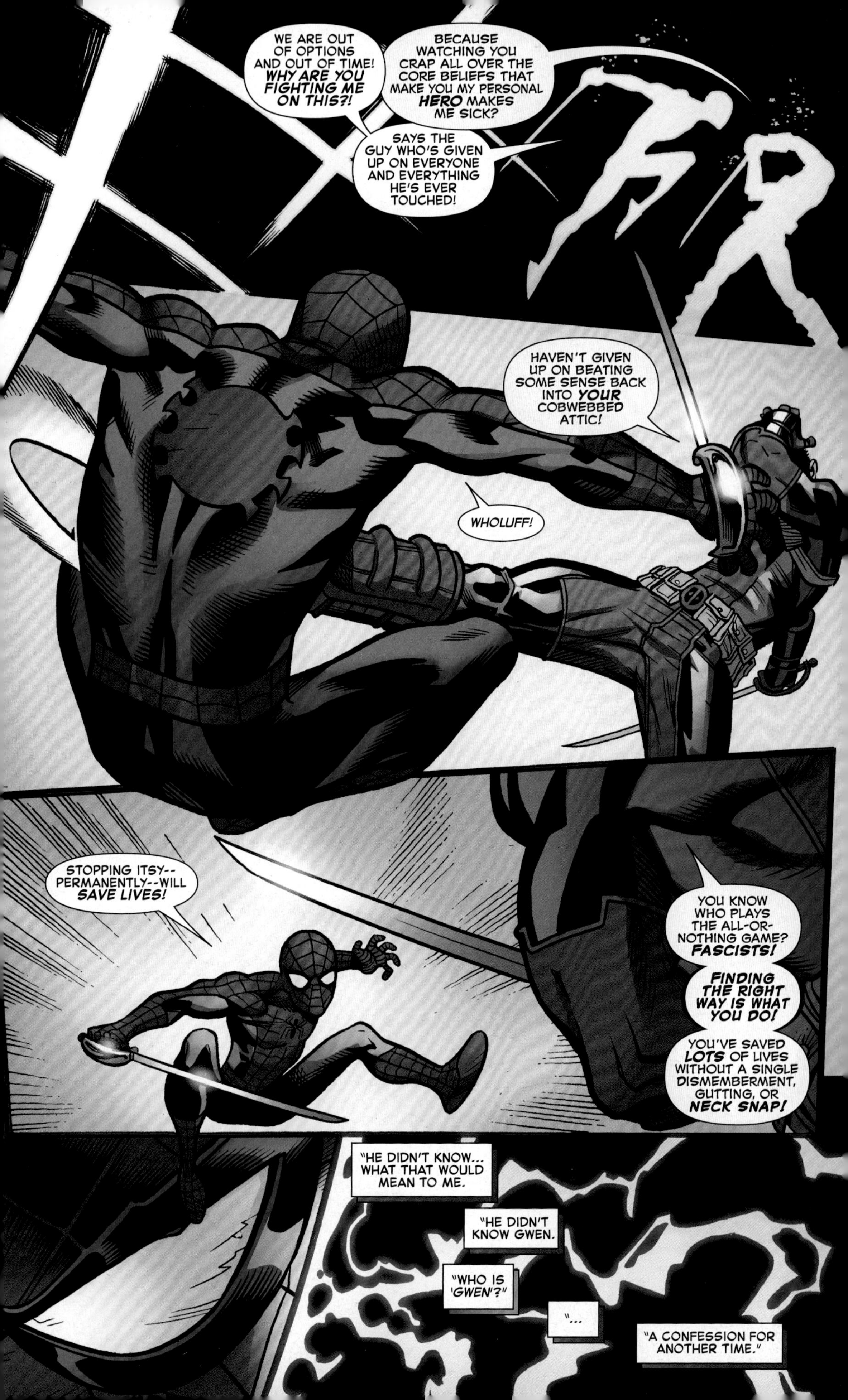
WE ARE OUT OF OPTIONS AND OUT OF TIME! WHY ARE YOU FIGHTING ME ON THIS?!
BECAUSE WATCHING YOU CRAP ALL OVER THE CORE BELIEFS THAT MAKE YOU MY PERSONAL HERO MAKES ME SICK?
SAYS THE GUY WHO'S GIVEN UP ON EVERYONE AND EVERYTHING HE'S EVER TOUCHED!
HAVEN'T GIVEN UP ON BEATING SOME SENSE BACK INTO YOUR COBWEBBED ATTIC!
WHOLUFF!
STOPPING ITSY--PERMANENTLY--WILL SAVE LIVES!
YOU KNOW WHO PLAYS THE ALL-OR-NOTHING GAME? FASCISTS!
FINDING THE RIGHT WAY IS WHAT YOU DO!
YOU'VE SAVED LOTS OF LIVES WITHOUT A SINGLE DISMEMBERMENT, GUTTING, OR NECK SNAP!
"HE DIDN'T KNOW... WHAT THAT WOULD MEAN TO ME.
"HE DIDN'T KNOW GWEN.
"WHO IS 'GWEN'?"
"...
"A CONFESSION FOR ANOTHER TIME."

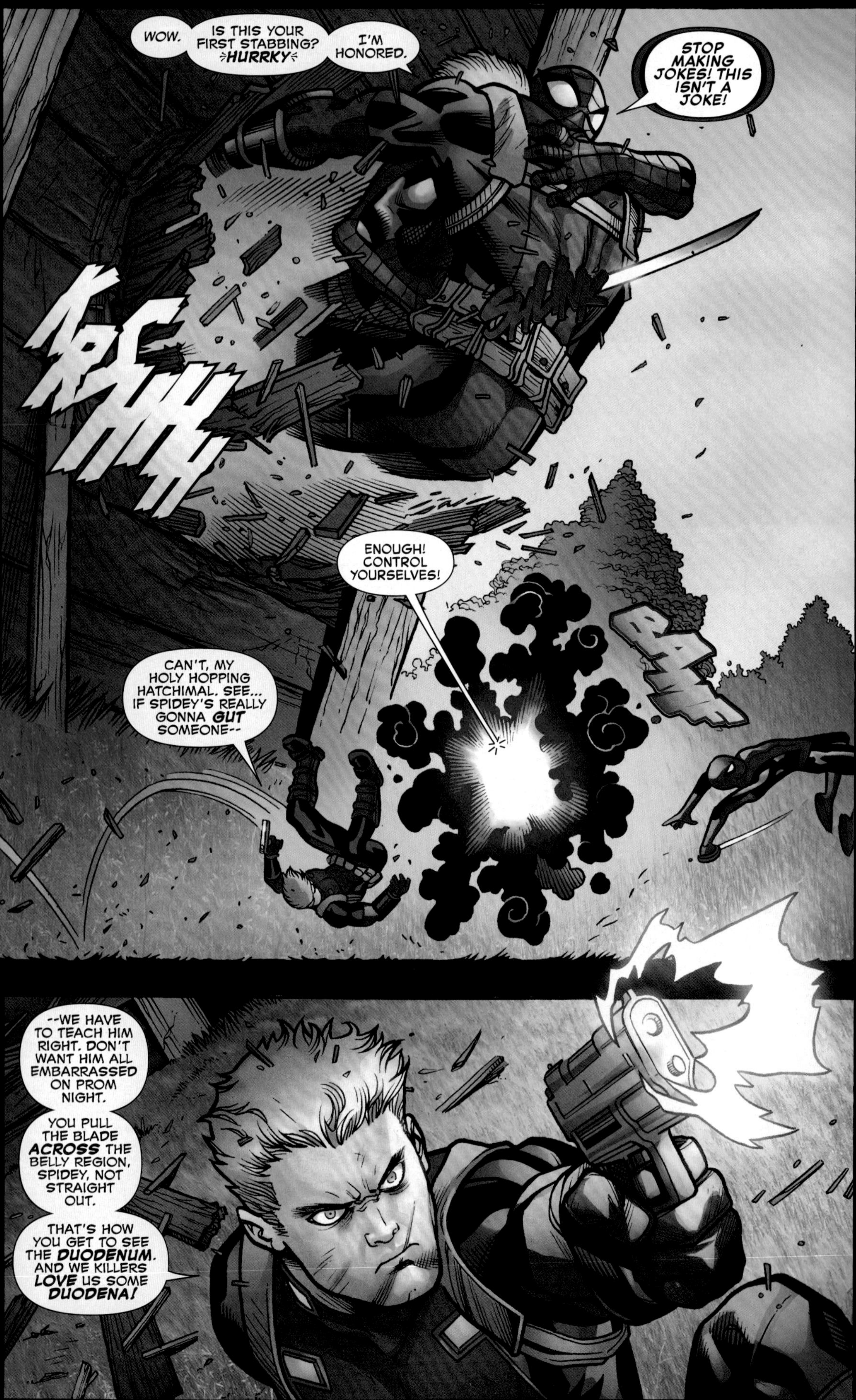
WOW.
IS THIS YOUR FIRST STABBING? *HURRKY*
I'M HONORED.
STOP MAKING JOKES! THIS ISN'T A JOKE!
ENOUGH! CONTROL YOURSELVES!
CAN'T, MY HOLY HOPPING HATCHIMAL. SEE... IF SPIDEY'S REALLY GONNA *GUT* SOMEONE--
--WE HAVE TO TEACH HIM RIGHT. DON'T WANT HIM ALL EMBARRASSED ON PROM NIGHT.
YOU PULL THE BLADE *ACROSS* THE BELLY REGION, SPIDEY, NOT STRAIGHT OUT.
THAT'S HOW YOU GET TO SEE THE *DUODENUM.* AND WE KILLERS *LOVE* US SOME *DUODENA!*

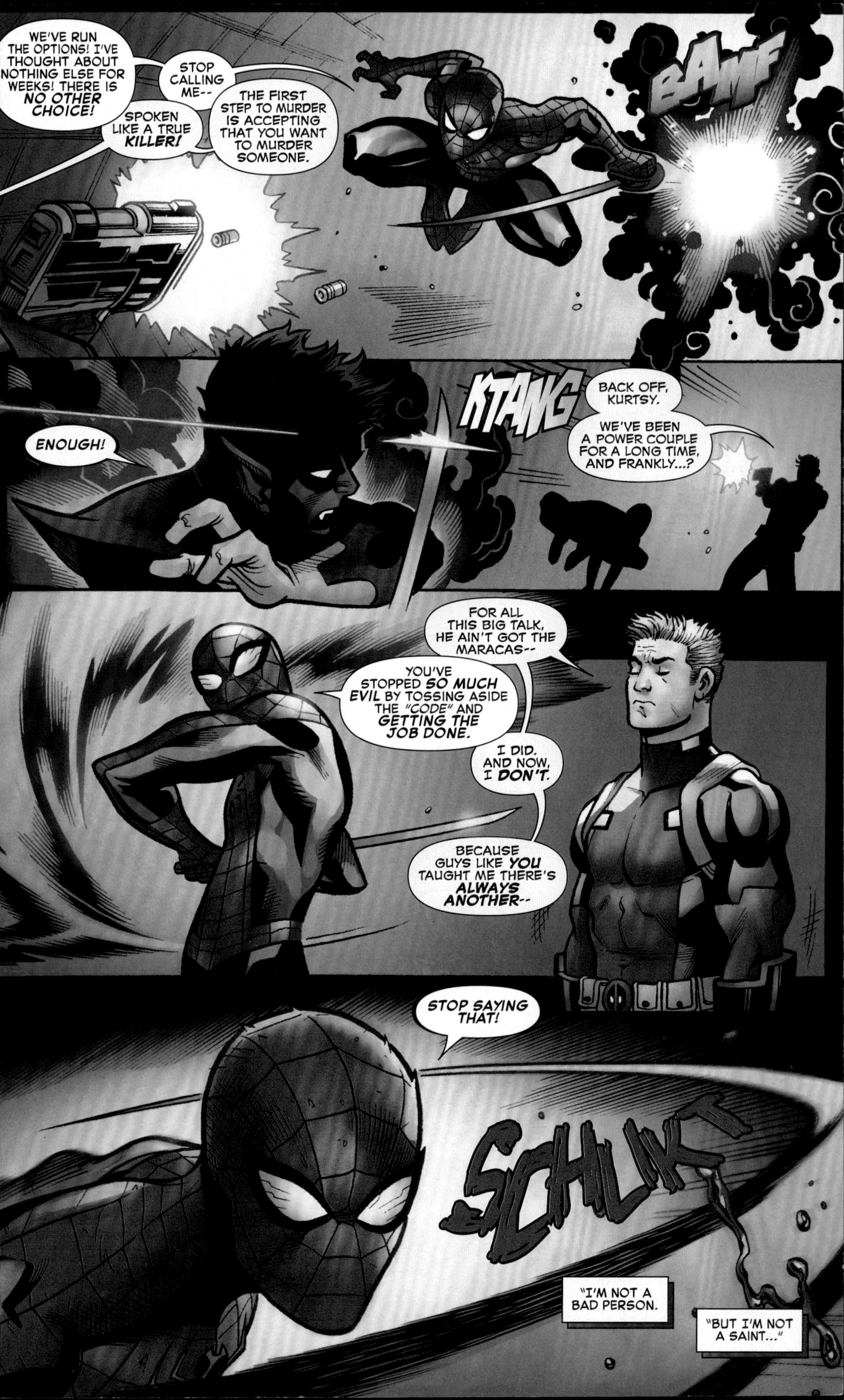

WE'VE RUN THE OPTIONS! I'VE THOUGHT ABOUT NOTHING ELSE FOR WEEKS! THERE IS NO OTHER CHOICE!
STOP CALLING ME--
SPOKEN LIKE A TRUE KILLER!
THE FIRST STEP TO MURDER IS ACCEPTING THAT YOU WANT TO MURDER SOMEONE.
BAMF
ENOUGH!
KTANG
BACK OFF, KURTSY.
WE'VE BEEN A POWER COUPLE FOR A LONG TIME, AND FRANKLY...?
FOR ALL THIS BIG TALK, HE AIN'T GOT THE MARACAS--
YOU'VE STOPPED SO MUCH EVIL BY TOSSING ASIDE THE "CODE" AND GETTING THE JOB DONE.
I DID. AND NOW, I DON'T.
BECAUSE GUYS LIKE YOU TAUGHT ME THERE'S ALWAYS ANOTHER--
STOP SAYING THAT!
SCHUKT
"I'M NOT A BAD PERSON.
"BUT I'M NOT A SAINT..."

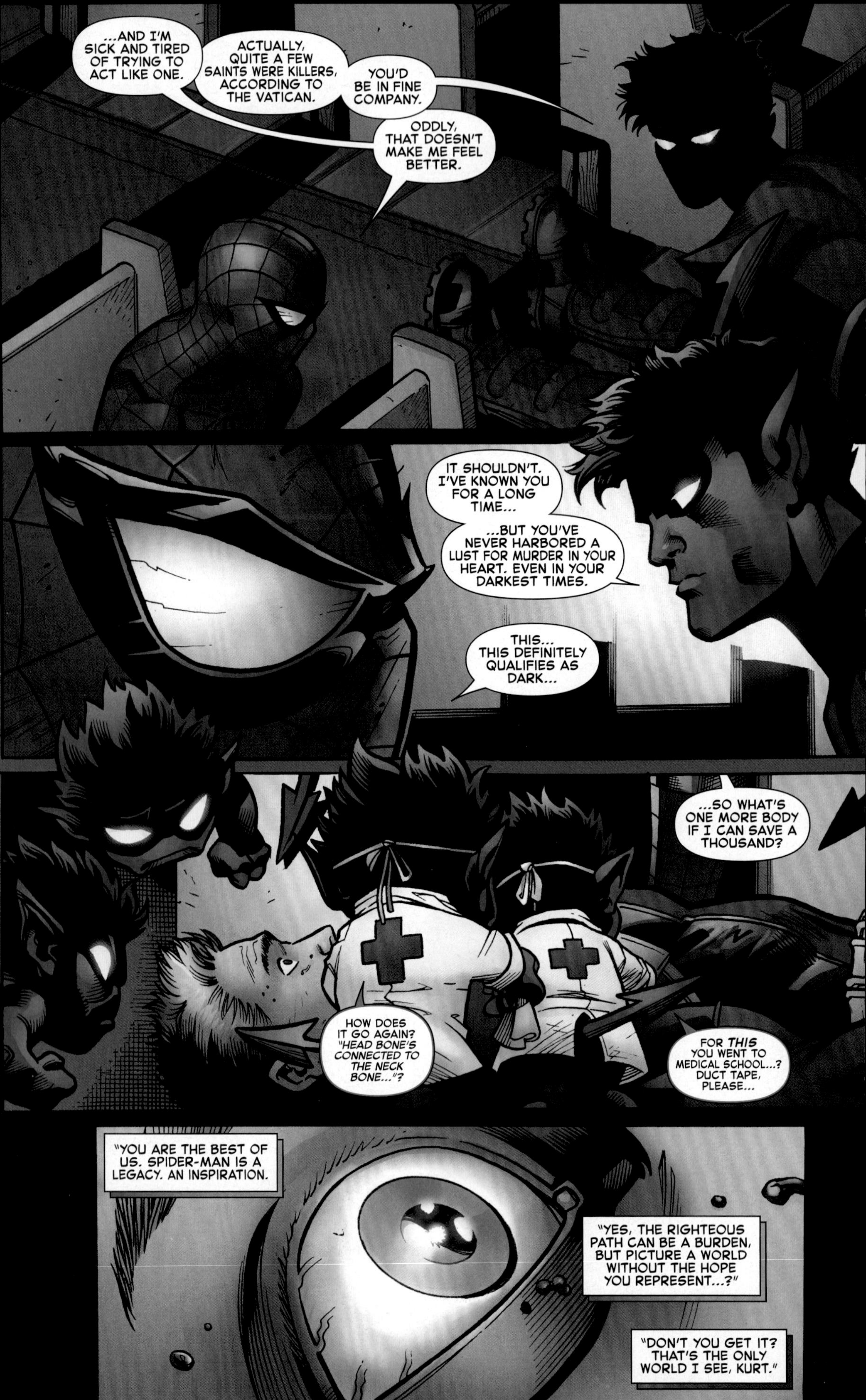
...AND I'M SICK AND TIRED OF TRYING TO ACT LIKE ONE.
ACTUALLY, QUITE A FEW SAINTS WERE KILLERS, ACCORDING TO THE VATICAN.
YOU'D BE IN FINE COMPANY.
ODDLY, THAT DOESN'T MAKE ME FEEL BETTER.
IT SHOULDN'T. I'VE KNOWN YOU FOR A LONG TIME...
...BUT YOU'VE NEVER HARBORED A LUST FOR MURDER IN YOUR HEART. EVEN IN YOUR DARKEST TIMES.
THIS... THIS DEFINITELY QUALIFIES AS DARK...
...SO WHAT'S ONE MORE BODY IF I CAN SAVE A THOUSAND?
HOW DOES IT GO AGAIN? "HEAD BONE'S CONNECTED TO THE NECK BONE..."?
FOR THIS YOU WENT TO MEDICAL SCHOOL...? DUCT TAPE, PLEASE...
"YOU ARE THE BEST OF US. SPIDER-MAN IS A LEGACY. AN INSPIRATION.
"YES, THE RIGHTEOUS PATH CAN BE A BURDEN, BUT PICTURE A WORLD WITHOUT THE HOPE YOU REPRESENT...?"
"DON'T YOU GET IT? THAT'S THE ONLY WORLD I SEE, KURT."

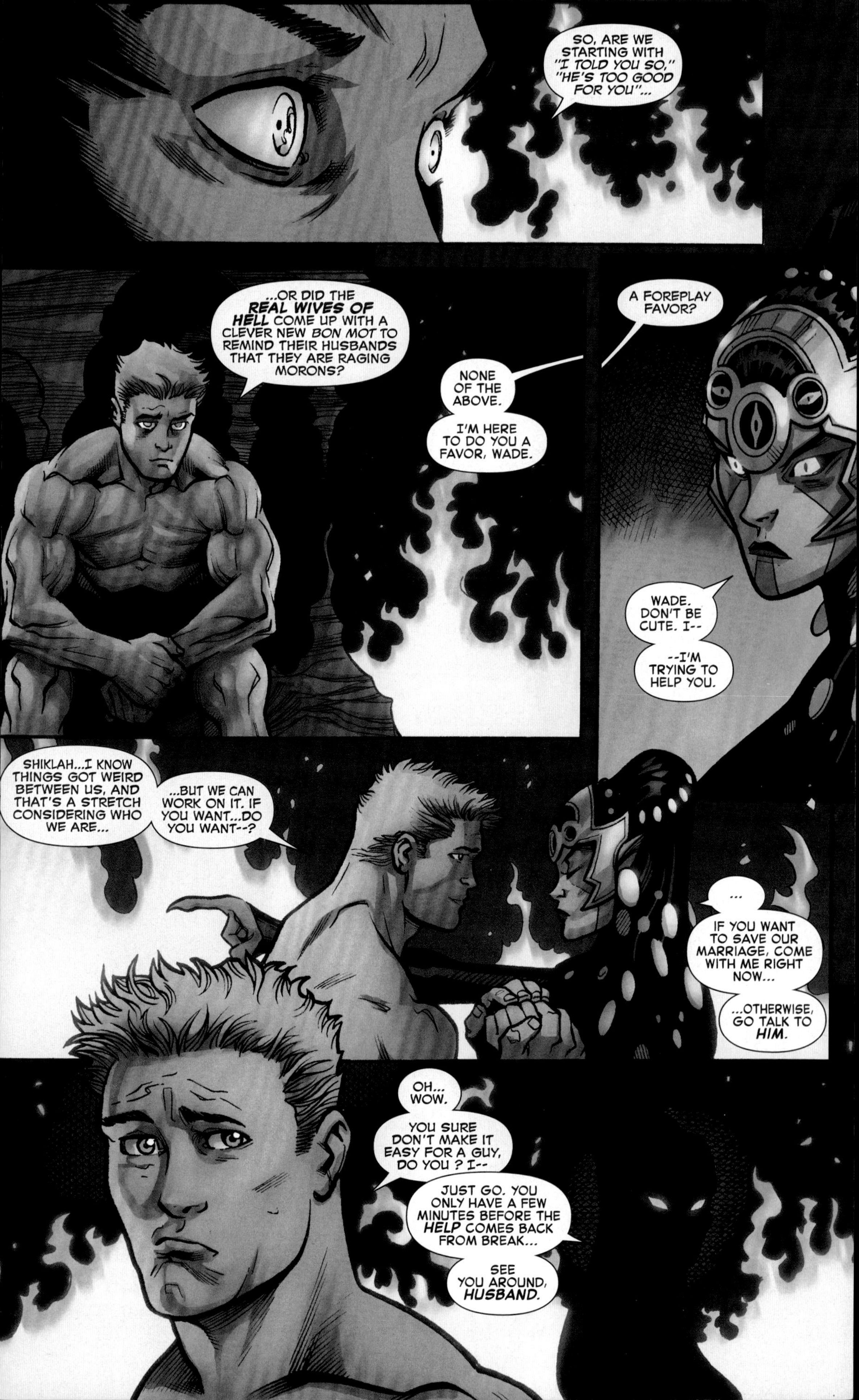
SO, ARE WE STARTING WITH "I TOLD YOU SO," "HE'S TOO GOOD FOR YOU"...
...OR DID THE REAL WIVES OF HELL COME UP WITH A CLEVER NEW BON MOT TO REMIND THEIR HUSBANDS THAT THEY ARE RAGING MORONS?
NONE OF THE ABOVE.
I'M HERE TO DO YOU A FAVOR, WADE.
A FOREPLAY FAVOR?
WADE. DON'T BE CUTE. I--
--I'M TRYING TO HELP YOU.
SHIKLAH...I KNOW THINGS GOT WEIRD BETWEEN US, AND THAT'S A STRETCH CONSIDERING WHO WE ARE...
...BUT WE CAN WORK ON IT. IF YOU WANT...DO YOU WANT--?
...
IF YOU WANT TO SAVE OUR MARRIAGE, COME WITH ME RIGHT NOW...
...OTHERWISE, GO TALK TO HIM.
OH... WOW.
YOU SURE DON'T MAKE IT EASY FOR A GUY, DO YOU? I--
JUST GO. YOU ONLY HAVE A FEW MINUTES BEFORE THE HELP COMES BACK FROM BREAK...
SEE YOU AROUND, HUSBAND.

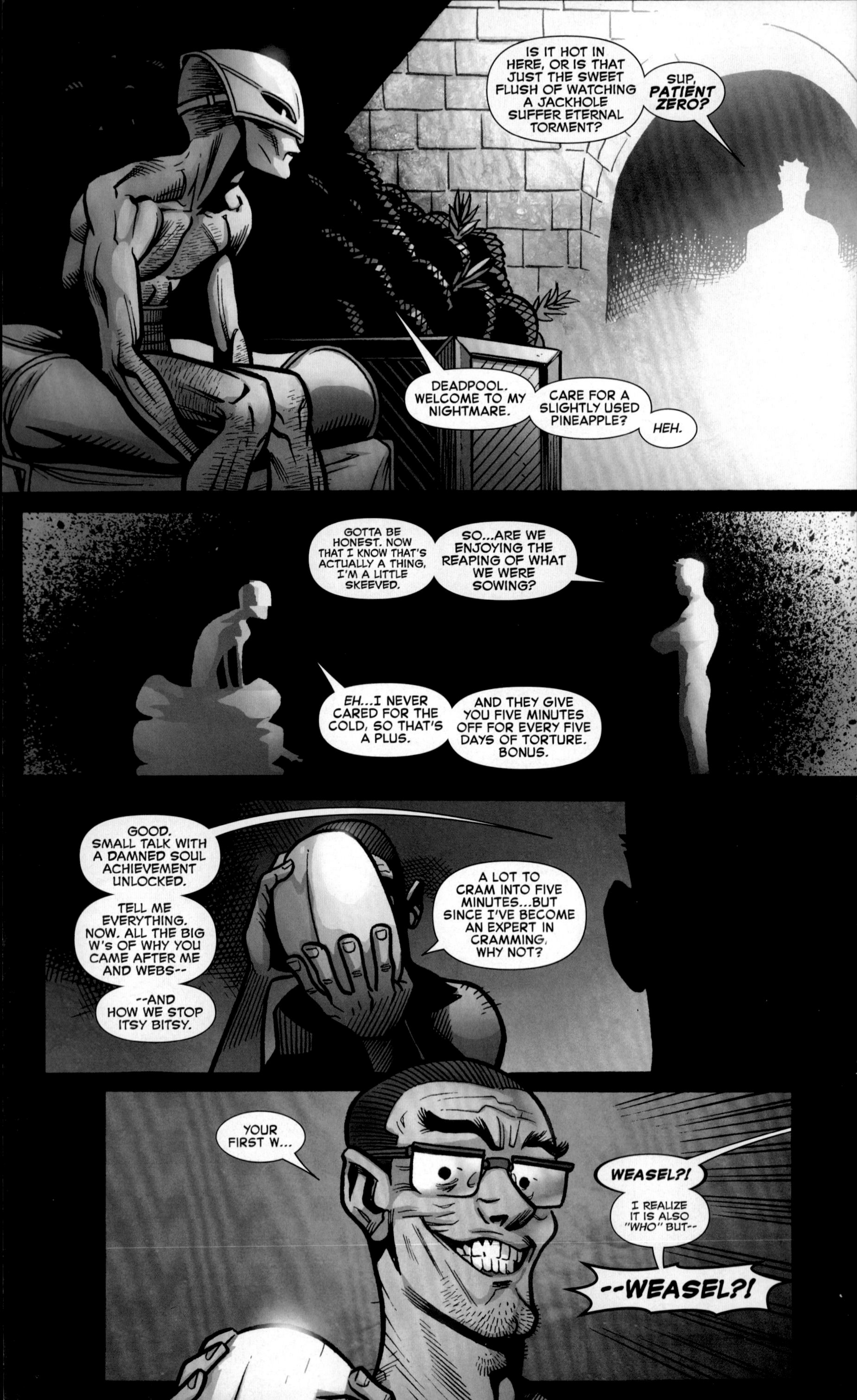
IS IT HOT IN HERE, OR IS THAT JUST THE SWEET FLUSH OF WATCHING A JACKHOLE SUFFER ETERNAL TORMENT?
SUP, PATIENT ZERO?
DEADPOOL. WELCOME TO MY NIGHTMARE.
CARE FOR A SLIGHTLY USED PINEAPPLE?
HEH.
GOTTA BE HONEST. NOW THAT I KNOW THAT'S ACTUALLY A THING, I'M A LITTLE SKEEVED.
SO...ARE WE ENJOYING THE REAPING OF WHAT WE WERE SOWING?
EH...I NEVER CARED FOR THE COLD, SO THAT'S A PLUS.
AND THEY GIVE YOU FIVE MINUTES OFF FOR EVERY FIVE DAYS OF TORTURE. BONUS.
GOOD. SMALL TALK WITH A DAMNED SOUL ACHIEVEMENT UNLOCKED.
TELL ME EVERYTHING. NOW. ALL THE BIG W'S OF WHY YOU CAME AFTER ME AND WEBS--
--AND HOW WE STOP ITSY BITSY.
A LOT TO CRAM INTO FIVE MINUTES...BUT SINCE I'VE BECOME AN EXPERT IN CRAMMING, WHY NOT?
YOUR FIRST W...
WEASEL?!
I REALIZE IT IS ALSO "WHO" BUT--
--WEASEL?!

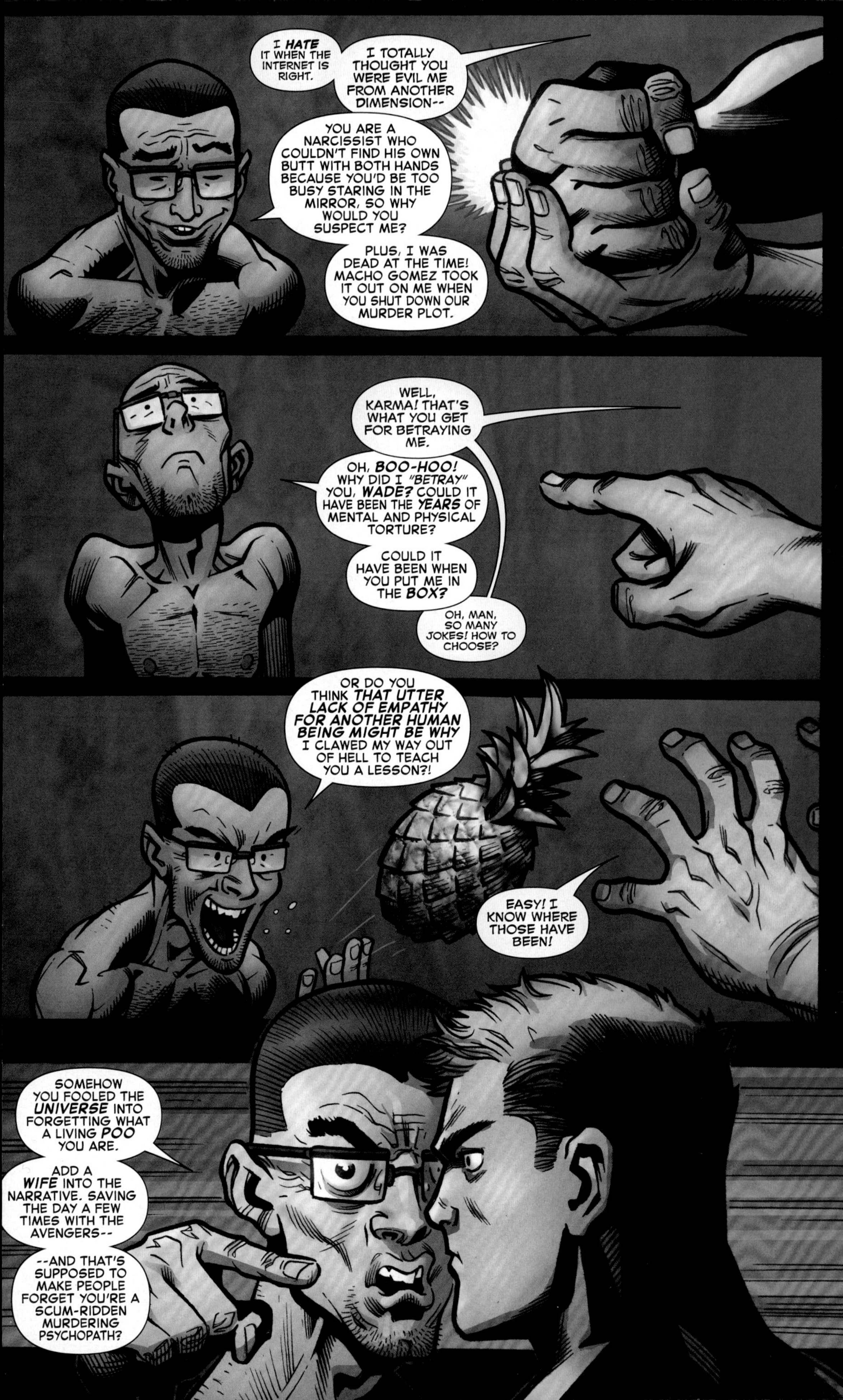
I *HATE* IT WHEN THE INTERNET IS RIGHT.
I TOTALLY THOUGHT YOU WERE EVIL ME FROM ANOTHER DIMENSION--
YOU ARE A NARCISSIST WHO COULDN'T FIND HIS OWN BUTT WITH BOTH HANDS BECAUSE YOU'D BE TOO BUSY STARING IN THE MIRROR, SO WHY WOULD YOU SUSPECT ME?
PLUS, I WAS DEAD AT THE TIME! MACHO GOMEZ TOOK IT OUT ON ME WHEN YOU SHUT DOWN OUR MURDER PLOT.
WELL, KARMA! THAT'S WHAT YOU GET FOR BETRAYING ME.
OH, *BOO-HOO!* WHY DID I *"BETRAY"* YOU, *WADE?* COULD IT HAVE BEEN THE *YEARS* OF MENTAL AND PHYSICAL TORTURE?
COULD IT HAVE BEEN WHEN YOU PUT ME IN THE *BOX?*
OH, MAN, SO MANY JOKES! HOW TO CHOOSE?
OR DO YOU THINK *THAT UTTER LACK OF EMPATHY FOR ANOTHER HUMAN BEING MIGHT BE WHY* I CLAWED MY WAY OUT OF HELL TO TEACH YOU A LESSON?!
EASY! I KNOW WHERE THOSE HAVE BEEN!
SOMEHOW YOU FOOLED THE *UNIVERSE* INTO FORGETTING WHAT A LIVING *POO* YOU ARE.
ADD A *WIFE* INTO THE NARRATIVE. SAVING THE DAY A FEW TIMES WITH THE AVENGERS--
--AND THAT'S SUPPOSED TO MAKE PEOPLE FORGET YOU'RE A SCUM-RIDDEN MURDERING PSYCHOPATH?

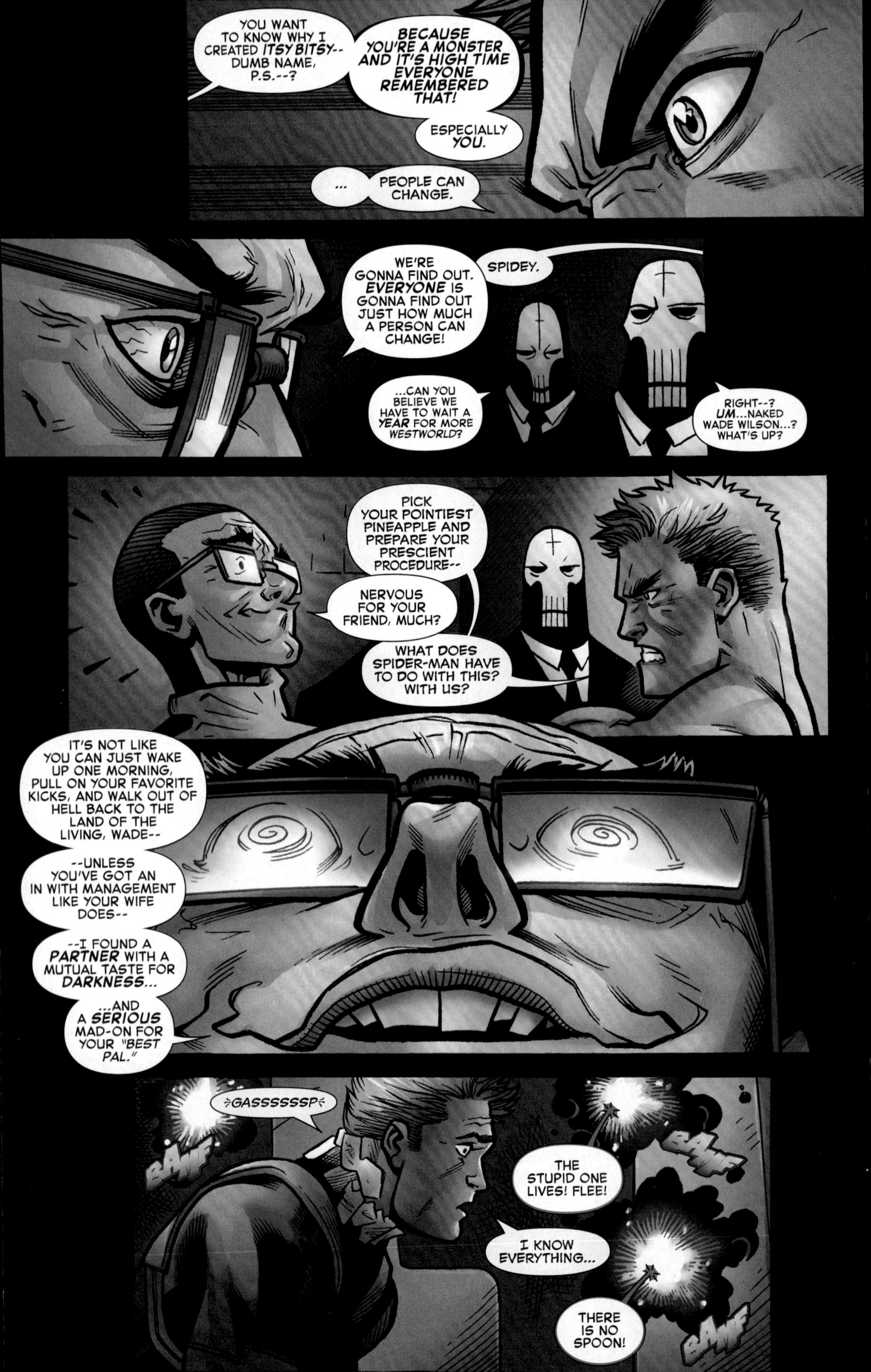
YOU WANT TO KNOW WHY I CREATED ITSY BITSY-- DUMB NAME, P.S.--?
BECAUSE YOU'RE A MONSTER AND IT'S HIGH TIME EVERYONE REMEMBERED THAT!
ESPECIALLY YOU.
...
PEOPLE CAN CHANGE.
WE'RE GONNA FIND OUT. EVERYONE IS GONNA FIND OUT JUST HOW MUCH A PERSON CAN CHANGE!
SPIDEY.
...CAN YOU BELIEVE WE HAVE TO WAIT A YEAR FOR MORE WESTWORLD?
RIGHT--? UM...NAKED WADE WILSON...? WHAT'S UP?
PICK YOUR POINTIEST PINEAPPLE AND PREPARE YOUR PRESCIENT PROCEDURE--
NERVOUS FOR YOUR FRIEND, MUCH?
WHAT DOES SPIDER-MAN HAVE TO DO WITH THIS? WITH US?
IT'S NOT LIKE YOU CAN JUST WAKE UP ONE MORNING, PULL ON YOUR FAVORITE KICKS, AND WALK OUT OF HELL BACK TO THE LAND OF THE LIVING, WADE--
--UNLESS YOU'VE GOT AN IN WITH MANAGEMENT LIKE YOUR WIFE DOES--
--I FOUND A PARTNER WITH A MUTUAL TASTE FOR DARKNESS...
...AND A SERIOUS MAD-ON FOR YOUR "BEST PAL."
GASSSSSSP
BAMF
BAMF
THE STUPID ONE LIVES! FLEE!
I KNOW EVERYTHING...
THERE IS NO SPOON!
BAMF

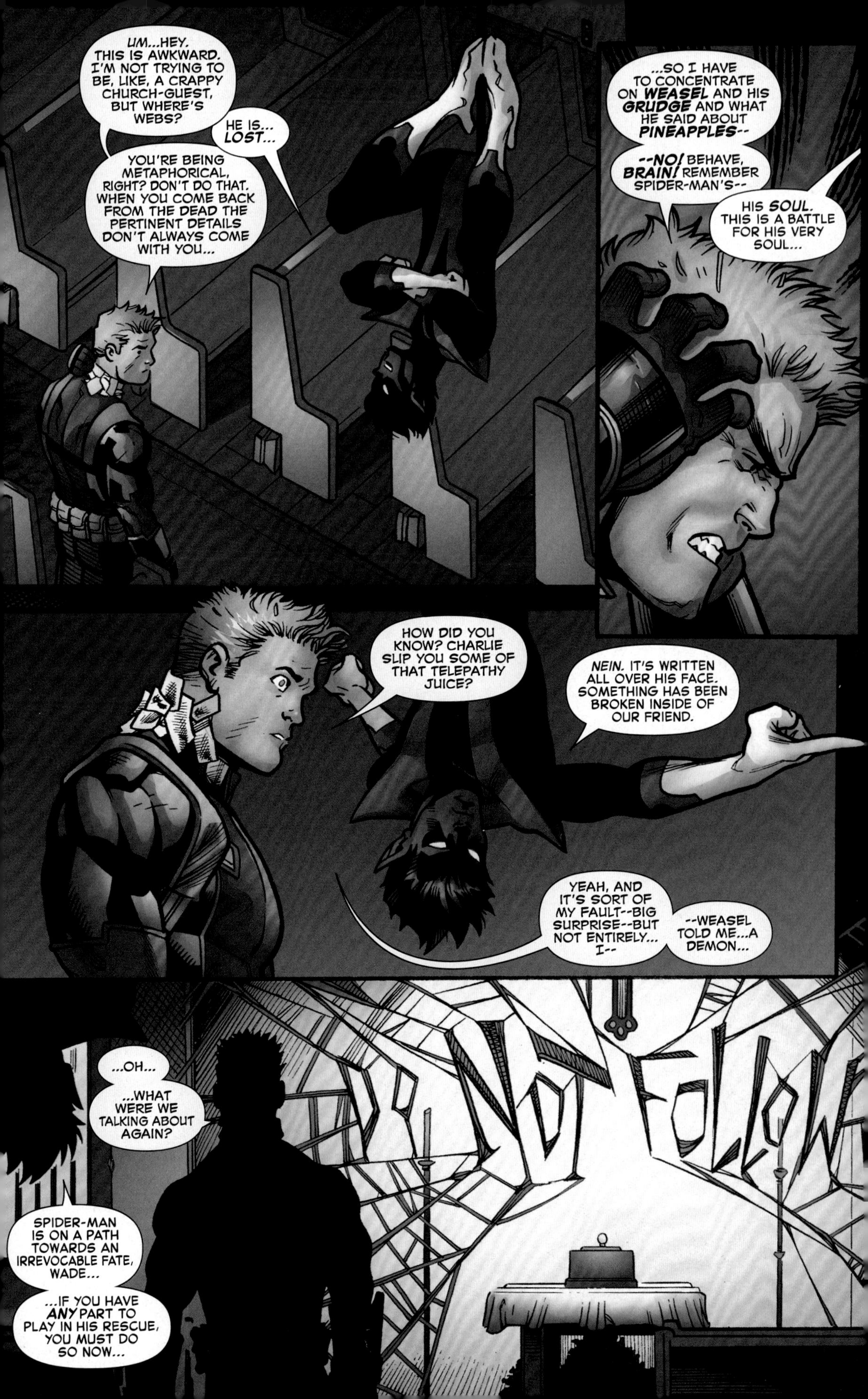
UM...HEY. THIS IS AWKWARD. I'M NOT TRYING TO BE, LIKE, A CRAPPY CHURCH-GUEST, BUT WHERE'S WEBS?
HE IS... LOST...
YOU'RE BEING METAPHORICAL, RIGHT? DON'T DO THAT. WHEN YOU COME BACK FROM THE DEAD THE PERTINENT DETAILS DON'T ALWAYS COME WITH YOU...
...SO I HAVE TO CONCENTRATE ON WEASEL AND HIS GRUDGE AND WHAT HE SAID ABOUT PINEAPPLES--
--NO! BEHAVE, BRAIN! REMEMBER SPIDER-MAN'S--
HIS SOUL. THIS IS A BATTLE FOR HIS VERY SOUL...
HOW DID YOU KNOW? CHARLIE SLIP YOU SOME OF THAT TELEPATHY JUICE?
NEIN. IT'S WRITTEN ALL OVER HIS FACE. SOMETHING HAS BEEN BROKEN INSIDE OF OUR FRIEND.
YEAH, AND IT'S SORT OF MY FAULT--BIG SURPRISE--BUT NOT ENTIRELY... I--
--WEASEL TOLD ME...A DEMON...
...OH...
...WHAT WERE WE TALKING ABOUT AGAIN?
SPIDER-MAN IS ON A PATH TOWARDS AN IRREVOCABLE FATE, WADE...
...IF YOU HAVE ANY PART TO PLAY IN HIS RESCUE, YOU MUST DO SO NOW...

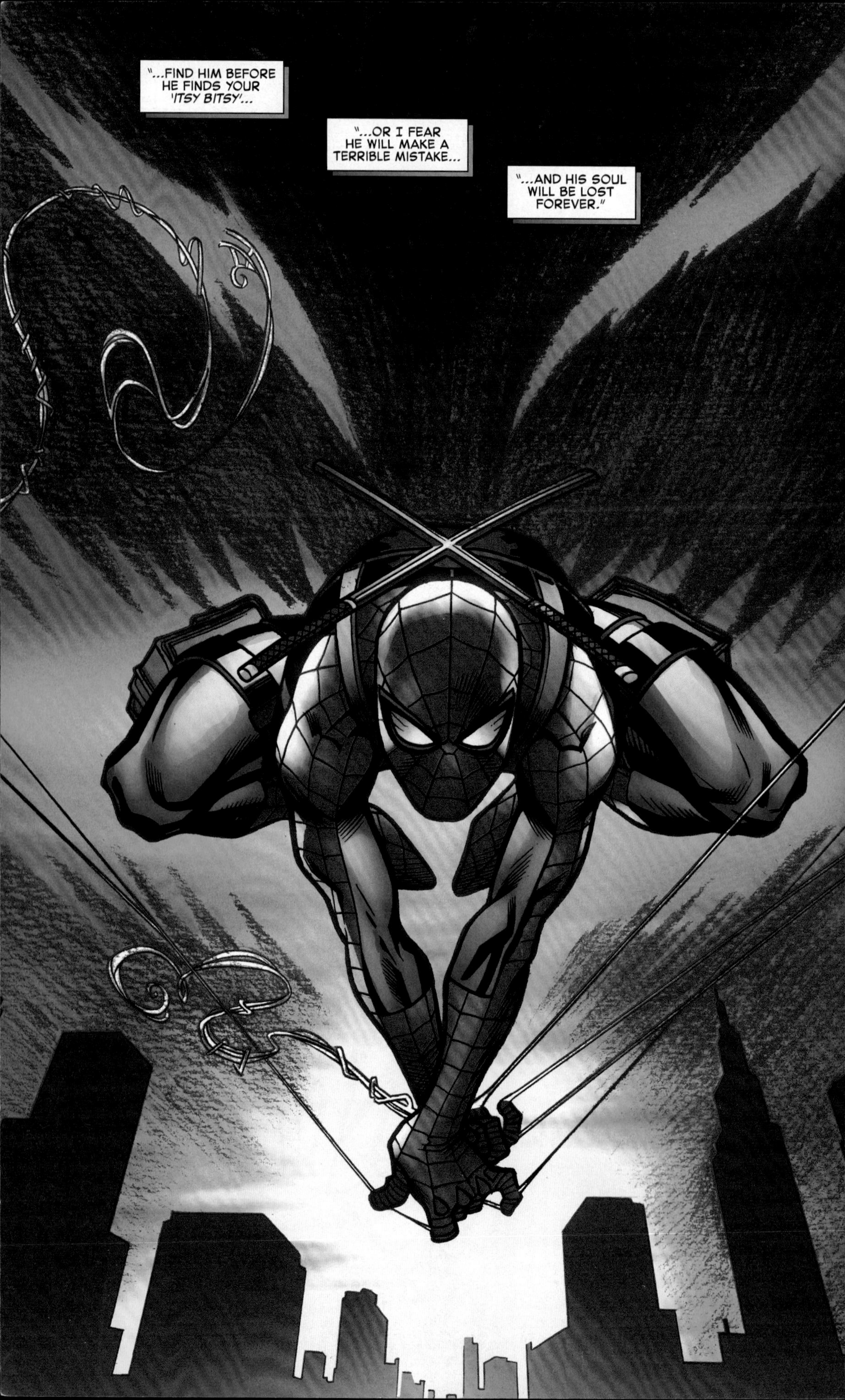
"...FIND HIM BEFORE HE FINDS YOUR 'ITSY BITSY'...
"...OR I FEAR HE WILL MAKE A TERRIBLE MISTAKE...
"...AND HIS SOUL WILL BE LOST FOREVER."

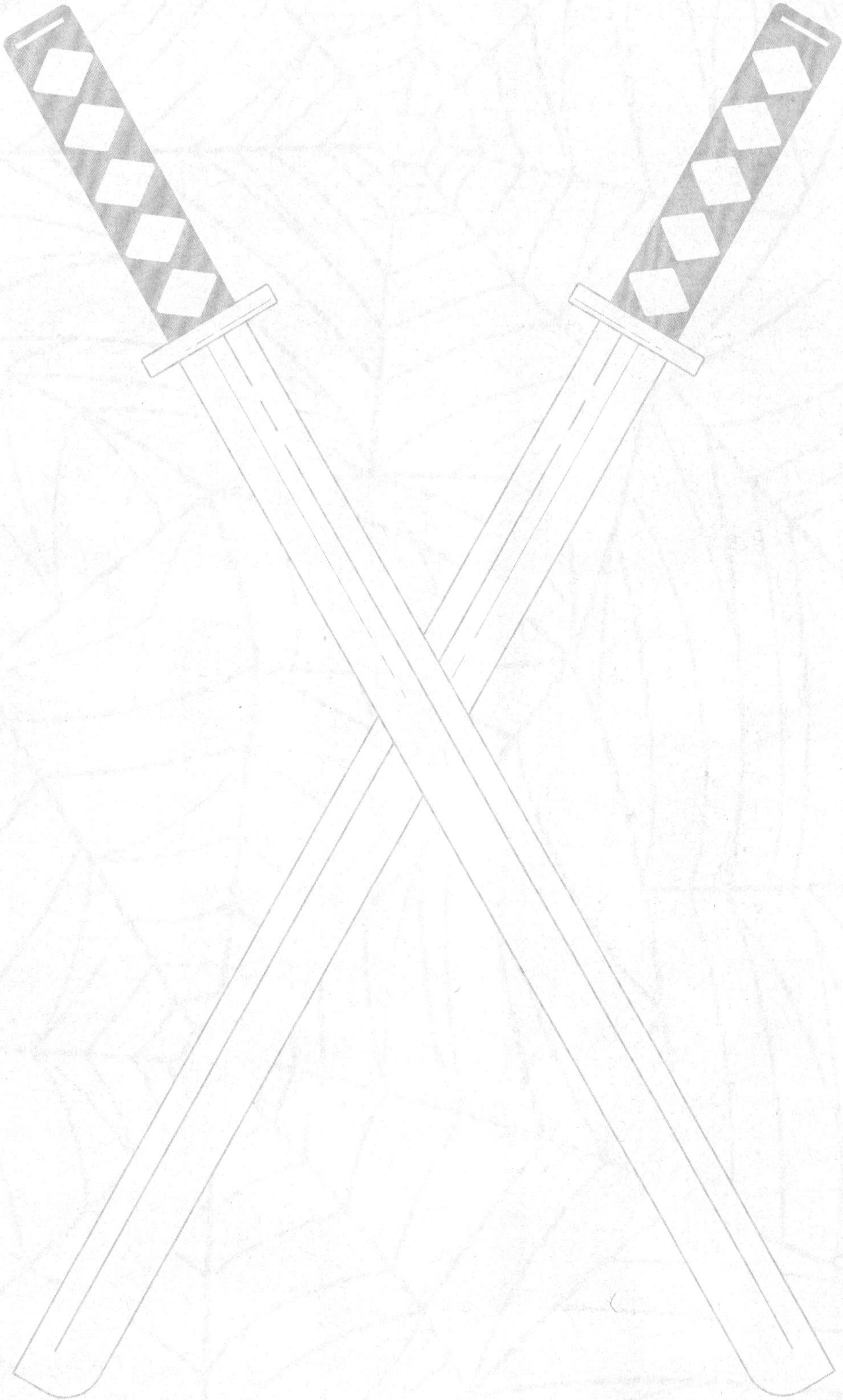

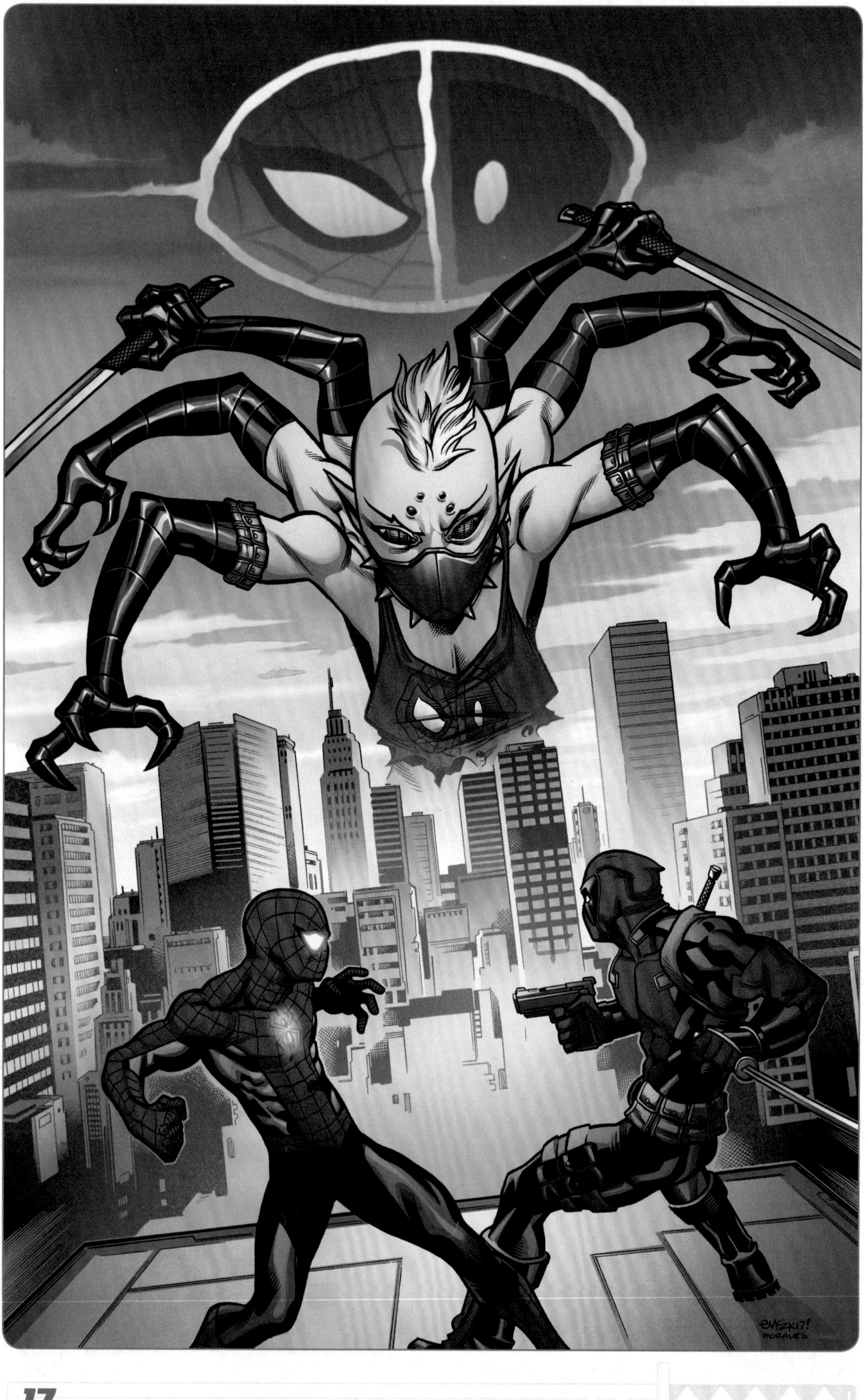

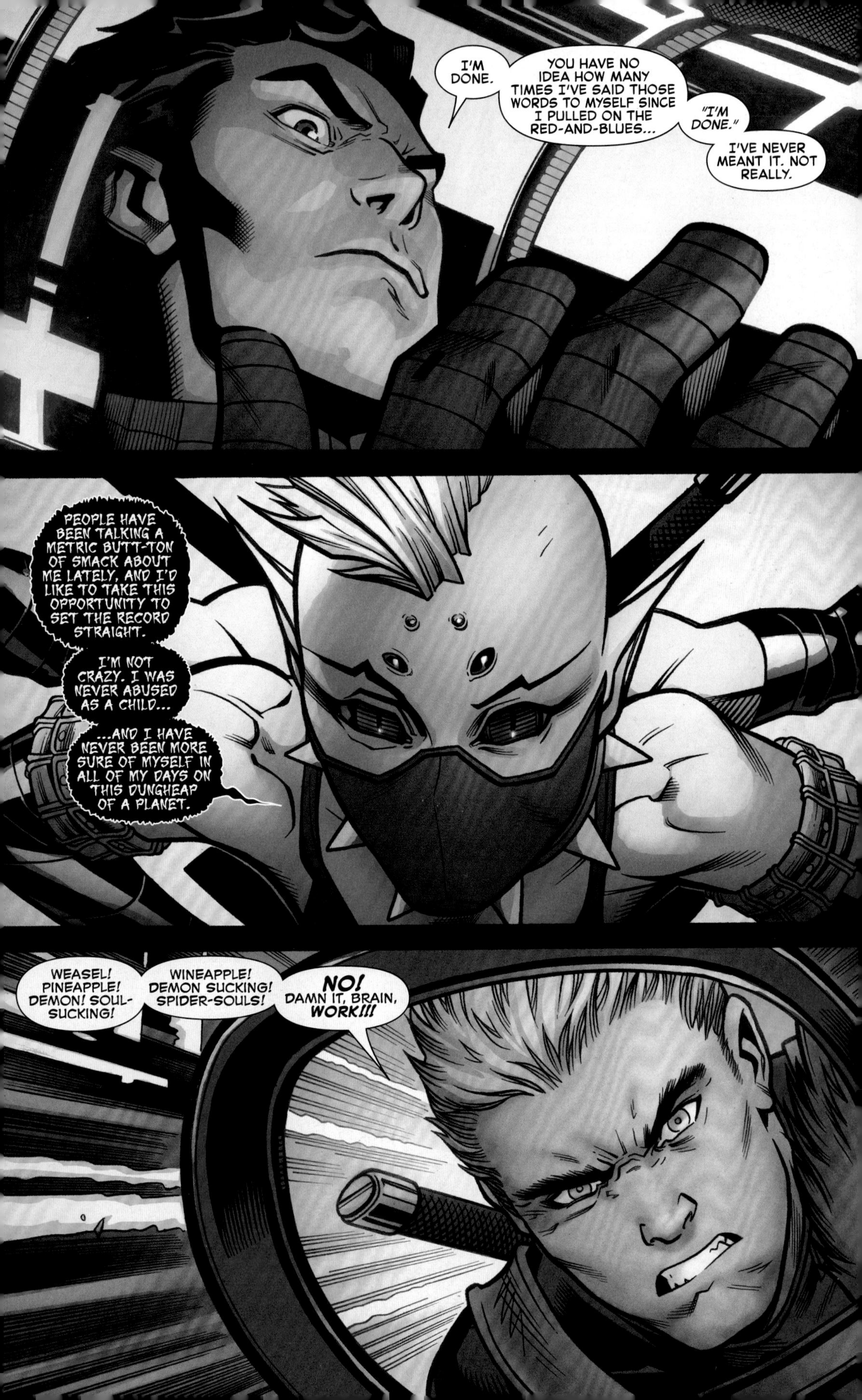
I'M DONE.
YOU HAVE NO IDEA HOW MANY TIMES I'VE SAID THOSE WORDS TO MYSELF SINCE I PULLED ON THE RED-AND-BLUES...
"I'M DONE."
I'VE NEVER MEANT IT. NOT REALLY.
PEOPLE HAVE BEEN TALKING A METRIC BUTT-TON OF SMACK ABOUT ME LATELY, AND I'D LIKE TO TAKE THIS OPPORTUNITY TO SET THE RECORD STRAIGHT.
I'M NOT CRAZY. I WAS NEVER ABUSED AS A CHILD...
...AND I HAVE NEVER BEEN MORE SURE OF MYSELF IN ALL OF MY DAYS ON THIS DUNGHEAP OF A PLANET.
WEASEL! PINEAPPLE! DEMON! SOUL-SUCKING!
WINEAPPLE! DEMON SUCKING! SPIDER-SOULS!
NO! DAMN IT, BRAIN, WORK!!!

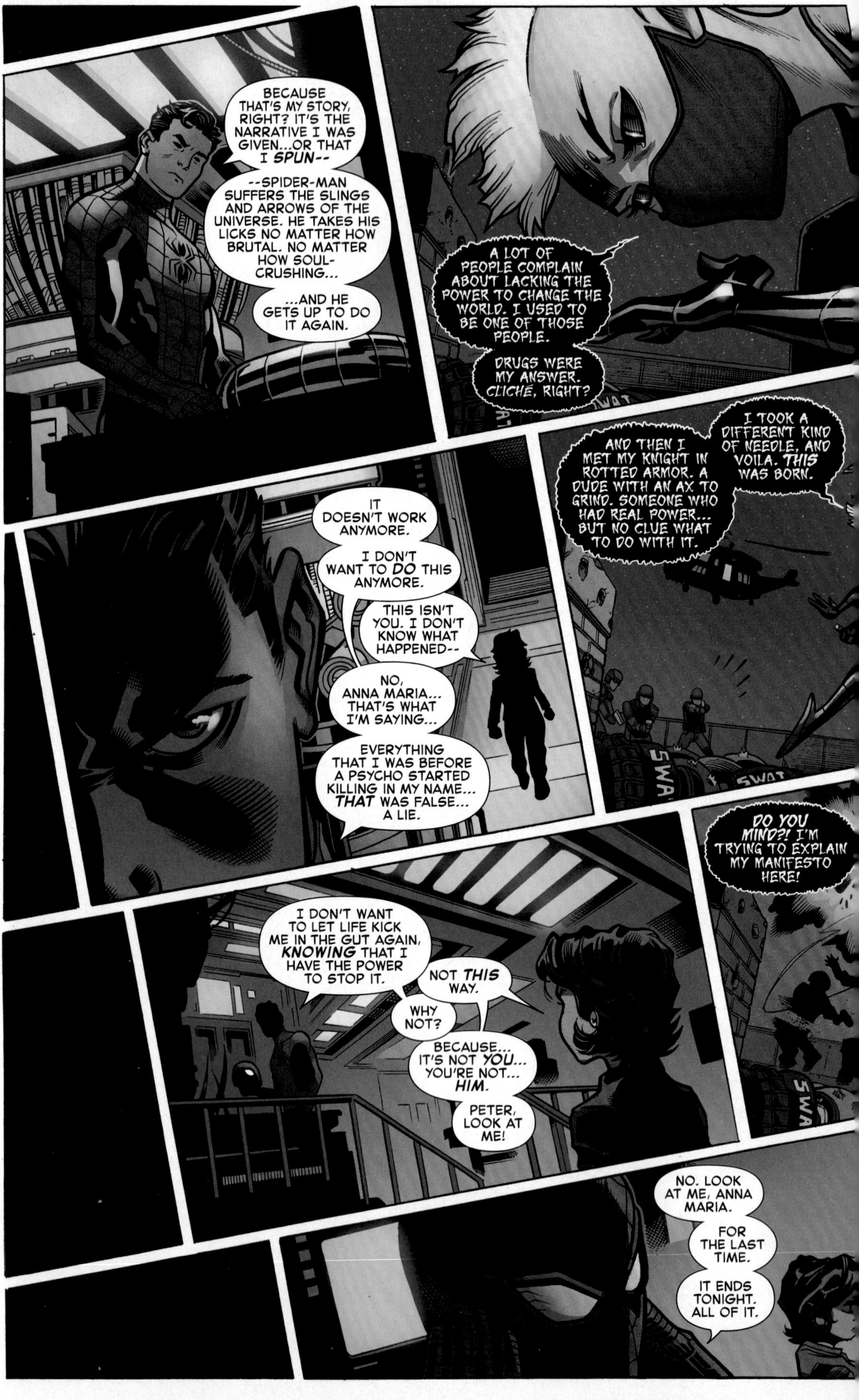
BECAUSE THAT'S MY STORY, RIGHT? IT'S THE NARRATIVE I WAS GIVEN...OR THAT I SPUN--
--SPIDER-MAN SUFFERS THE SLINGS AND ARROWS OF THE UNIVERSE. HE TAKES HIS LICKS NO MATTER HOW BRUTAL. NO MATTER HOW SOUL-CRUSHING...
...AND HE GETS UP TO DO IT AGAIN.
A LOT OF PEOPLE COMPLAIN ABOUT LACKING THE POWER TO CHANGE THE WORLD. I USED TO BE ONE OF THOSE PEOPLE.
DRUGS WERE MY ANSWER. CLICHÉ, RIGHT?
IT DOESN'T WORK ANYMORE.
I DON'T WANT TO DO THIS ANYMORE.
THIS ISN'T YOU. I DON'T KNOW WHAT HAPPENED--
NO, ANNA MARIA... THAT'S WHAT I'M SAYING...
EVERYTHING THAT I WAS BEFORE A PSYCHO STARTED KILLING IN MY NAME... THAT WAS FALSE... A LIE.
AND THEN I MET MY KNIGHT IN ROTTED ARMOR. A DUDE WITH AN AX TO GRIND. SOMEONE WHO HAD REAL POWER... BUT NO CLUE WHAT TO DO WITH IT.
I TOOK A DIFFERENT KIND OF NEEDLE, AND VOILA. THIS WAS BORN.
SWAT
DO YOU MIND?! I'M TRYING TO EXPLAIN MY MANIFESTO HERE!
I DON'T WANT TO LET LIFE KICK ME IN THE GUT AGAIN, KNOWING THAT I HAVE THE POWER TO STOP IT.
NOT THIS WAY.
WHY NOT?
BECAUSE... IT'S NOT YOU... YOU'RE NOT... HIM.
PETER, LOOK AT ME!
NO. LOOK AT ME, ANNA MARIA.
FOR THE LAST TIME.
IT ENDS TONIGHT. ALL OF IT.

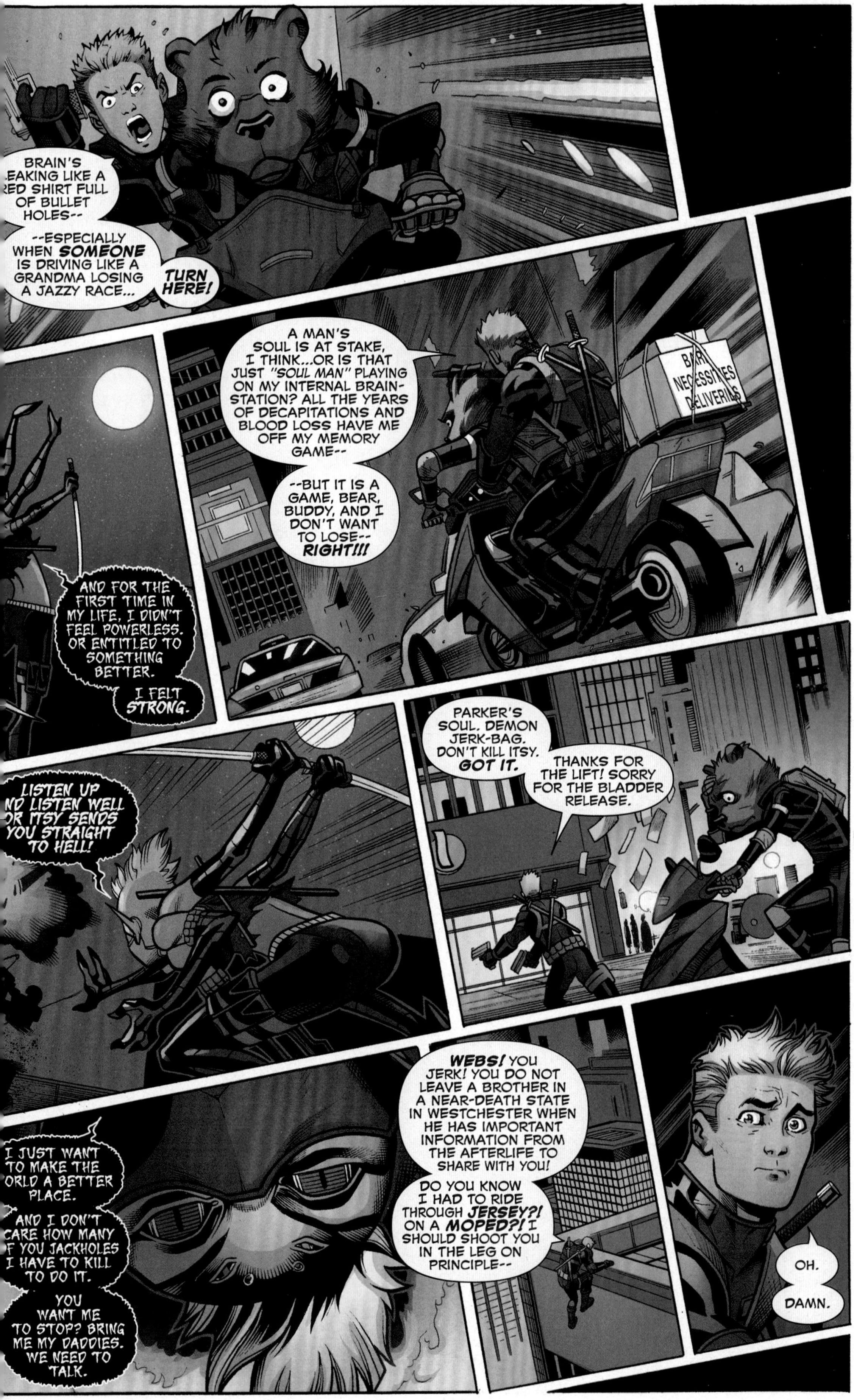
BRAIN'S EAKING LIKE A RED SHIRT FULL OF BULLET HOLES--
--ESPECIALLY WHEN SOMEONE IS DRIVING LIKE A GRANDMA LOSING A JAZZY RACE...
TURN HERE!
A MAN'S SOUL IS AT STAKE, I THINK...OR IS THAT JUST "SOUL MAN" PLAYING ON MY INTERNAL BRAIN-STATION? ALL THE YEARS OF DECAPITATIONS AND BLOOD LOSS HAVE ME OFF MY MEMORY GAME--
--BUT IT IS A GAME, BEAR, BUDDY, AND I DON'T WANT TO LOSE--RIGHT!!!
AND FOR THE FIRST TIME IN MY LIFE, I DIDN'T FEEL POWERLESS. OR ENTITLED TO SOMETHING BETTER.
I FELT STRONG.
LISTEN UP ND LISTEN WELL OR ITSY SENDS YOU STRAIGHT TO HELL!
PARKER'S SOUL. DEMON JERK-BAG. DON'T KILL ITSY. GOT IT.
THANKS FOR THE LIFT! SORRY FOR THE BLADDER RELEASE.
I JUST WANT TO MAKE THE ORLD A BETTER PLACE.
AND I DON'T CARE HOW MANY F YOU JACKHOLES I HAVE TO KILL TO DO IT.
YOU WANT ME TO STOP? BRING ME MY DADDIES. WE NEED TO TALK.
WEBS! YOU JERK! YOU DO NOT LEAVE A BROTHER IN A NEAR-DEATH STATE IN WESTCHESTER WHEN HE HAS IMPORTANT INFORMATION FROM THE AFTERLIFE TO SHARE WITH YOU!
DO YOU KNOW I HAD TO RIDE THROUGH JERSEY?! ON A MOPED?! I SHOULD SHOOT YOU IN THE LEG ON PRINCIPLE--
OH.
DAMN.

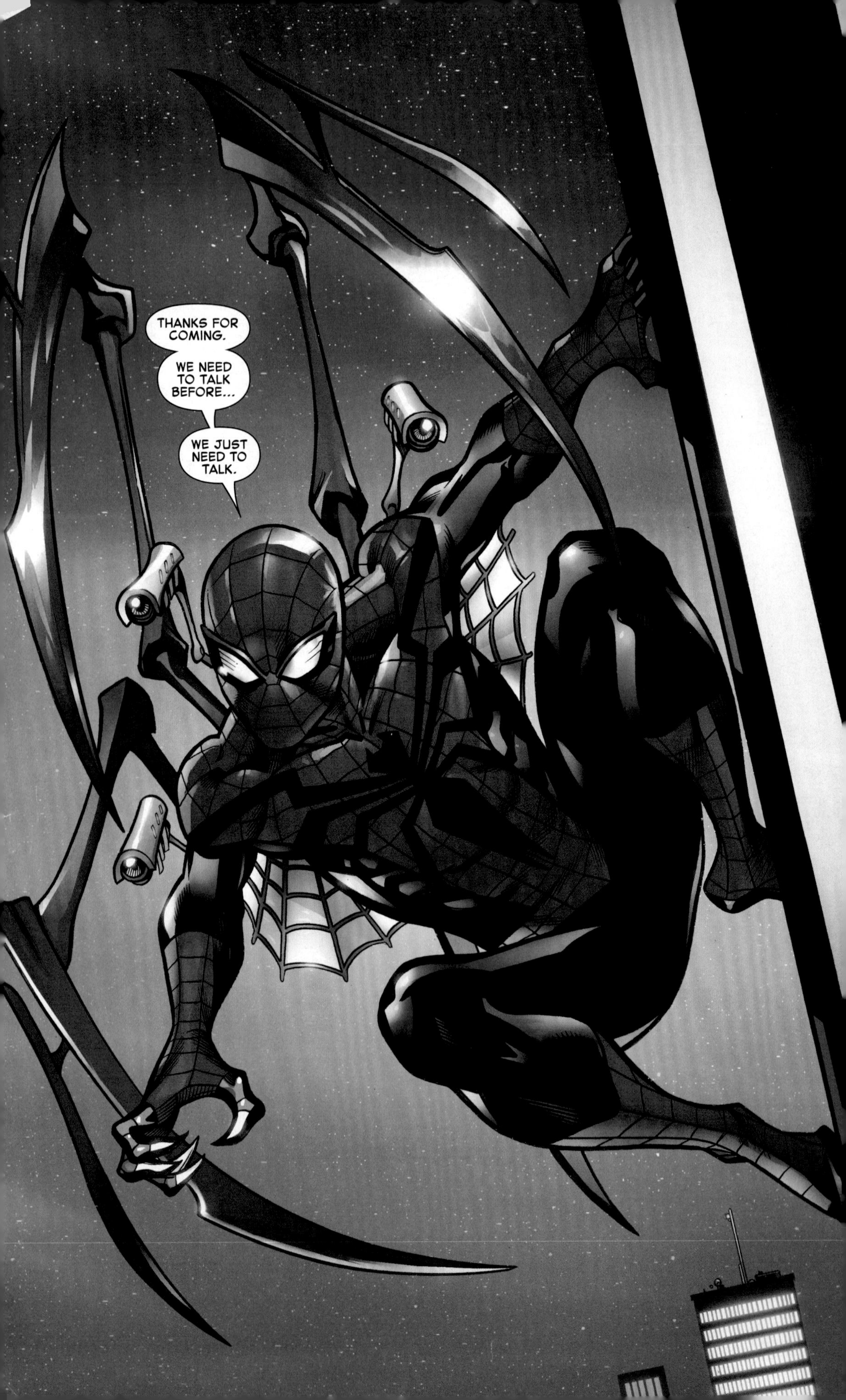
THANKS FOR COMING.
WE NEED TO TALK BEFORE...
WE JUST NEED TO TALK.

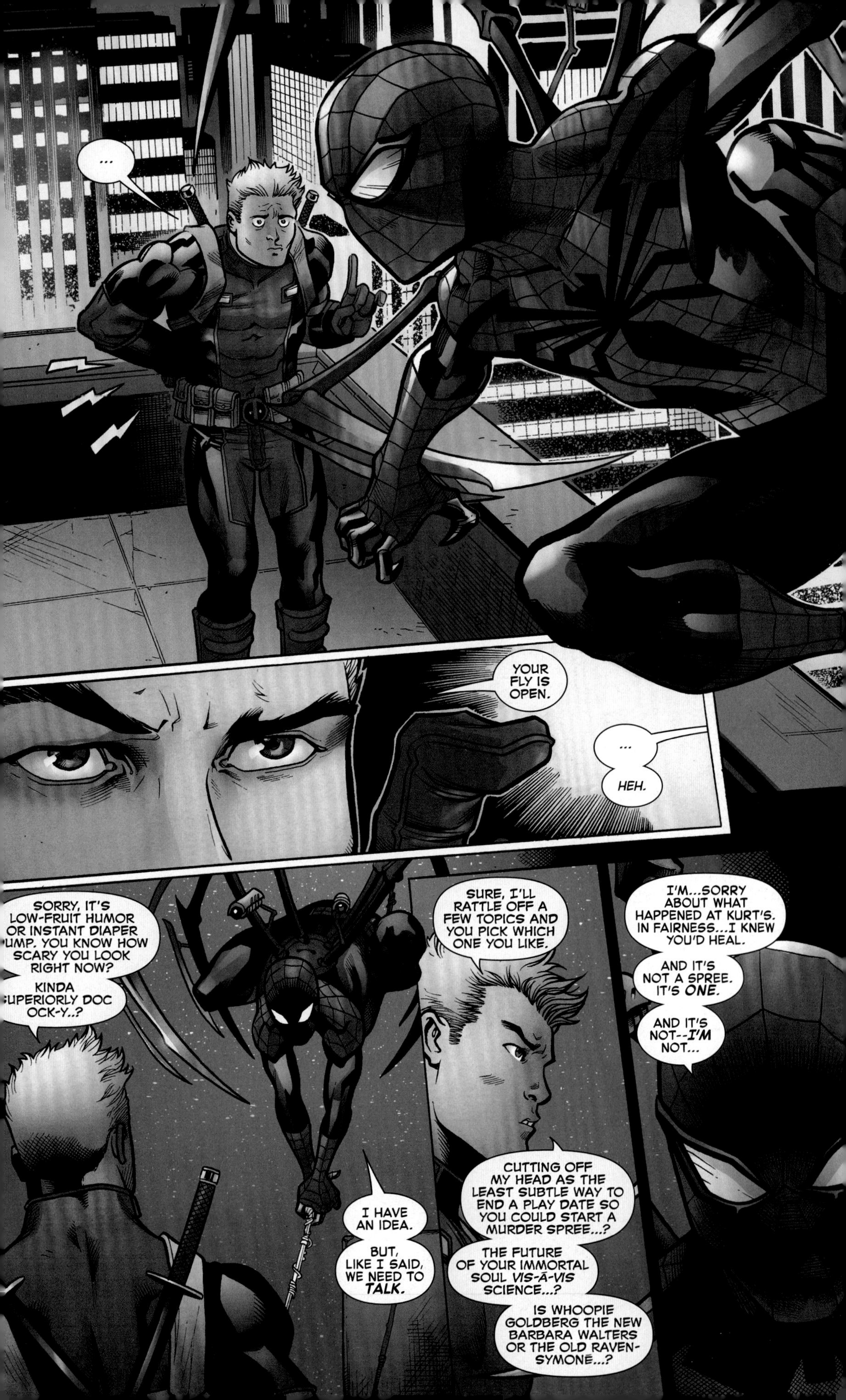
...
YOUR FLY IS OPEN.
...
HEH.
SORRY, IT'S LOW-FRUIT HUMOR OR INSTANT DIAPER DUMP. YOU KNOW HOW SCARY YOU LOOK RIGHT NOW?
KINDA SUPERIORLY DOC OCK-Y..?
I HAVE AN IDEA.
BUT, LIKE I SAID, WE NEED TO TALK.
SURE, I'LL RATTLE OFF A FEW TOPICS AND YOU PICK WHICH ONE YOU LIKE.
CUTTING OFF MY HEAD AS THE LEAST SUBTLE WAY TO END A PLAY DATE SO YOU COULD START A MURDER SPREE...?
THE FUTURE OF YOUR IMMORTAL SOUL VIS-À-VIS SCIENCE...?
IS WHOOPIE GOLDBERG THE NEW BARBARA WALTERS OR THE OLD RAVEN-SYMONE...?
I'M...SORRY ABOUT WHAT HAPPENED AT KURT'S. IN FAIRNESS...I KNEW YOU'D HEAL.
AND IT'S NOT A SPREE. IT'S ONE.
AND IT'S NOT--I'M NOT...

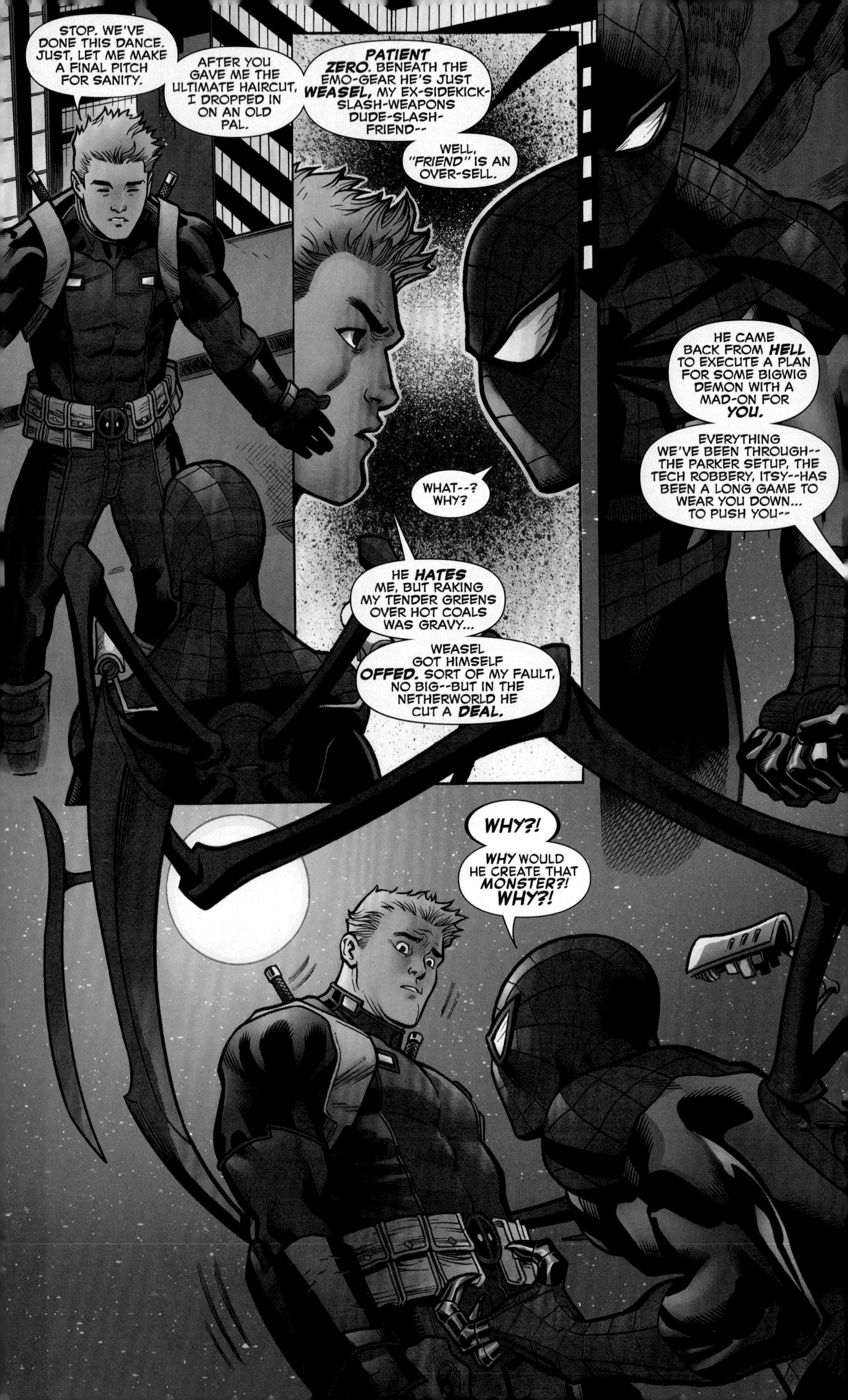
STOP. WE'VE DONE THIS DANCE. JUST, LET ME MAKE A FINAL PITCH FOR SANITY.
AFTER YOU GAVE ME THE ULTIMATE HAIRCUT, I DROPPED IN ON AN OLD PAL.
PATIENT ZERO. BENEATH THE EMO-GEAR HE'S JUST WEASEL, MY EX-SIDEKICK-SLASH-WEAPONS DUDE-SLASH-FRIEND--
WELL, "FRIEND" IS AN OVER-SELL.
WHAT--? WHY?
HE HATES ME, BUT RAKING MY TENDER GREENS OVER HOT COALS WAS GRAVY...
WEASEL GOT HIMSELF OFFED. SORT OF MY FAULT, NO BIG--BUT IN THE NETHERWORLD HE CUT A DEAL.
HE CAME BACK FROM HELL TO EXECUTE A PLAN FOR SOME BIGWIG DEMON WITH A MAD-ON FOR YOU.
EVERYTHING WE'VE BEEN THROUGH-- THE PARKER SETUP, THE TECH ROBBERY, ITSY--HAS BEEN A LONG GAME TO WEAR YOU DOWN... TO PUSH YOU--
WHY?!
WHY WOULD HE CREATE THAT MONSTER?! WHY?!

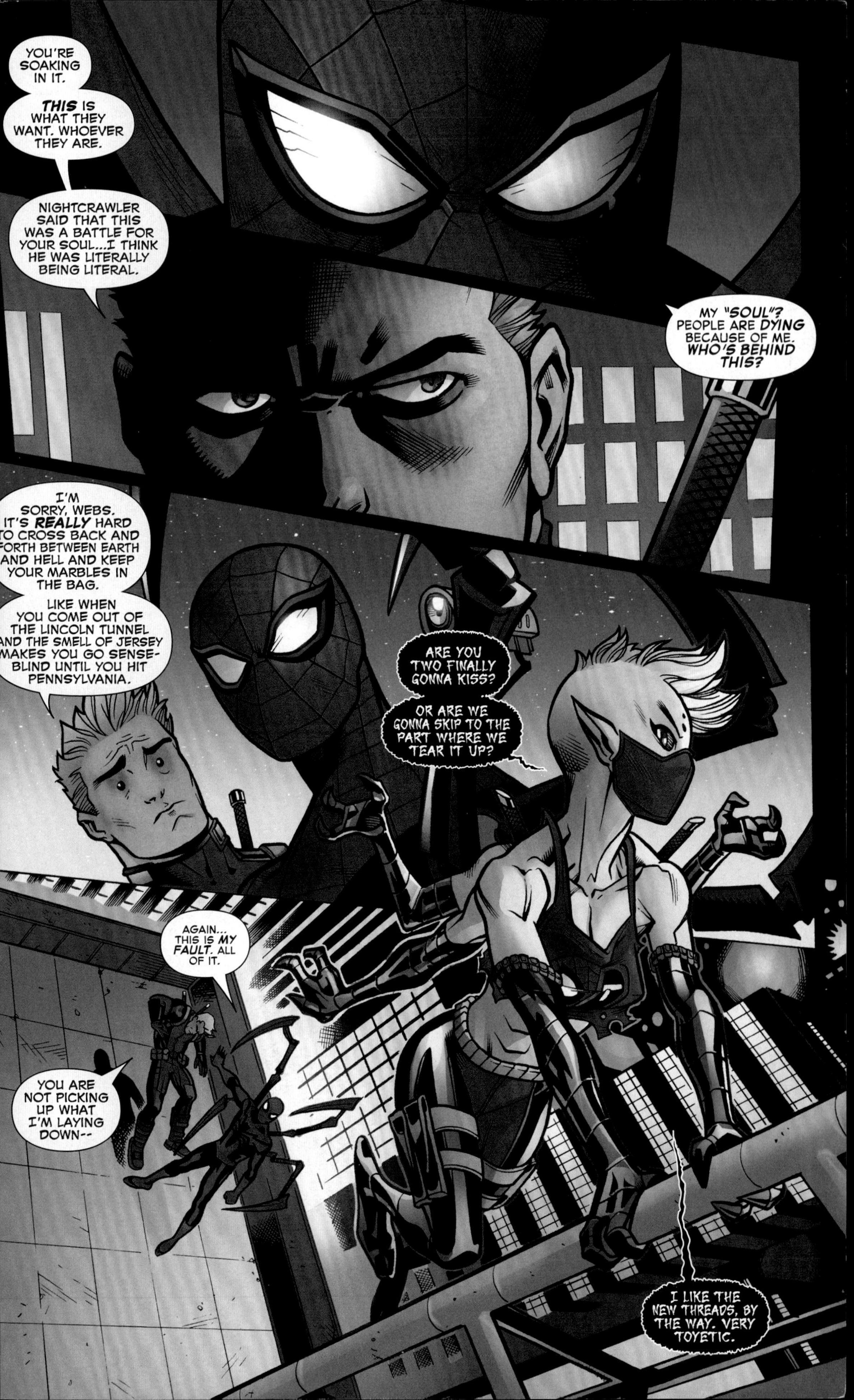
YOU'RE SOAKING IN IT.
THIS IS WHAT THEY WANT. WHOEVER THEY ARE.
NIGHTCRAWLER SAID THAT THIS WAS A BATTLE FOR YOUR SOUL...I THINK HE WAS LITERALLY BEING LITERAL.
MY "SOUL"? PEOPLE ARE DYING BECAUSE OF ME. WHO'S BEHIND THIS?
I'M SORRY, WEBS. IT'S REALLY HARD TO CROSS BACK AND FORTH BETWEEN EARTH AND HELL AND KEEP YOUR MARBLES IN THE BAG.
LIKE WHEN YOU COME OUT OF THE LINCOLN TUNNEL AND THE SMELL OF JERSEY MAKES YOU GO SENSE-BLIND UNTIL YOU HIT PENNSYLVANIA.
ARE YOU TWO FINALLY GONNA KISS?
OR ARE WE GONNA SKIP TO THE PART WHERE WE TEAR IT UP?
AGAIN... THIS IS MY FAULT. ALL OF IT.
YOU ARE NOT PICKING UP WHAT I'M LAYING DOWN--
I LIKE THE NEW THREADS, BY THE WAY. VERY TOYETIC.

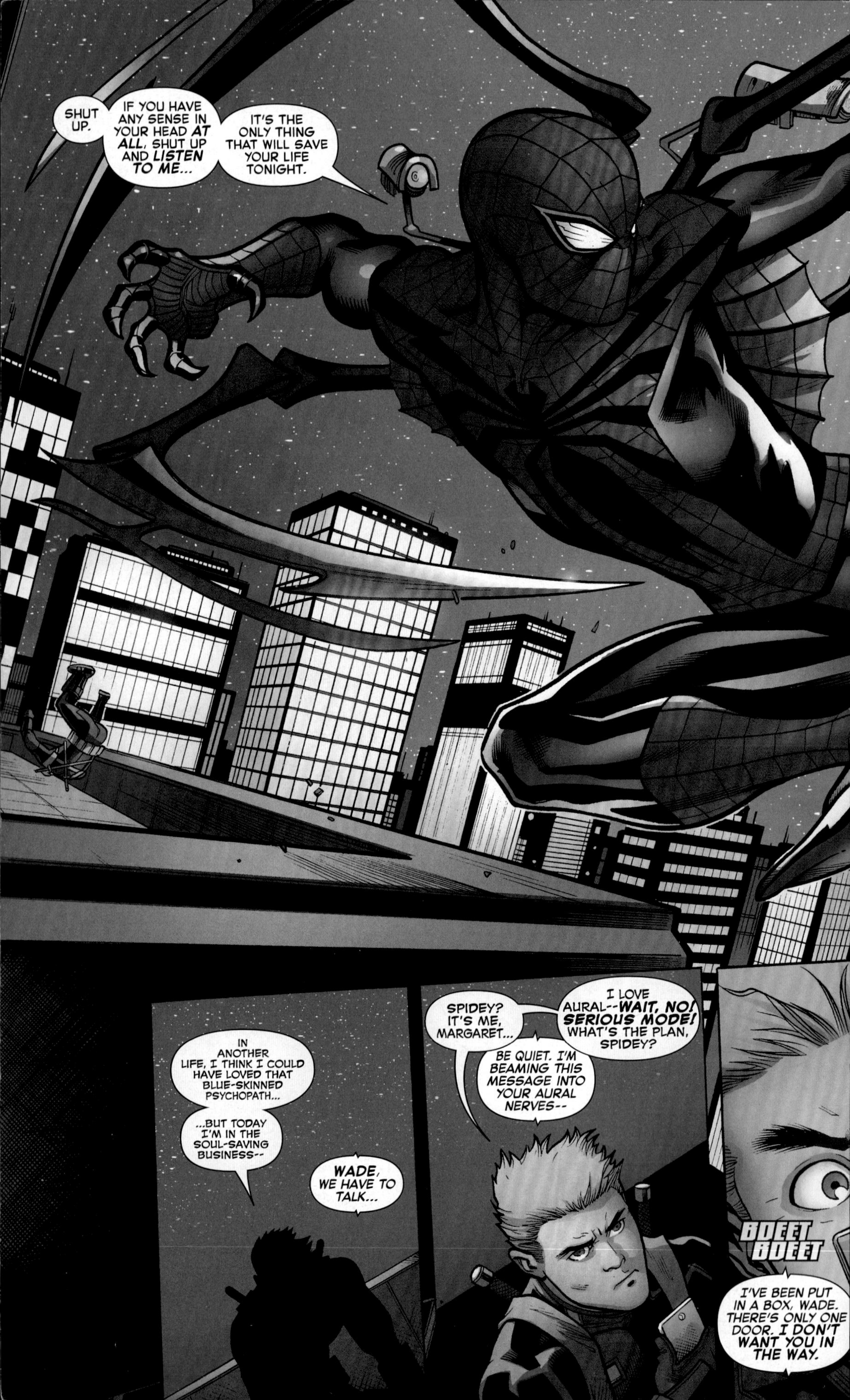
SHUT UP.
IF YOU HAVE ANY SENSE IN YOUR HEAD **AT ALL**, SHUT UP AND **LISTEN TO ME...**
IT'S THE ONLY THING THAT WILL SAVE YOUR LIFE TONIGHT.
IN ANOTHER LIFE, I THINK I COULD HAVE LOVED THAT BLUE-SKINNED PSYCHOPATH...
...BUT TODAY I'M IN THE SOUL-SAVING BUSINESS--
WADE, WE HAVE TO TALK...
SPIDEY? IT'S ME, MARGARET...
I LOVE AURAL--**WAIT, NO! SERIOUS MODE!** WHAT'S THE PLAN, SPIDEY?
BE QUIET. I'M BEAMING THIS MESSAGE INTO YOUR AURAL NERVES--
BDEET BDEET
I'VE BEEN PUT IN A BOX, WADE. THERE'S ONLY ONE DOOR. **I DON'T WANT YOU IN THE WAY.**

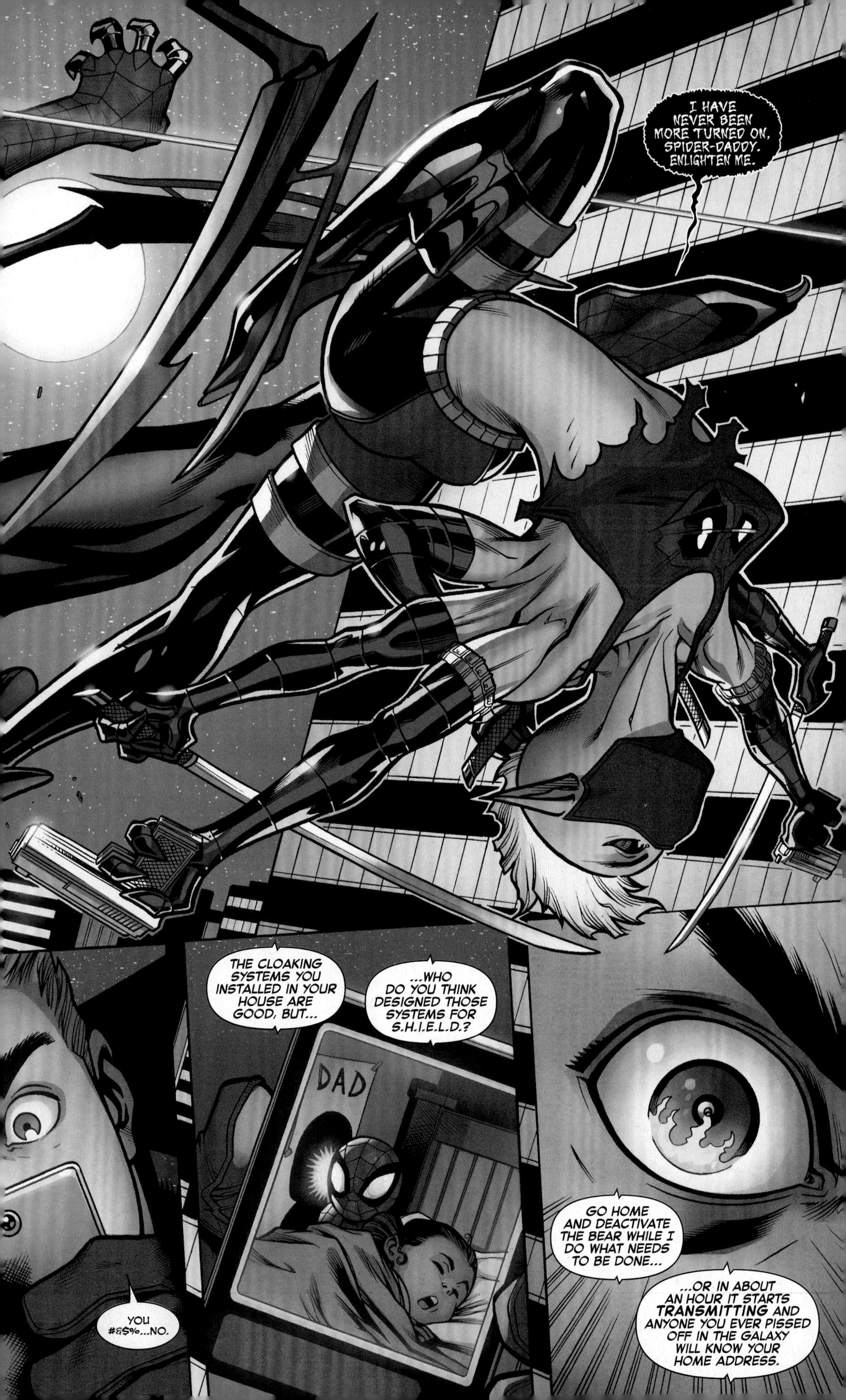
I HAVE NEVER BEEN MORE TURNED ON, SPIDER-DADDY. ENLIGHTEN ME.
THE CLOAKING SYSTEMS YOU INSTALLED IN YOUR HOUSE ARE GOOD, BUT...
...WHO DO YOU THINK DESIGNED THOSE SYSTEMS FOR S.H.I.E.L.D.?
DAD
YOU #&$%...NO.
GO HOME AND DEACTIVATE THE BEAR WHILE I DO WHAT NEEDS TO BE DONE...
...OR IN ABOUT AN HOUR IT STARTS TRANSMITTING AND ANYONE YOU EVER PISSED OFF IN THE GALAXY WILL KNOW YOUR HOME ADDRESS.

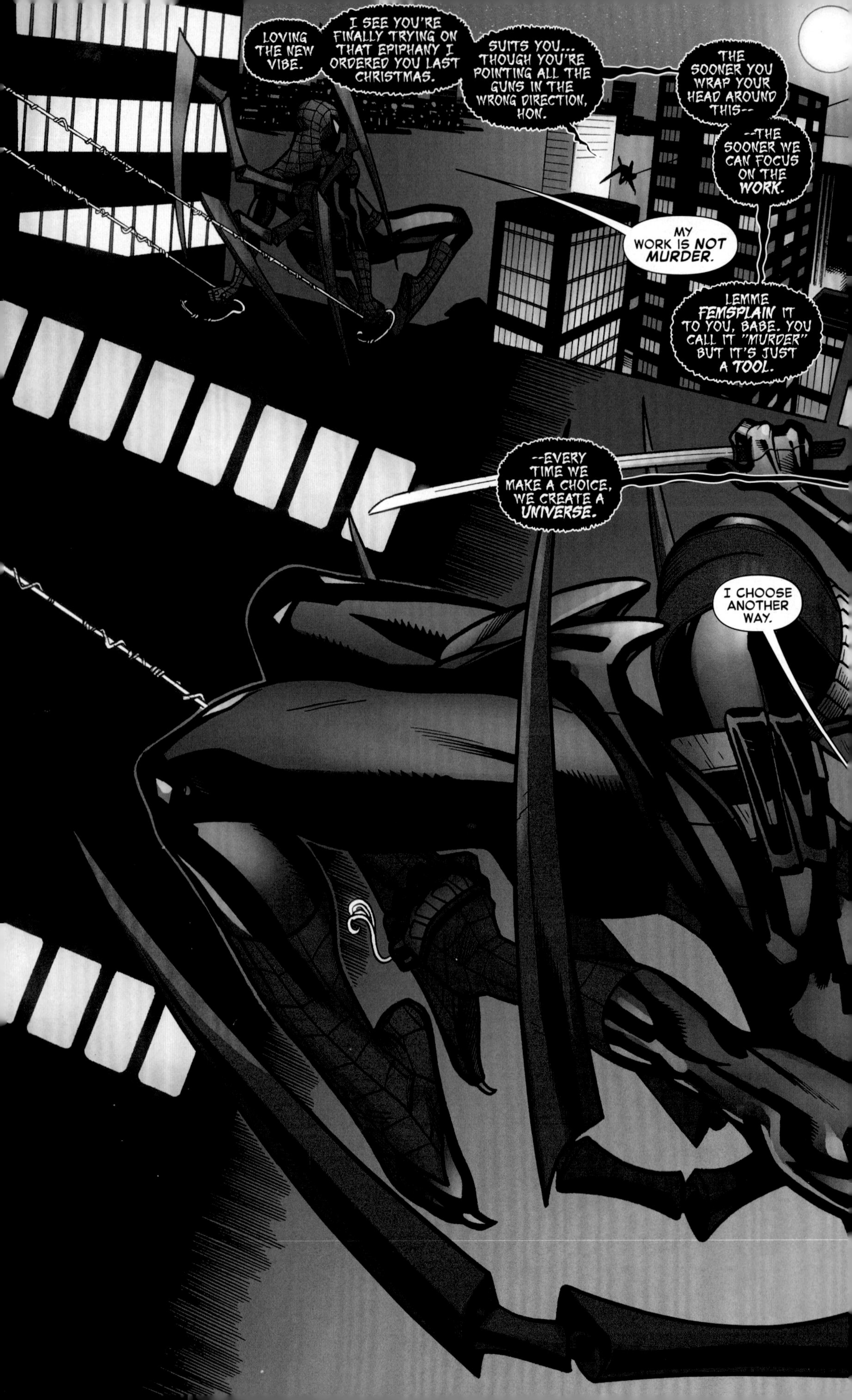
LOVING THE NEW VIBE.
I SEE YOU'RE FINALLY TRYING ON THAT EPIPHANY I ORDERED YOU LAST CHRISTMAS.
SUITS YOU... THOUGH YOU'RE POINTING ALL THE GUNS IN THE WRONG DIRECTION, HON.
THE SOONER YOU WRAP YOUR HEAD AROUND THIS--
--THE SOONER WE CAN FOCUS ON THE WORK.
MY WORK IS NOT MURDER.
LEMME FEMSPLAIN IT TO YOU, BABE. YOU CALL IT "MURDER" BUT IT'S JUST A TOOL.
--EVERY TIME WE MAKE A CHOICE, WE CREATE A UNIVERSE.
I CHOOSE ANOTHER WAY.

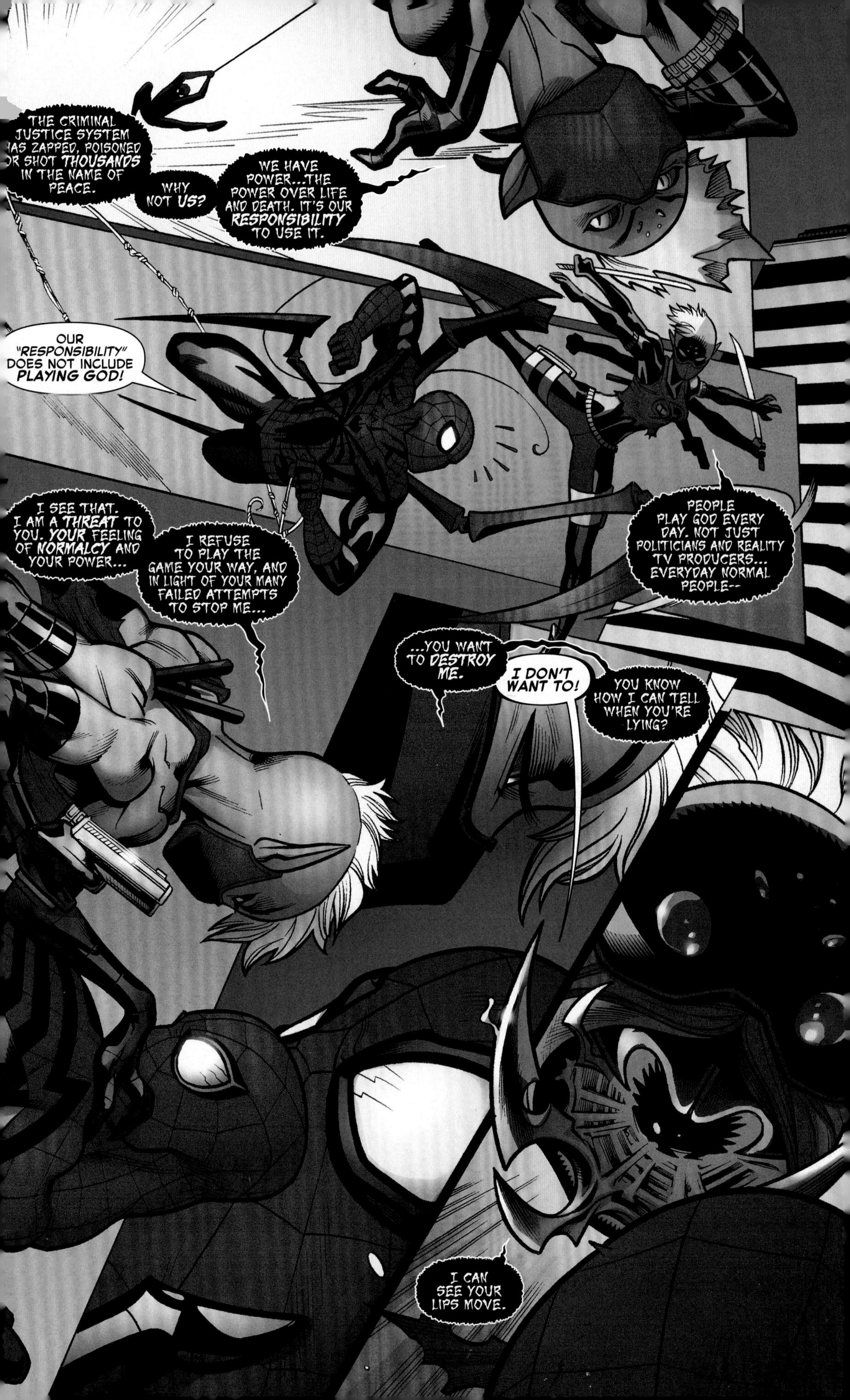
THE CRIMINAL JUSTICE SYSTEM HAS ZAPPED, POISONED OR SHOT THOUSANDS IN THE NAME OF PEACE.
WHY NOT US?
WE HAVE POWER...THE POWER OVER LIFE AND DEATH. IT'S OUR RESPONSIBILITY TO USE IT.
OUR "RESPONSIBILITY" DOES NOT INCLUDE PLAYING GOD!
PEOPLE PLAY GOD EVERY DAY. NOT JUST POLITICIANS AND REALITY TV PRODUCERS... EVERYDAY NORMAL PEOPLE--
I SEE THAT. I AM A THREAT TO YOU. YOUR FEELING OF NORMALCY AND YOUR POWER...
I REFUSE TO PLAY THE GAME YOUR WAY, AND IN LIGHT OF YOUR MANY FAILED ATTEMPTS TO STOP ME...
...YOU WANT TO DESTROY ME.
I DON'T WANT TO!
YOU KNOW HOW I CAN TELL WHEN YOU'RE LYING?
I CAN SEE YOUR LIPS MOVE.

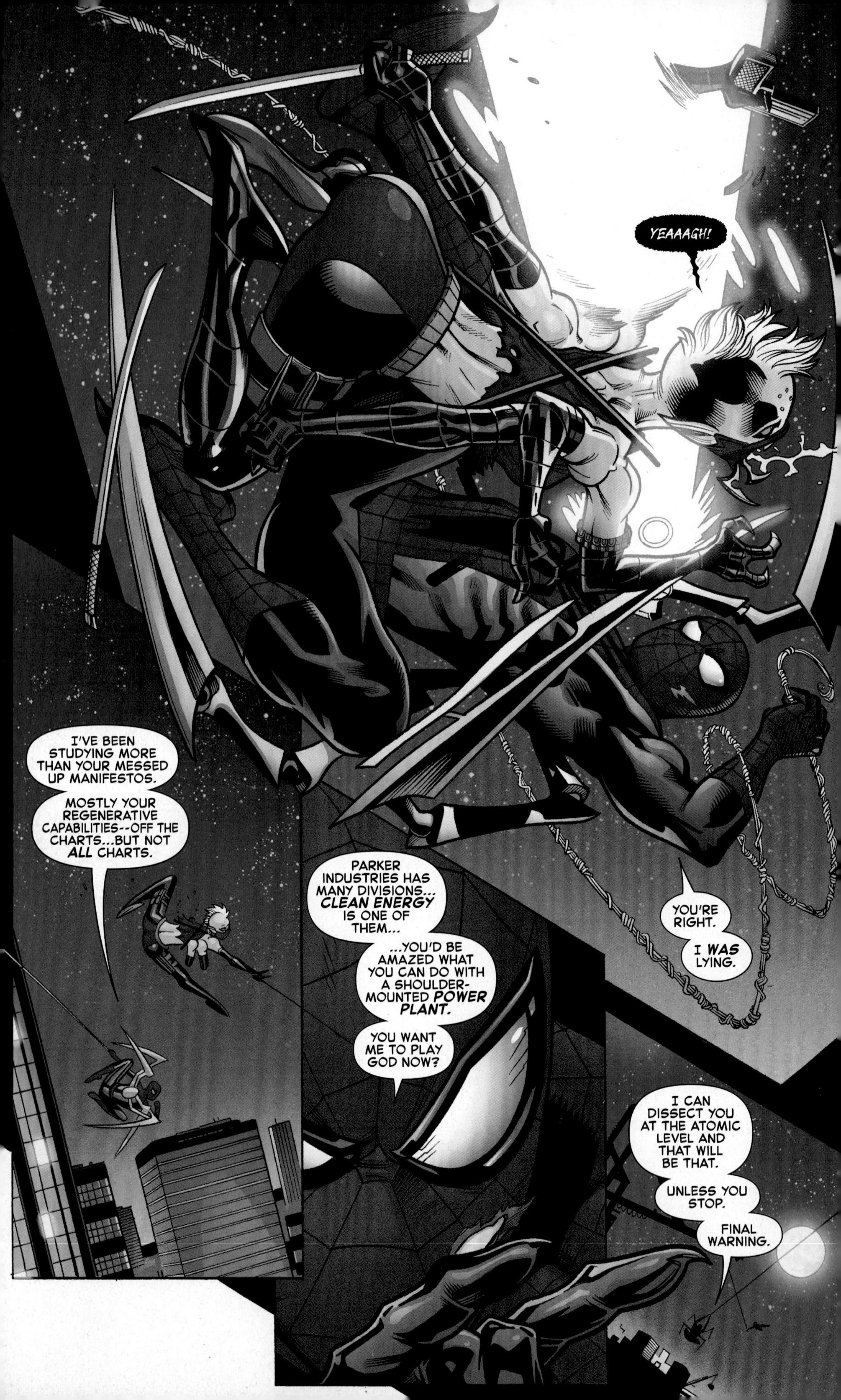
YEAAAGH!
I'VE BEEN STUDYING MORE THAN YOUR MESSED UP MANIFESTOS.
MOSTLY YOUR REGENERATIVE CAPABILITIES--OFF THE CHARTS...BUT NOT ALL CHARTS.
PARKER INDUSTRIES HAS MANY DIVISIONS... CLEAN ENERGY IS ONE OF THEM...
...YOU'D BE AMAZED WHAT YOU CAN DO WITH A SHOULDER-MOUNTED POWER PLANT.
YOU WANT ME TO PLAY GOD NOW?
YOU'RE RIGHT.
I WAS LYING.
I CAN DISSECT YOU AT THE ATOMIC LEVEL AND THAT WILL BE THAT.
UNLESS YOU STOP.
FINAL WARNING.

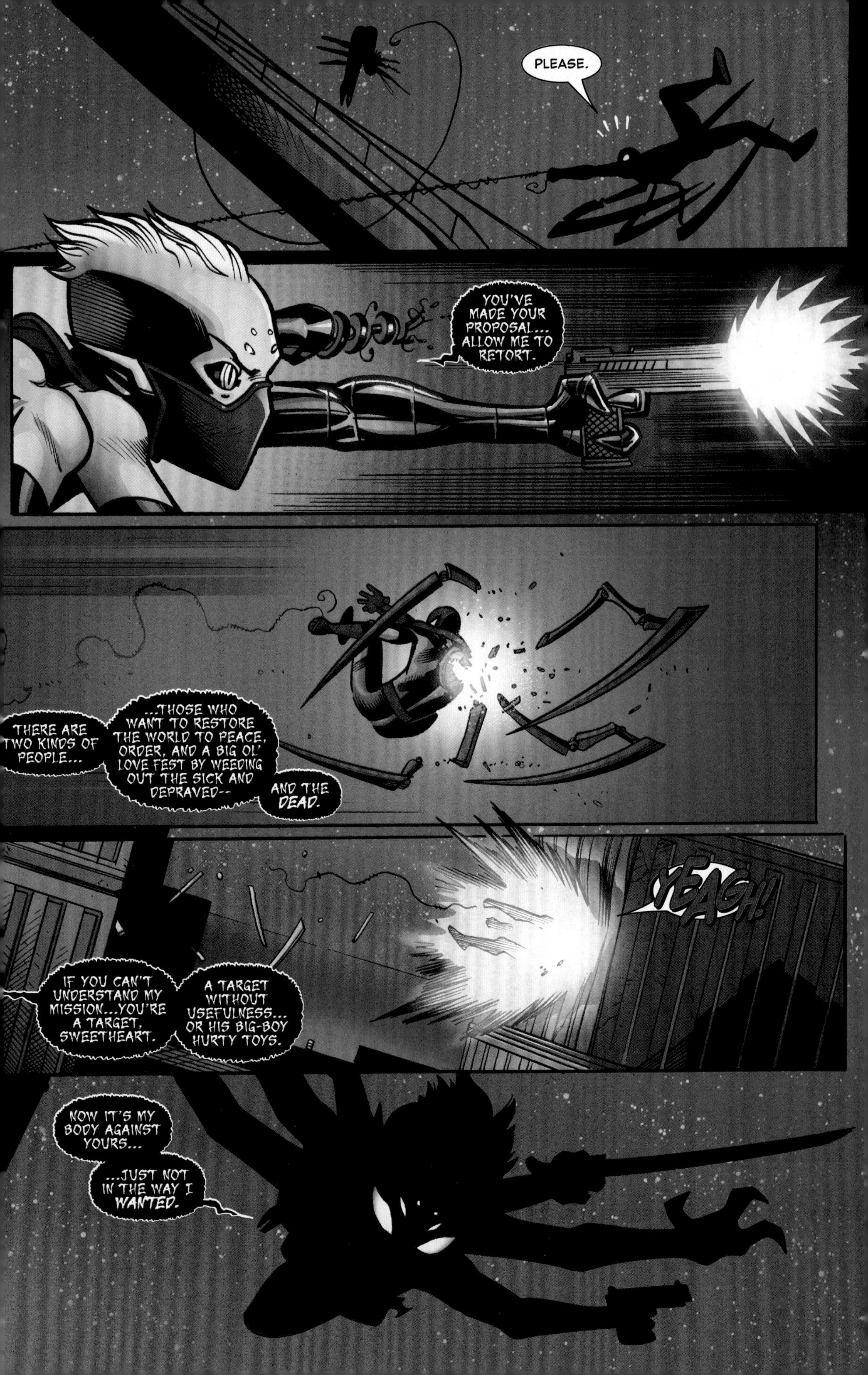
PLEASE.
YOU'VE MADE YOUR PROPOSAL... ALLOW ME TO RETORT.
THERE ARE TWO KINDS OF PEOPLE...
...THOSE WHO WANT TO RESTORE THE WORLD TO PEACE, ORDER, AND A BIG OL' LOVE FEST BY WEEDING OUT THE SICK AND DEPRAVED--
AND THE DEAD.
YEAGH!
IF YOU CAN'T UNDERSTAND MY MISSION...YOU'RE A TARGET, SWEETHEART.
A TARGET WITHOUT USEFULNESS... OR HIS BIG-BOY HURTY TOYS.
NOW IT'S MY BODY AGAINST YOURS...
...JUST NOT IN THE WAY I WANTED.

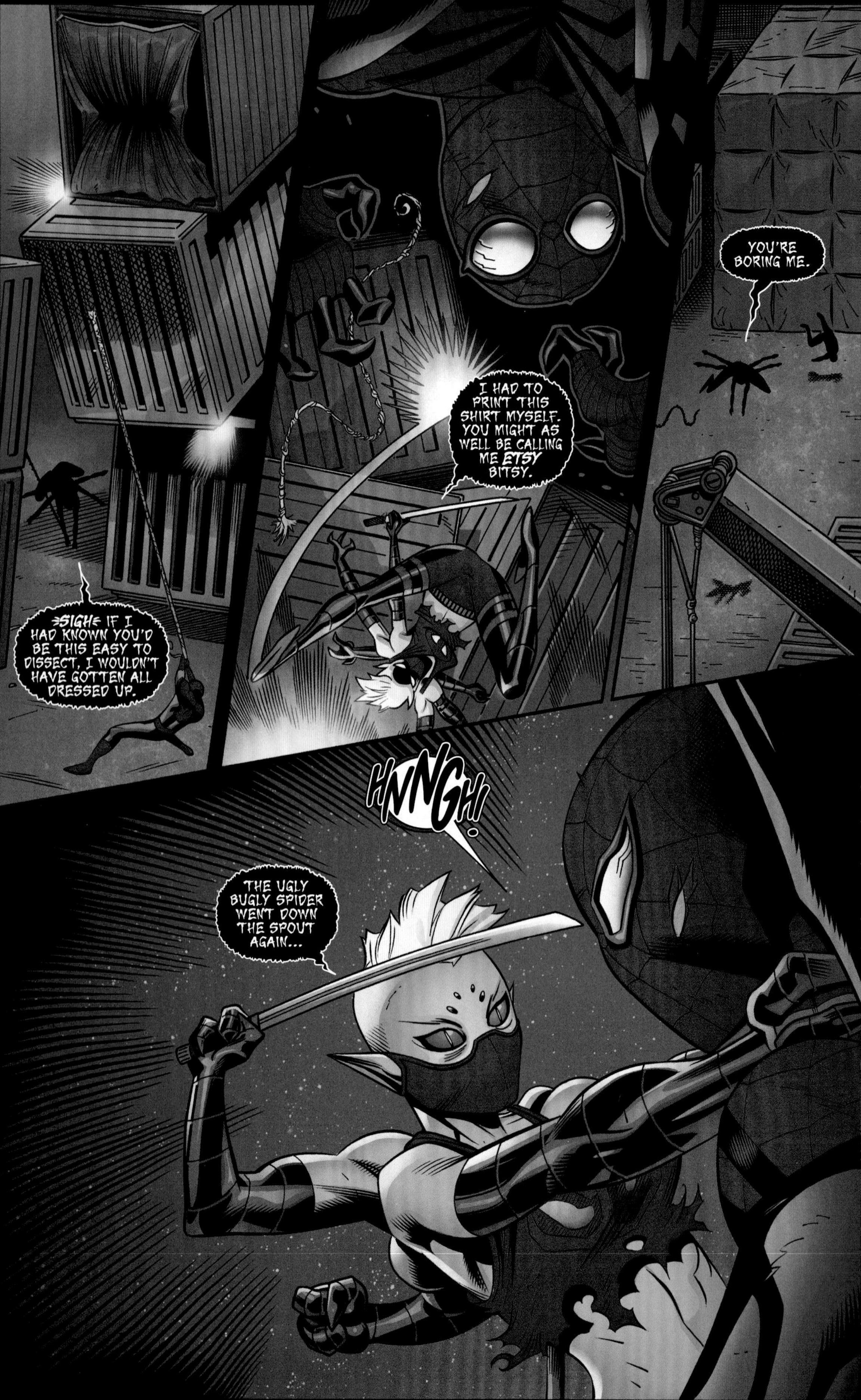

≈SIGH≈ IF I HAD KNOWN YOU'D BE THIS EASY TO DISSECT, I WOULDN'T HAVE GOTTEN ALL DRESSED UP.
I HAD TO PRINT THIS SHIRT MYSELF. YOU MIGHT AS WELL BE CALLING ME ETSY BITSY.
YOU'RE BORING ME.
HNNGH!
THE UGLY BUGLY SPIDER WENT DOWN THE SPOUT AGAIN...

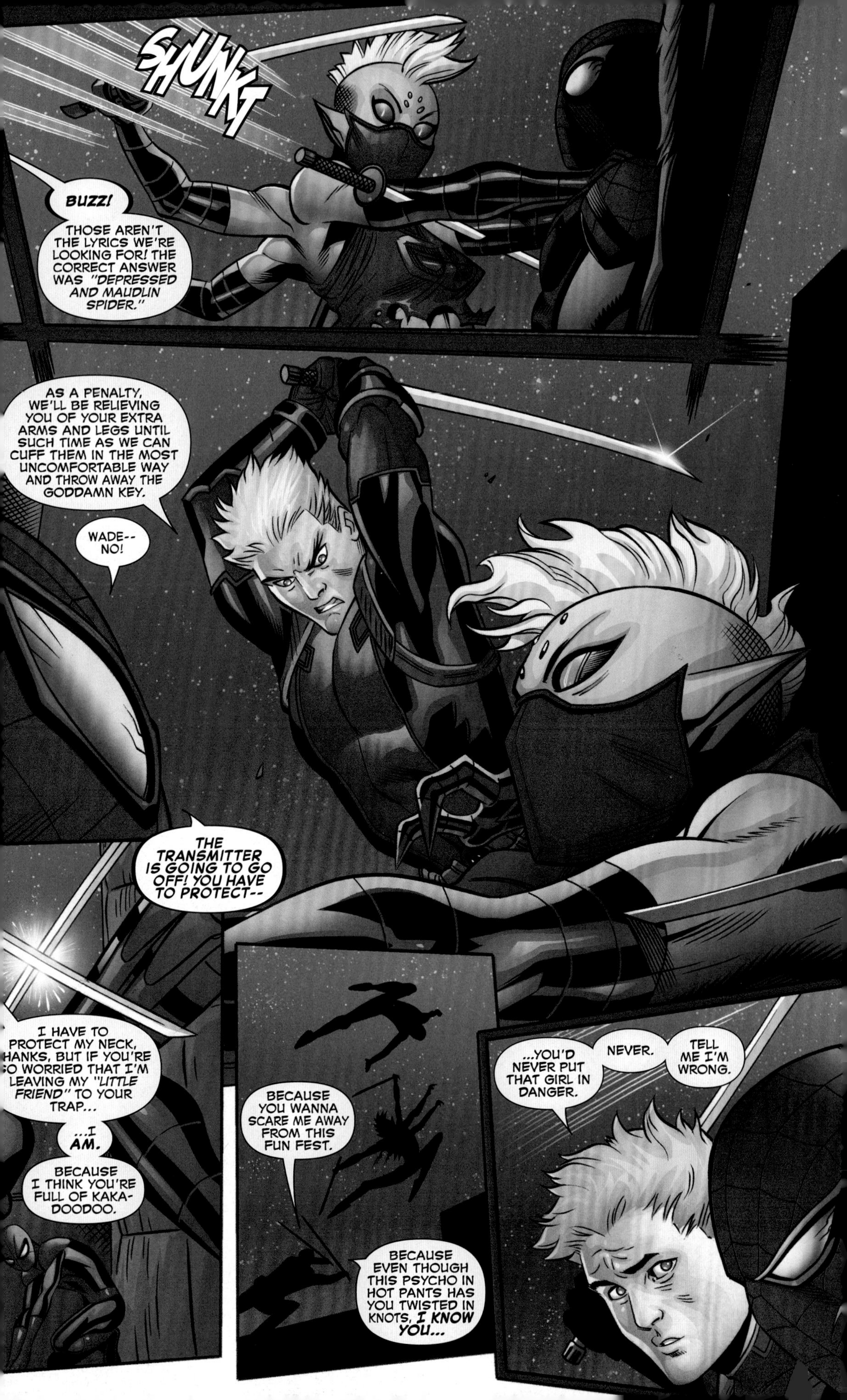
SHUNK!
BUZZ!
THOSE AREN'T THE LYRICS WE'RE LOOKING FOR! THE CORRECT ANSWER WAS "DEPRESSED AND MAUDLIN SPIDER."
AS A PENALTY, WE'LL BE RELIEVING YOU OF YOUR EXTRA ARMS AND LEGS UNTIL SUCH TIME AS WE CAN CUFF THEM IN THE MOST UNCOMFORTABLE WAY AND THROW AWAY THE GODDAMN KEY.
WADE-- NO!
THE TRANSMITTER IS GOING TO GO OFF! YOU HAVE TO PROTECT--
I HAVE TO PROTECT MY NECK, THANKS, BUT IF YOU'RE SO WORRIED THAT I'M LEAVING MY "LITTLE FRIEND" TO YOUR TRAP...
...I AM.
BECAUSE I THINK YOU'RE FULL OF KAKA-DOODOO.
BECAUSE YOU WANNA SCARE ME AWAY FROM THIS FUN FEST.
BECAUSE EVEN THOUGH THIS PSYCHO IN HOT PANTS HAS YOU TWISTED IN KNOTS, I KNOW YOU...
...YOU'D NEVER PUT THAT GIRL IN DANGER.
NEVER.
TELL ME I'M WRONG.

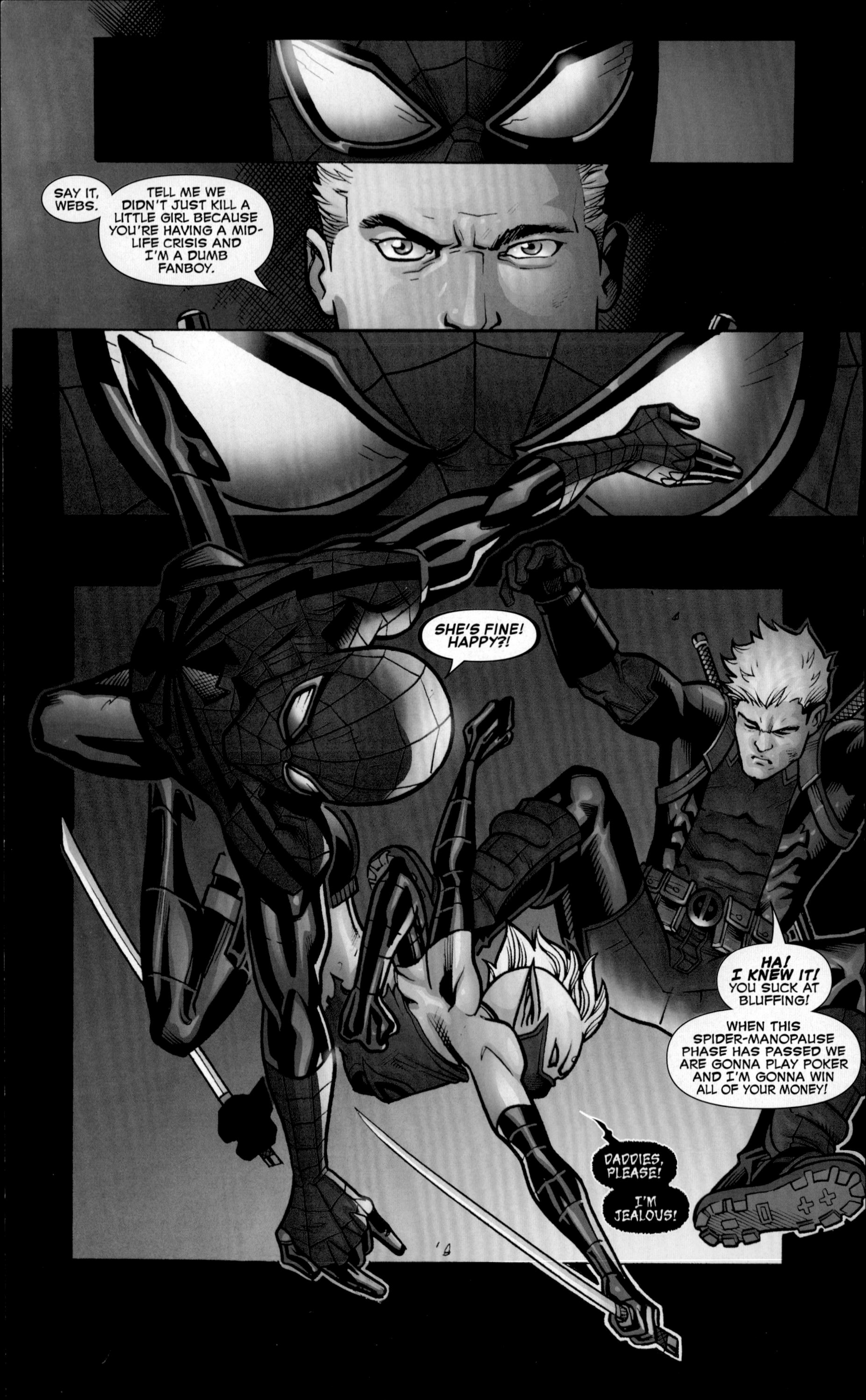
SAY IT, WEBS.
TELL ME WE DIDN'T JUST KILL A LITTLE GIRL BECAUSE YOU'RE HAVING A MID-LIFE CRISIS AND I'M A DUMB FANBOY.
SHE'S FINE! HAPPY?!
HA! I KNEW IT! YOU SUCK AT BLUFFING!
WHEN THIS SPIDER-MANOPAUSE PHASE HAS PASSED WE ARE GONNA PLAY POKER AND I'M GONNA WIN ALL OF YOUR MONEY!
DADDIES, PLEASE!
I'M JEALOUS!

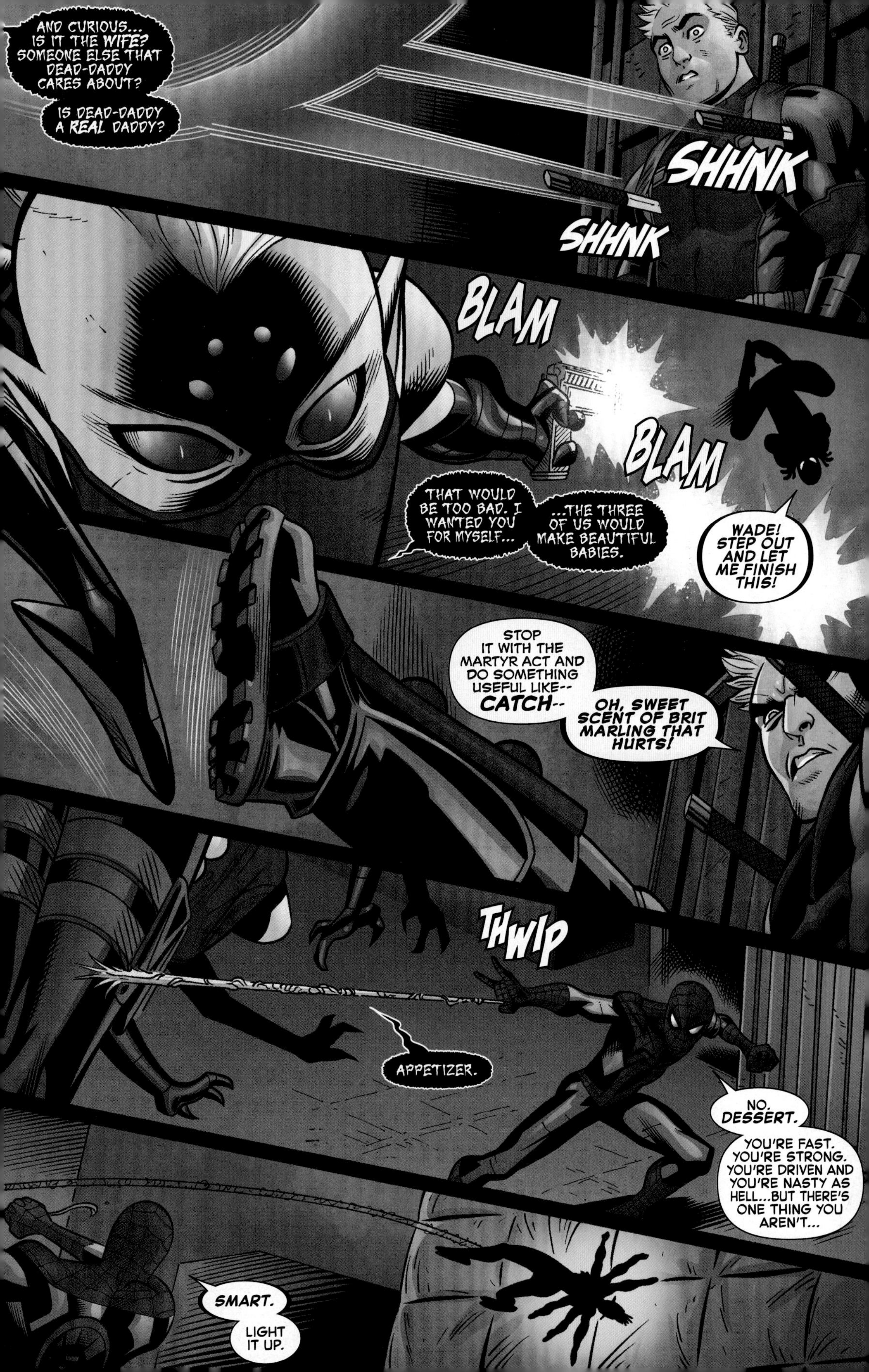
AND CURIOUS... IS IT THE WIFE? SOMEONE ELSE THAT DEAD-DADDY CARES ABOUT?
IS DEAD-DADDY A REAL DADDY?
SHHNK
SHHNK
BLAM
BLAM
THAT WOULD BE TOO BAD. I WANTED YOU FOR MYSELF...
...THE THREE OF US WOULD MAKE BEAUTIFUL BABIES.
WADE! STEP OUT AND LET ME FINISH THIS!
STOP IT WITH THE MARTYR ACT AND DO SOMETHING USEFUL LIKE-- CATCH--
OH, SWEET SCENT OF BRIT MARLING THAT HURTS!
THWIP
APPETIZER.
NO. DESSERT.
YOU'RE FAST. YOU'RE STRONG. YOU'RE DRIVEN AND YOU'RE NASTY AS HELL...BUT THERE'S ONE THING YOU AREN'T...
SMART.
LIGHT IT UP.

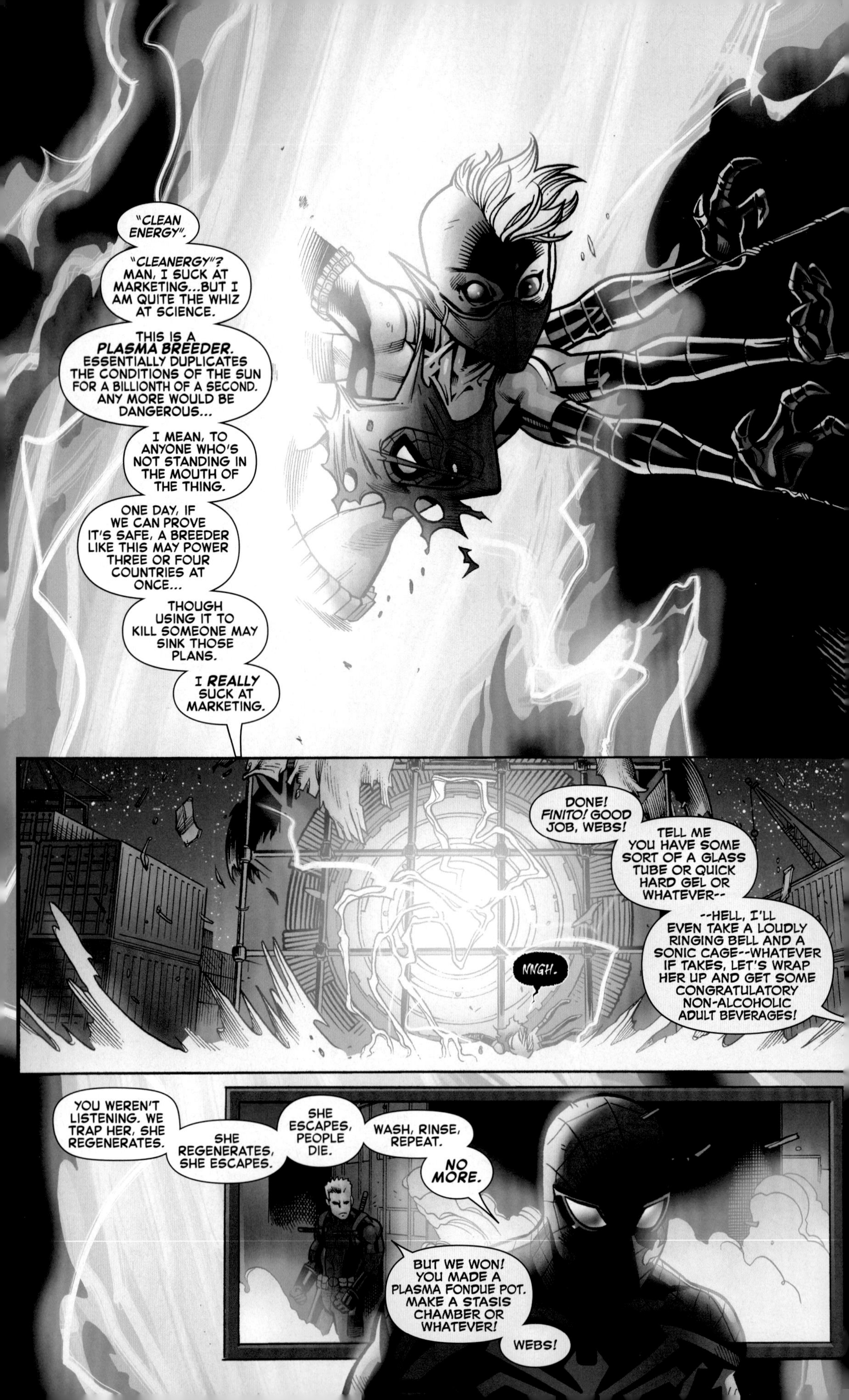

"CLEAN ENERGY".
"CLEANERGY"? MAN, I SUCK AT MARKETING...BUT I AM QUITE THE WHIZ AT SCIENCE.
THIS IS A PLASMA BREEDER. ESSENTIALLY DUPLICATES THE CONDITIONS OF THE SUN FOR A BILLIONTH OF A SECOND. ANY MORE WOULD BE DANGEROUS...
I MEAN, TO ANYONE WHO'S NOT STANDING IN THE MOUTH OF THE THING.
ONE DAY, IF WE CAN PROVE IT'S SAFE, A BREEDER LIKE THIS MAY POWER THREE OR FOUR COUNTRIES AT ONCE...
THOUGH USING IT TO KILL SOMEONE MAY SINK THOSE PLANS.
I REALLY SUCK AT MARKETING.
DONE! FINITO! GOOD JOB, WEBS!
TELL ME YOU HAVE SOME SORT OF A GLASS TUBE OR QUICK HARD GEL OR WHATEVER--
--HELL, I'LL EVEN TAKE A LOUDLY RINGING BELL AND A SONIC CAGE--WHATEVER IF TAKES, LET'S WRAP HER UP AND GET SOME CONGRATULATORY NON-ALCOHOLIC ADULT BEVERAGES!
NNGH.
YOU WEREN'T LISTENING. WE TRAP HER, SHE REGENERATES.
SHE REGENERATES, SHE ESCAPES.
SHE ESCAPES, PEOPLE DIE.
WASH, RINSE, REPEAT.
NO MORE.
BUT WE WON! YOU MADE A PLASMA FONDUE POT. MAKE A STASIS CHAMBER OR WHATEVER!
WEBS!

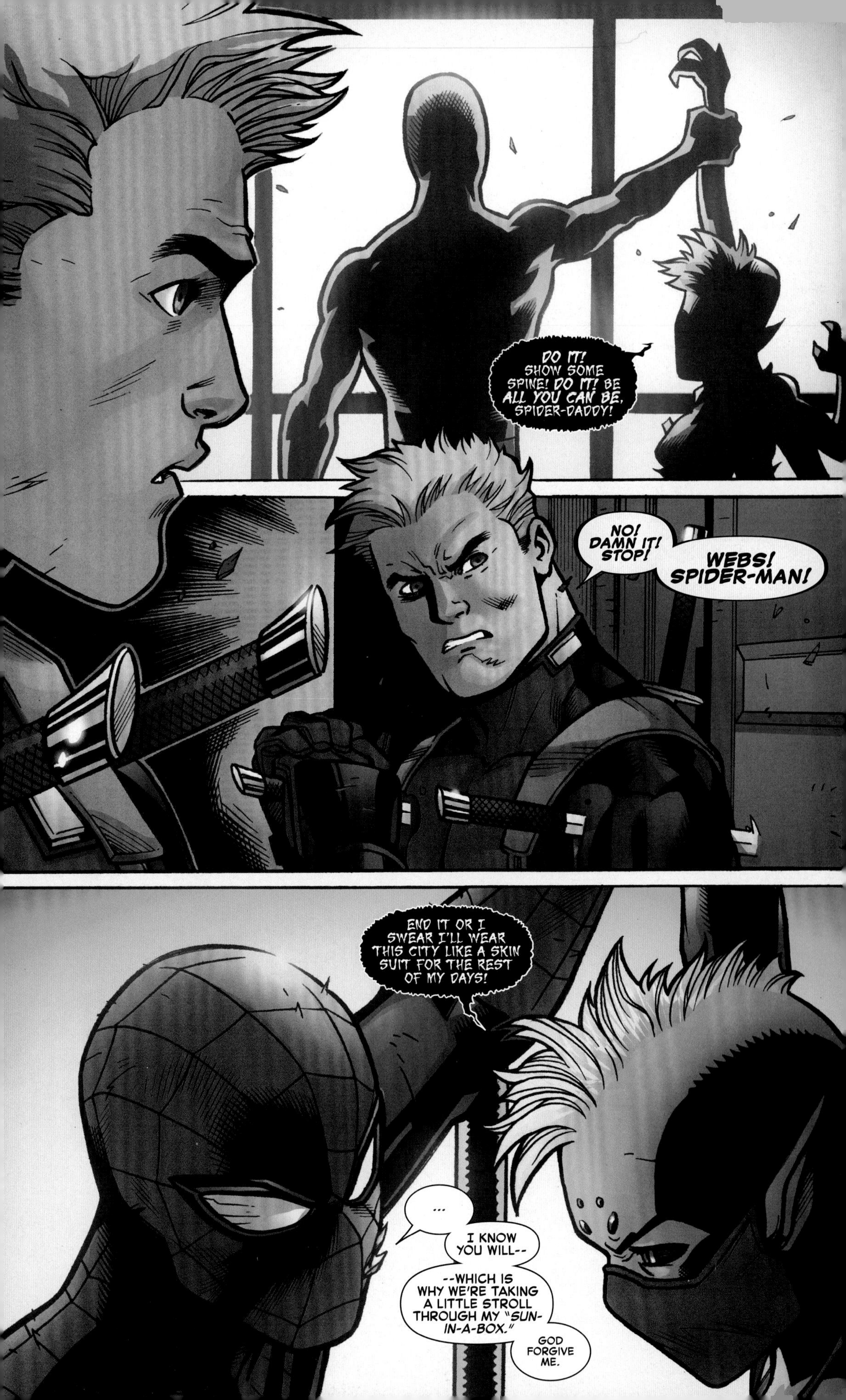
DO IT! SHOW SOME SPINE! DO IT! BE ALL YOU CAN BE, SPIDER-DADDY!
NO! DAMN IT! STOP!
WEBS! SPIDER-MAN!
END IT OR I SWEAR I'LL WEAR THIS CITY LIKE A SKIN SUIT FOR THE REST OF MY DAYS!
...
I KNOW YOU WILL--
--WHICH IS WHY WE'RE TAKING A LITTLE STROLL THROUGH MY "SUN-IN-A-BOX."
GOD FORGIVE ME.

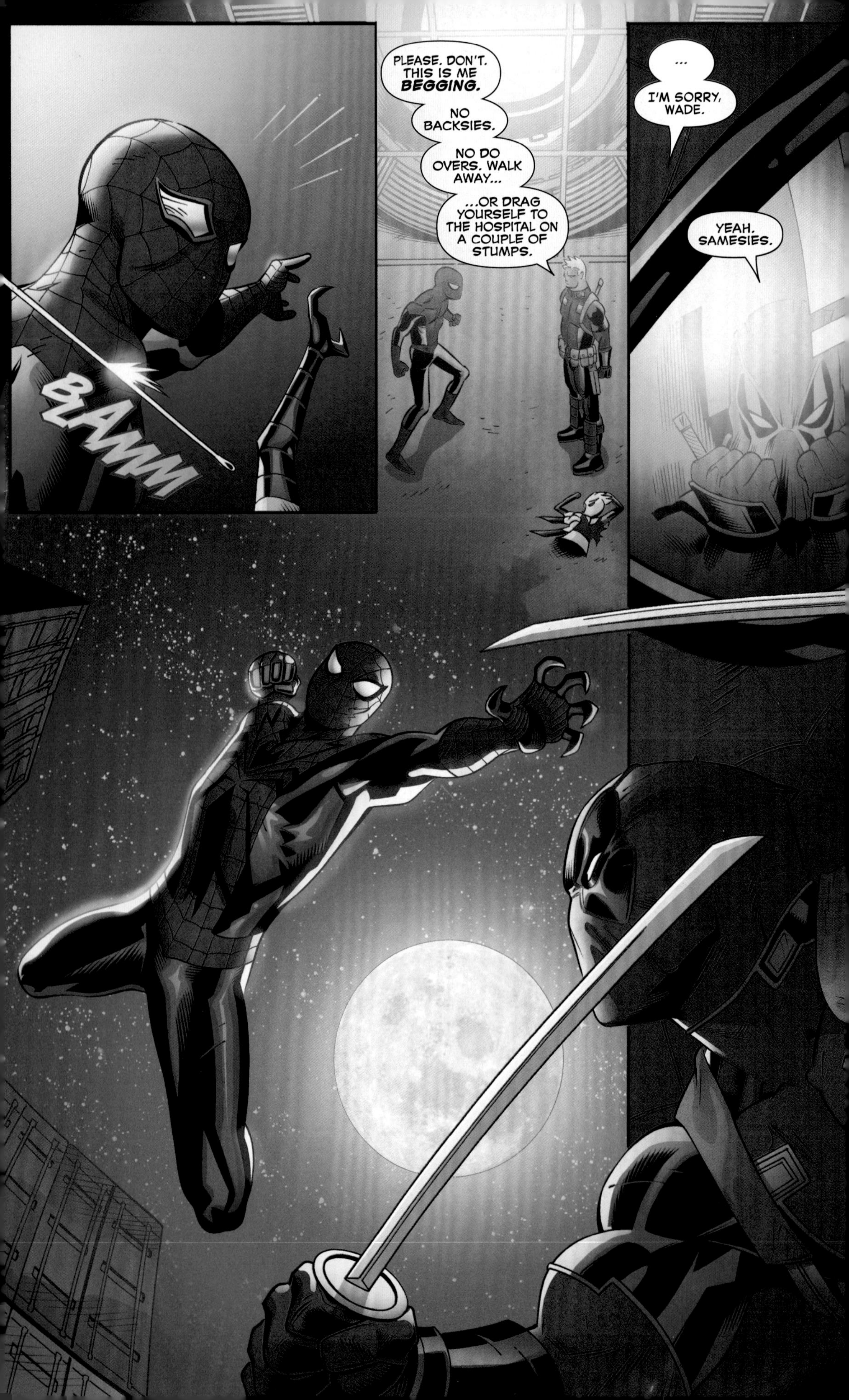
BLAMM
PLEASE. DON'T. THIS IS ME **BEGGING.**
NO BACKSIES.
NO DO OVERS. WALK AWAY...
...OR DRAG YOURSELF TO THE HOSPITAL ON A COUPLE OF STUMPS.
...
I'M SORRY, WADE.
YEAH. SAMESIES.

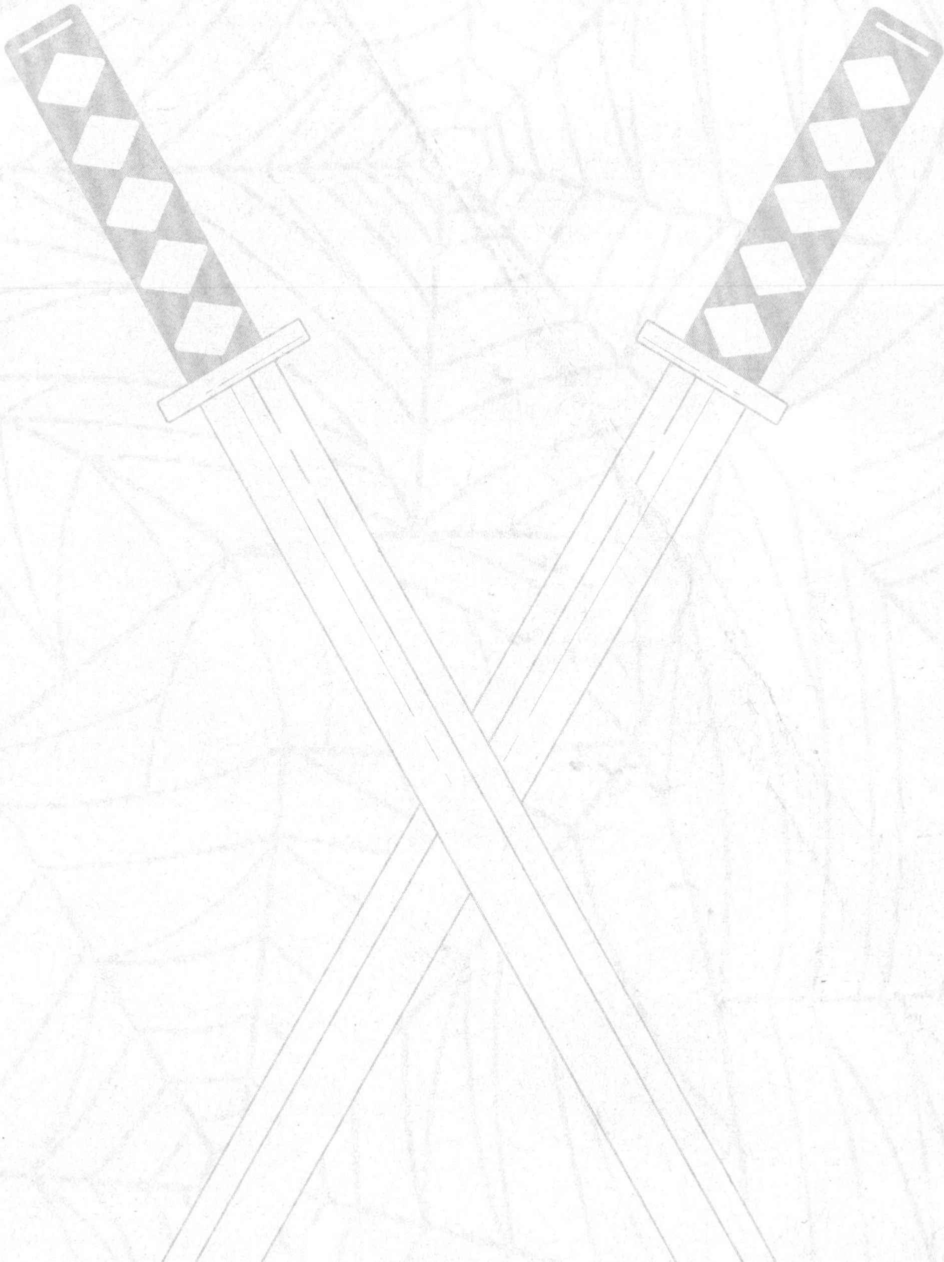

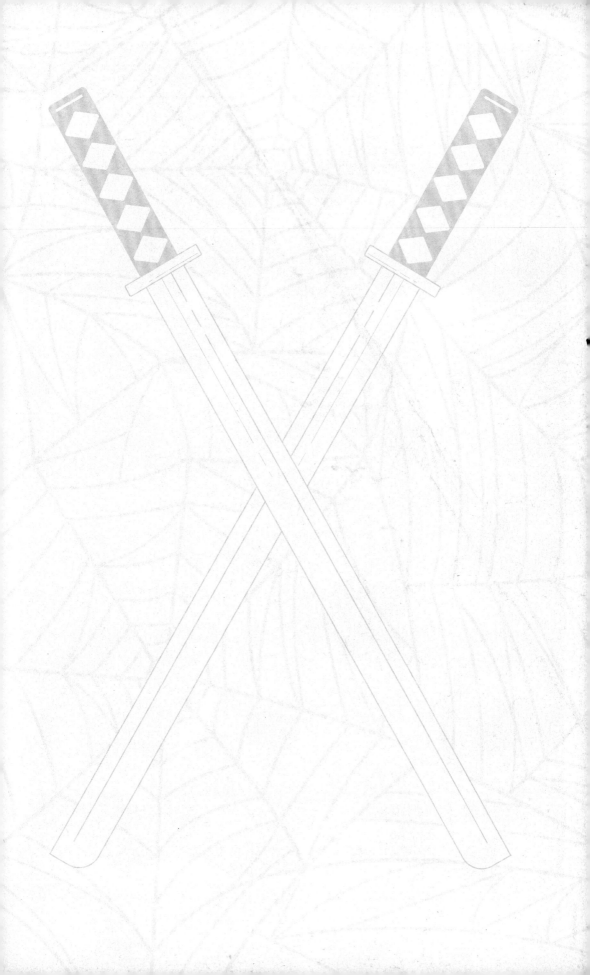

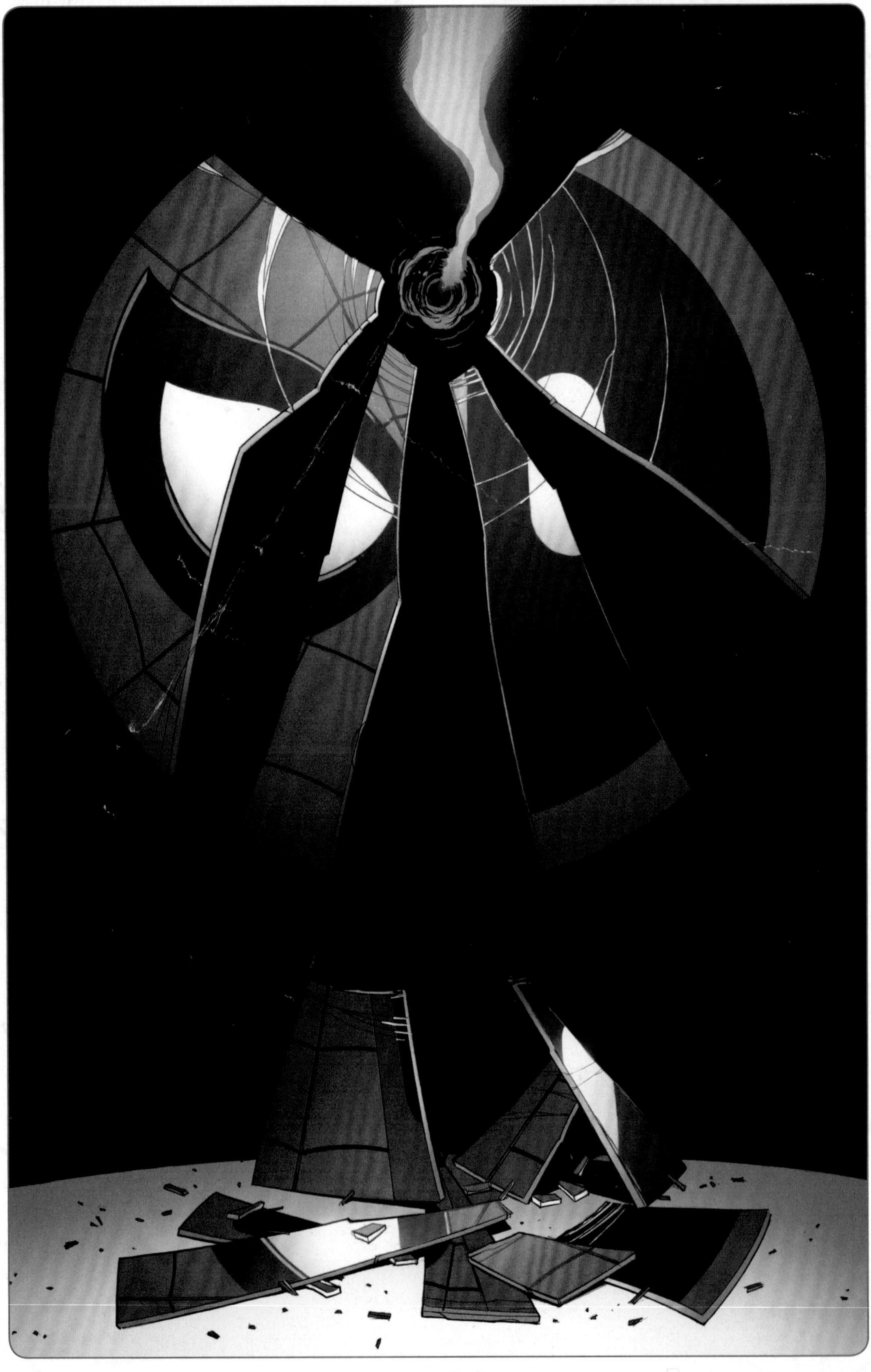

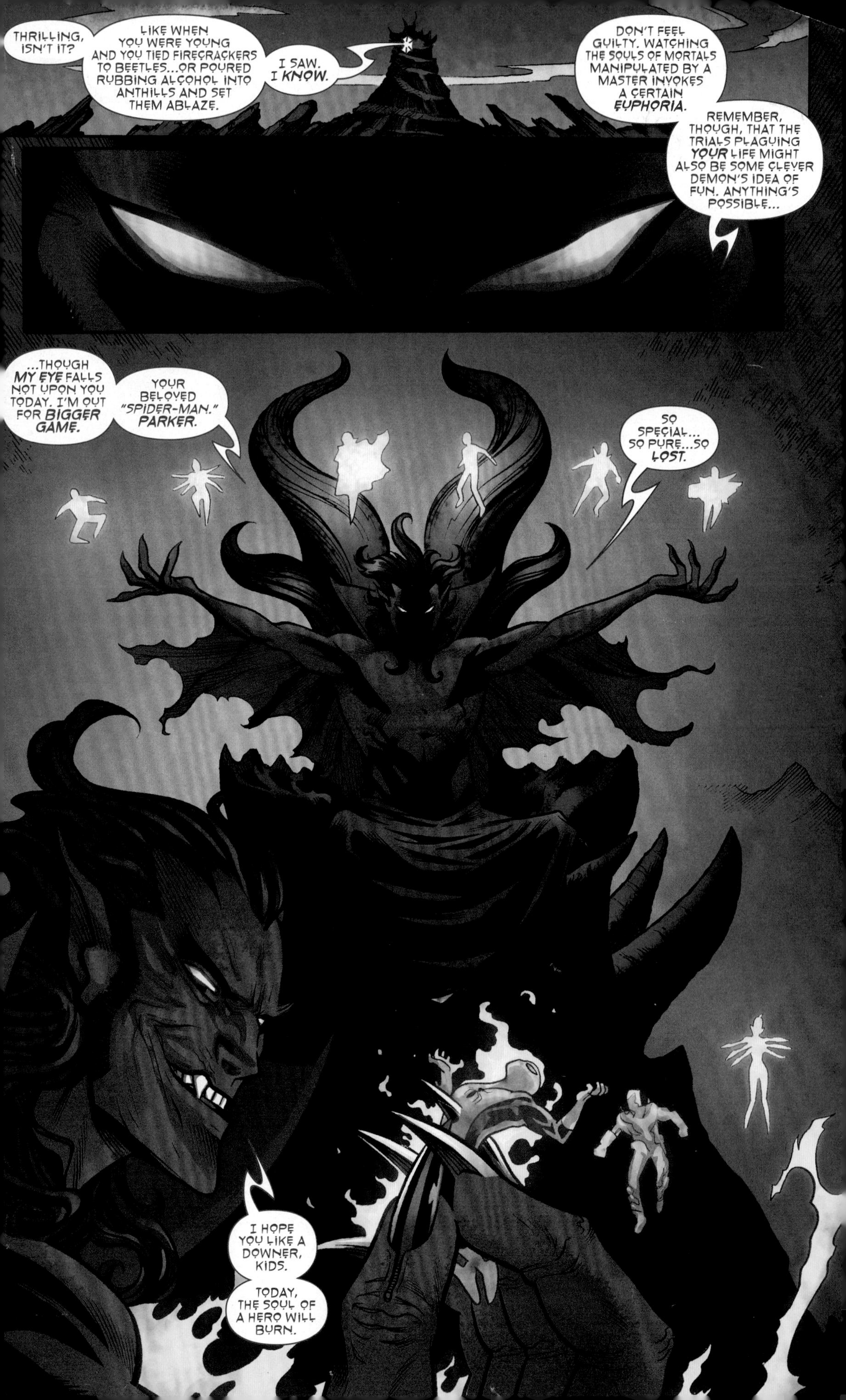
THRILLING, ISN'T IT?
LIKE WHEN YOU WERE YOUNG AND YOU TIED FIRECRACKERS TO BEETLES...OR POURED RUBBING ALCOHOL INTO ANTHILLS AND SET THEM ABLAZE.
I SAW. I KNOW.
DON'T FEEL GUILTY. WATCHING THE SOULS OF MORTALS MANIPULATED BY A MASTER INVOKES A CERTAIN EUPHORIA.
REMEMBER, THOUGH, THAT THE TRIALS PLAGUING YOUR LIFE MIGHT ALSO BE SOME CLEVER DEMON'S IDEA OF FUN. ANYTHING'S POSSIBLE...
...THOUGH MY EYE FALLS NOT UPON YOU TODAY. I'M OUT FOR BIGGER GAME.
YOUR BELOVED "SPIDER-MAN." PARKER.
SO SPECIAL... SO PURE...SO LOST.
I HOPE YOU LIKE A DOWNER, KIDS.
TODAY, THE SOUL OF A HERO WILL BURN.

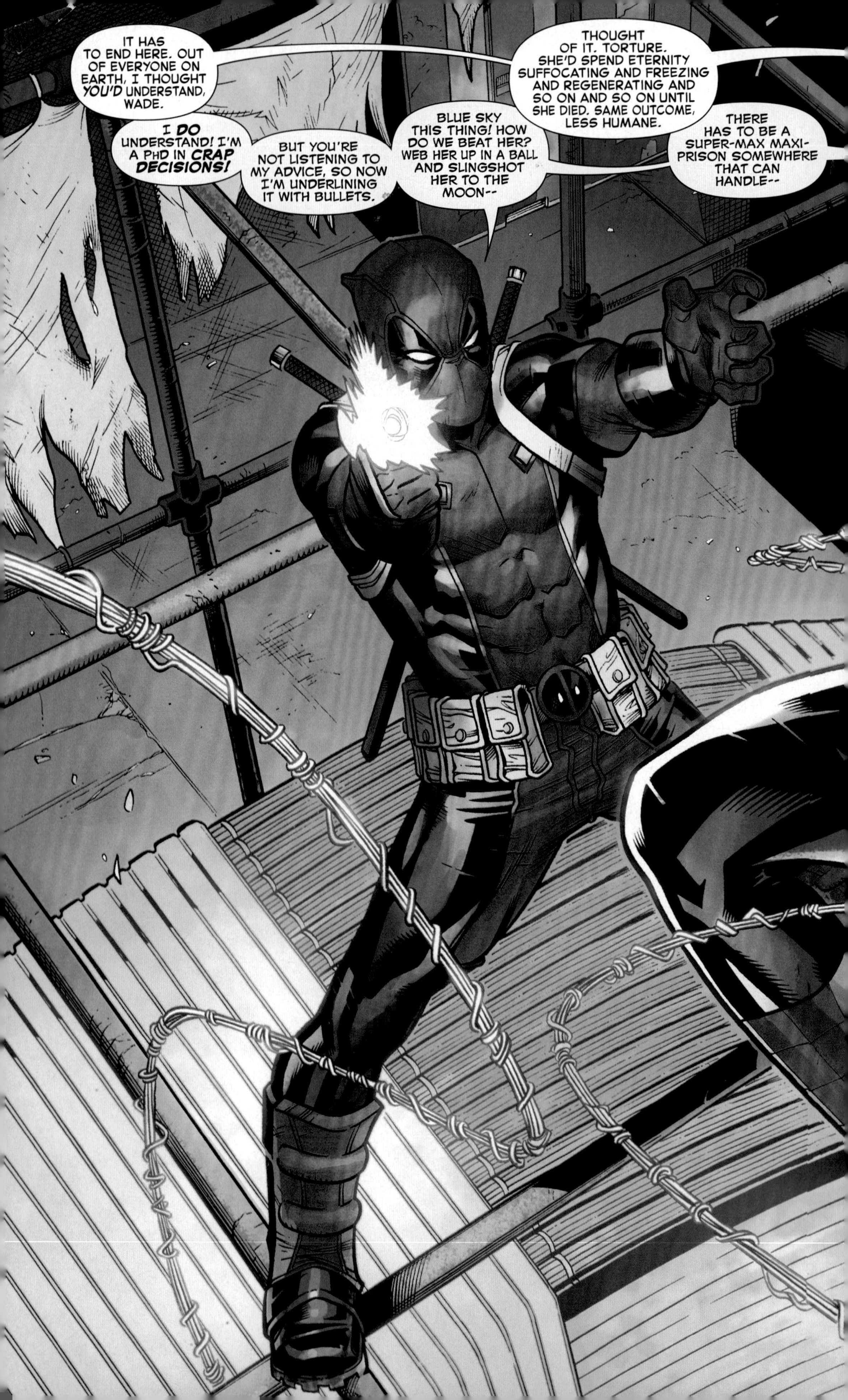
IT HAS TO END HERE. OUT OF EVERYONE ON EARTH, I THOUGHT *YOU'D* UNDERSTAND, WADE.
I ***DO*** UNDERSTAND! I'M A PHD IN ***CRAP DECISIONS!***
BUT YOU'RE NOT LISTENING TO MY ADVICE, SO NOW I'M UNDERLINING IT WITH BULLETS.
BLUE SKY THIS THING! HOW DO WE BEAT HER? WEB HER UP IN A BALL AND SLINGSHOT HER TO THE MOON--
THOUGHT OF IT. TORTURE. SHE'D SPEND ETERNITY SUFFOCATING AND FREEZING AND REGENERATING AND SO ON AND SO ON UNTIL SHE DIED. SAME OUTCOME, LESS HUMANE.
THERE HAS TO BE A SUPER-MAX MAXI-PRISON SOMEWHERE THAT CAN HANDLE--

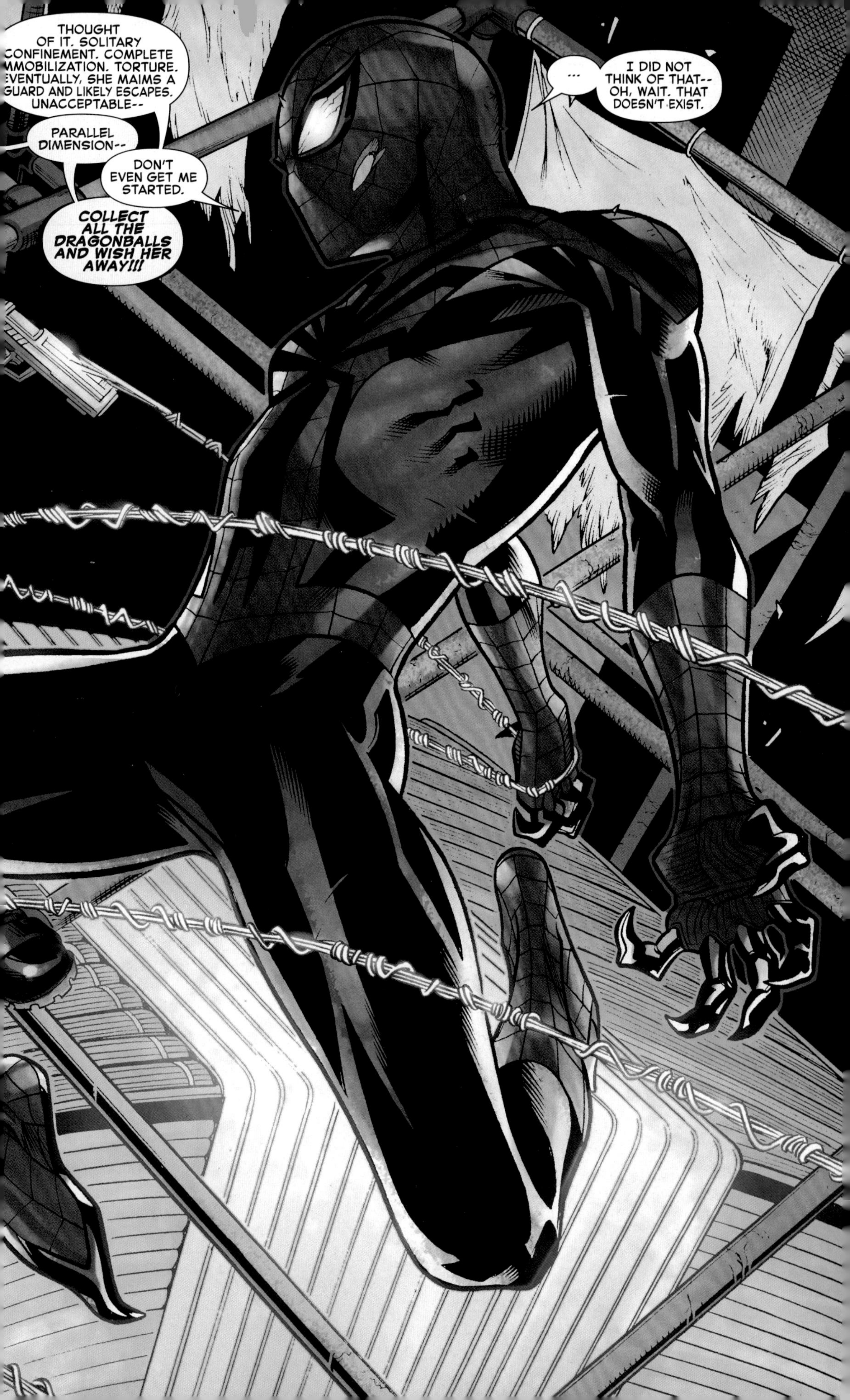

THOUGHT OF IT. SOLITARY CONFINEMENT. COMPLETE MMOBILIZATION. TORTURE. EVENTUALLY, SHE MAIMS A GUARD AND LIKELY ESCAPES. UNACCEPTABLE--
PARALLEL DIMENSION--
DON'T EVEN GET ME STARTED.
COLLECT ALL THE DRAGONBALLS AND WISH HER AWAY!!!
...
I DID NOT THINK OF THAT-- OH, WAIT. THAT DOESN'T EXIST.

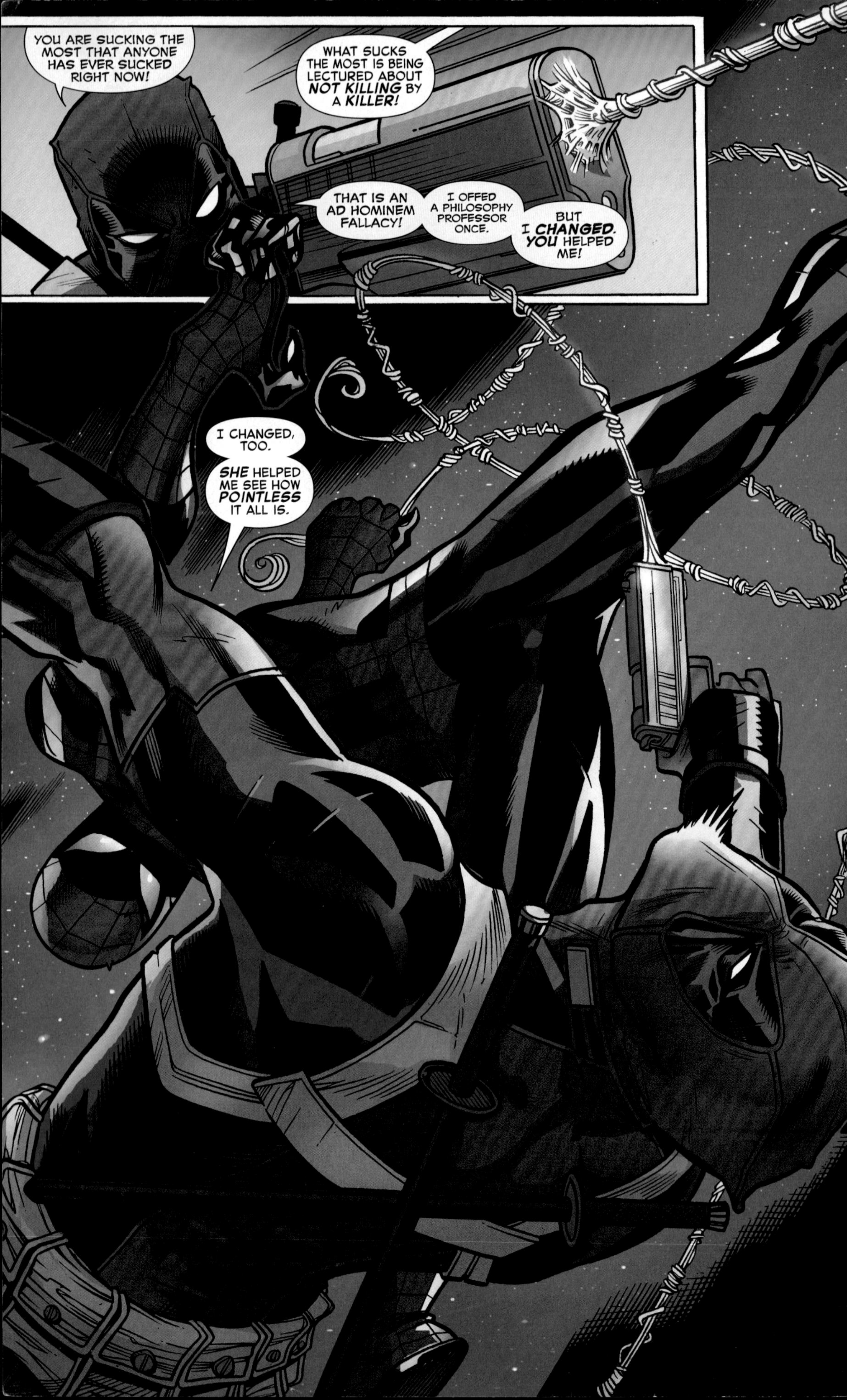
YOU ARE SUCKING THE MOST THAT ANYONE HAS EVER SUCKED RIGHT NOW!
WHAT SUCKS THE MOST IS BEING LECTURED ABOUT **NOT KILLING** BY A **KILLER!**
THAT IS AN AD HOMINEM FALLACY!
I OFFED A PHILOSOPHY PROFESSOR ONCE.
BUT I **CHANGED. YOU** HELPED ME!
I CHANGED, TOO.
SHE HELPED ME SEE HOW **POINTLESS** IT ALL IS.

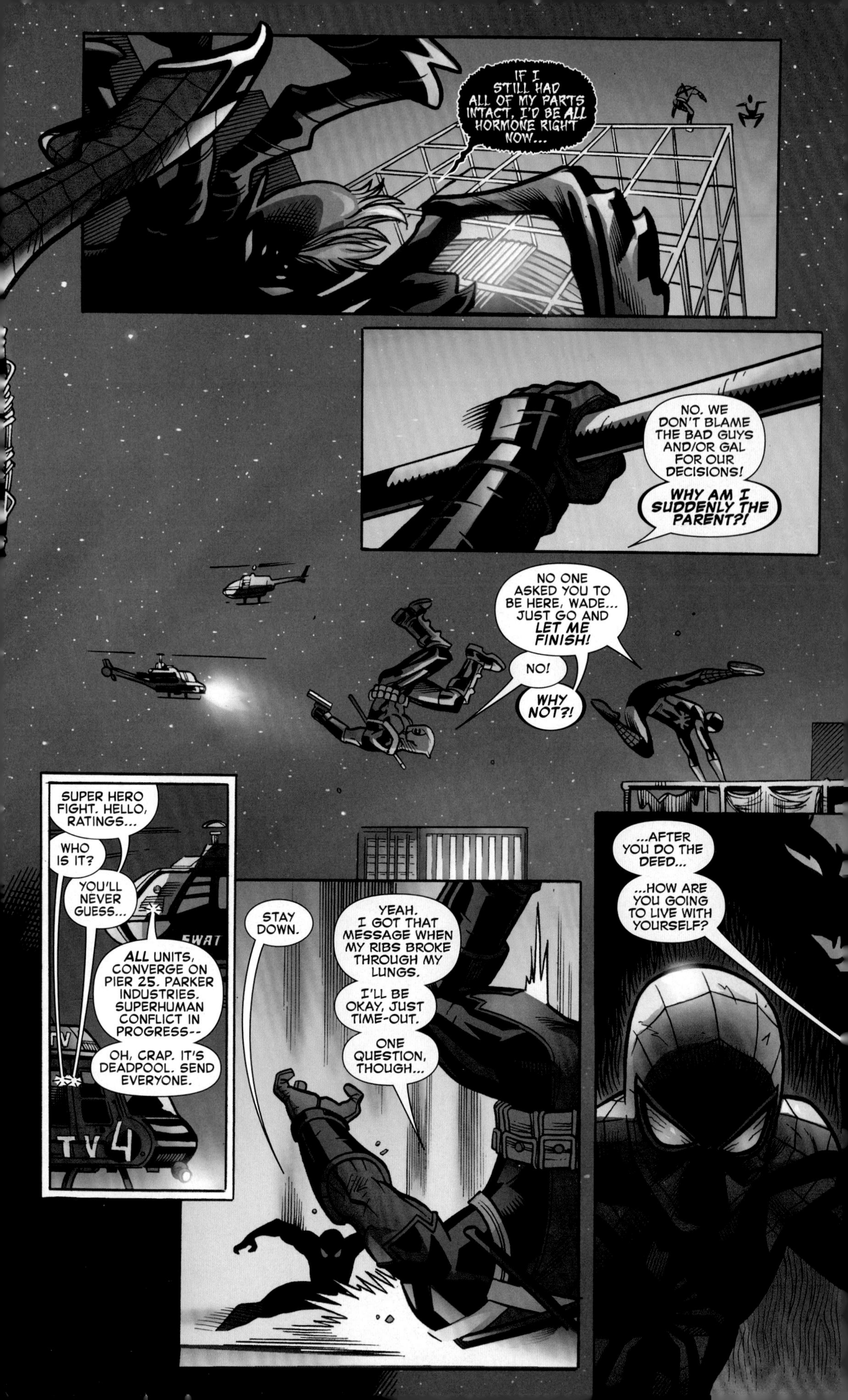
IF I STILL HAD ALL OF MY PARTS INTACT, I'D BE ALL HORMONE RIGHT NOW...
NO. WE DON'T BLAME THE BAD GUYS AND/OR GAL FOR OUR DECISIONS!
WHY AM I SUDDENLY THE PARENT?!
NO ONE ASKED YOU TO BE HERE, WADE... JUST GO AND LET ME FINISH!
NO!
WHY NOT?!
SUPER HERO FIGHT. HELLO, RATINGS...
WHO IS IT?
YOU'LL NEVER GUESS...
ALL UNITS, CONVERGE ON PIER 25. PARKER INDUSTRIES. SUPERHUMAN CONFLICT IN PROGRESS--
OH, CRAP. IT'S DEADPOOL. SEND EVERYONE.
TV 4
SWAT
STAY DOWN.
YEAH. I GOT THAT MESSAGE WHEN MY RIBS BROKE THROUGH MY LUNGS.
I'LL BE OKAY, JUST TIME-OUT.
ONE QUESTION, THOUGH...
...AFTER YOU DO THE DEED...
...HOW ARE YOU GOING TO LIVE WITH YOURSELF?

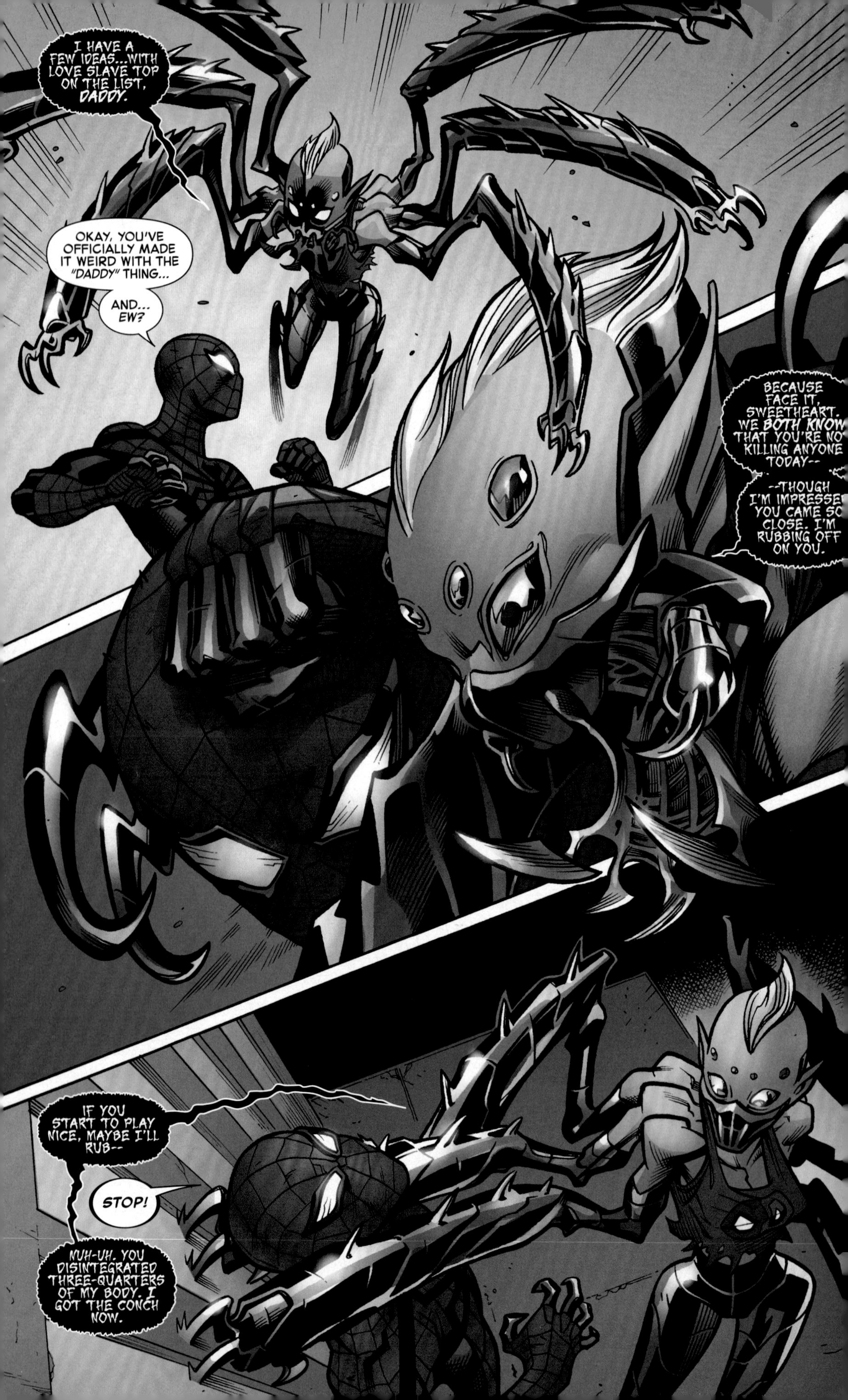

I HAVE A FEW IDEAS...WITH LOVE SLAVE TOP ON THE LIST, DADDY.
OKAY, YOU'VE OFFICIALLY MADE IT WEIRD WITH THE "DADDY" THING...
AND... EW?
BECAUSE FACE IT, SWEETHEART. WE BOTH KNOW THAT YOU'RE NOT KILLING ANYONE TODAY--
--THOUGH I'M IMPRESSED YOU CAME SO CLOSE. I'M RUBBING OFF ON YOU.
IF YOU START TO PLAY NICE, MAYBE I'LL RUB--
STOP!
NUH-UH. YOU DISINTEGRATED THREE-QUARTERS OF MY BODY. I GOT THE CONCH NOW.

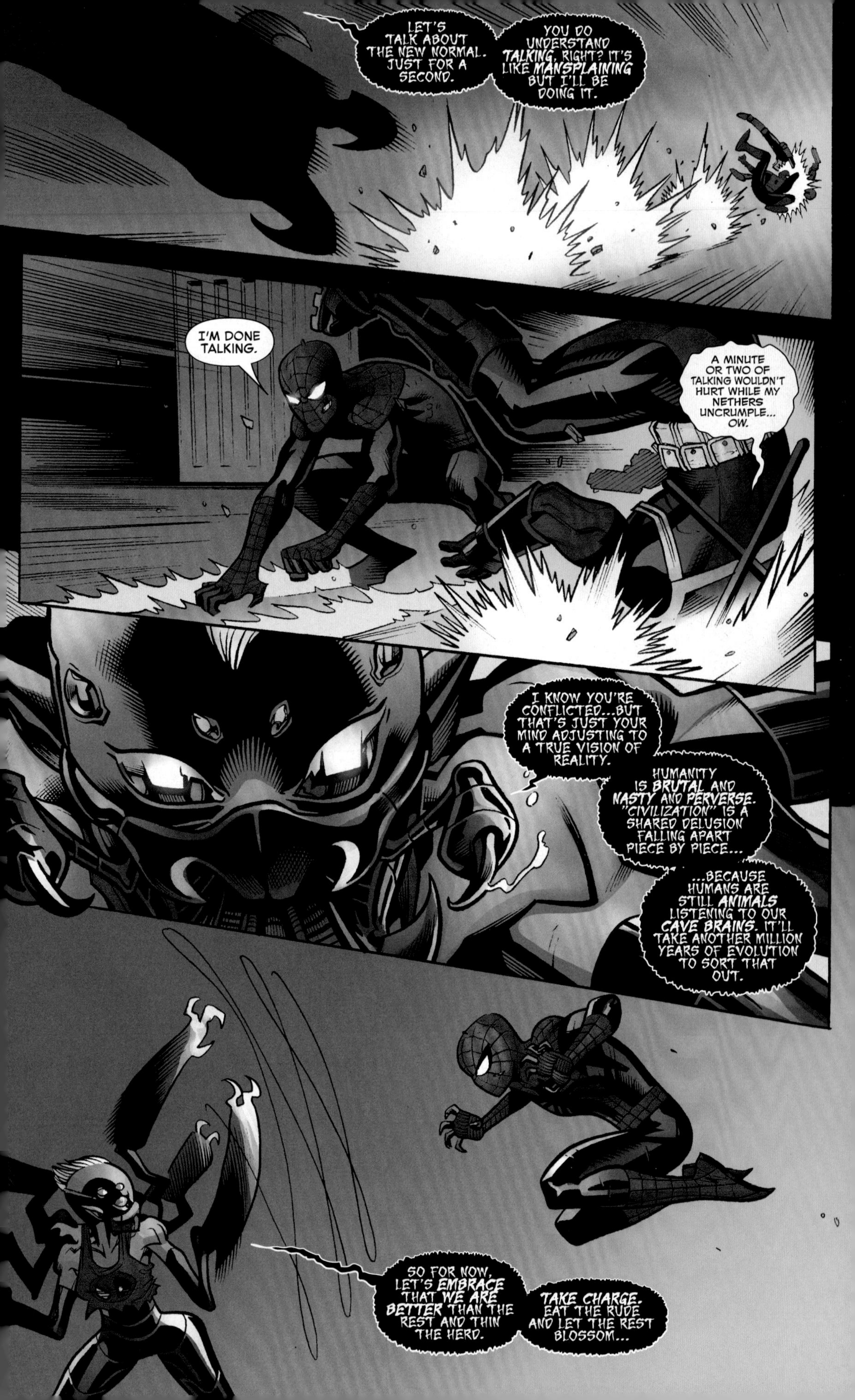
LET'S TALK ABOUT THE NEW NORMAL. JUST FOR A SECOND.
YOU DO UNDERSTAND TALKING, RIGHT? IT'S LIKE MANSPLAINING BUT I'LL BE DOING IT.
I'M DONE TALKING.
A MINUTE OR TWO OF TALKING WOULDN'T HURT WHILE MY NETHERS UNCRUMPLE... OW.
I KNOW YOU'RE CONFLICTED...BUT THAT'S JUST YOUR MIND ADJUSTING TO A TRUE VISION OF REALITY.
HUMANITY IS BRUTAL AND NASTY AND PERVERSE. "CIVILIZATION" IS A SHARED DELUSION FALLING APART PIECE BY PIECE...
...BECAUSE HUMANS ARE STILL ANIMALS LISTENING TO OUR CAVE BRAINS. IT'LL TAKE ANOTHER MILLION YEARS OF EVOLUTION TO SORT THAT OUT.
SO FOR NOW, LET'S EMBRACE THAT WE ARE BETTER THAN THE REST AND THIN THE HERD.
TAKE CHARGE. EAT THE RUDE AND LET THE REST BLOSSOM...

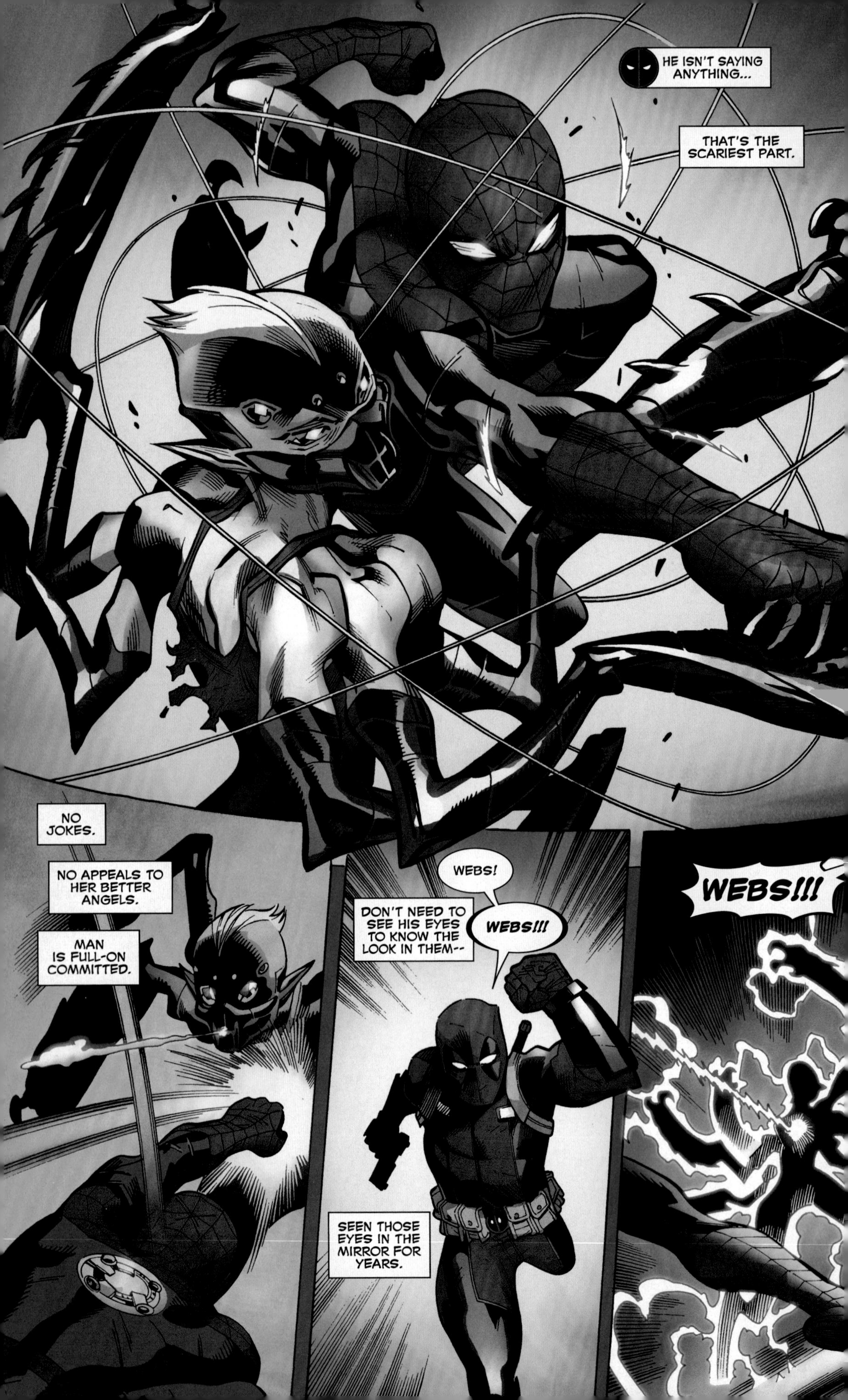
HE ISN'T SAYING ANYTHING...
THAT'S THE SCARIEST PART.
NO JOKES.
NO APPEALS TO HER BETTER ANGELS.
MAN IS FULL-ON COMMITTED.
DON'T NEED TO SEE HIS EYES TO KNOW THE LOOK IN THEM--
WEBS!
WEBS!!!
SEEN THOSE EYES IN THE MIRROR FOR YEARS.
WEBS!!!

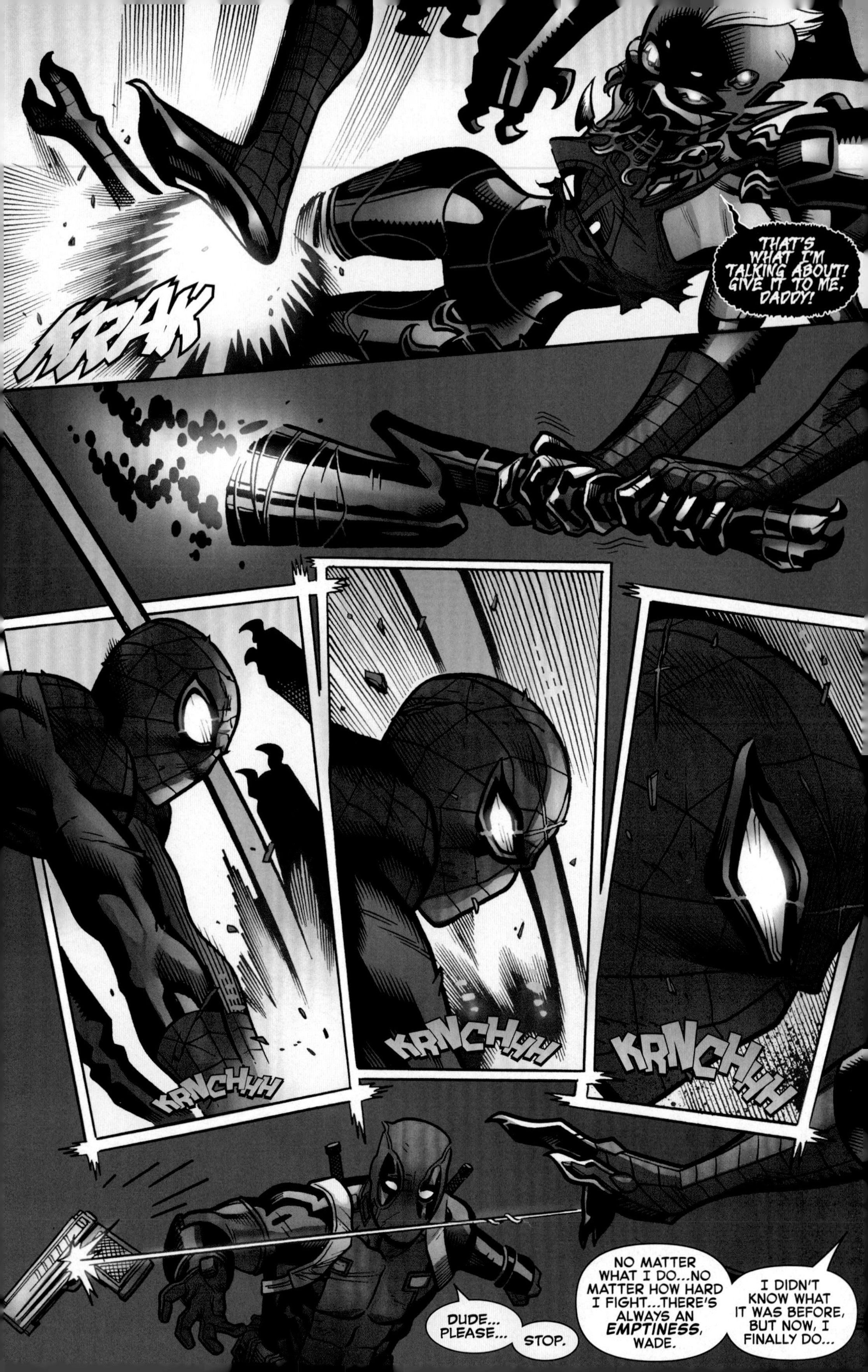
THAT'S WHAT I'M TALKING ABOUT! GIVE IT TO ME, DADDY!
KRAK
KRNCHHH
KRNCHHH
KRNCHHH
DUDE... PLEASE...
STOP.
NO MATTER WHAT I DO...NO MATTER HOW HARD I FIGHT...THERE'S ALWAYS AN **EMPTINESS**, WADE.
I DIDN'T KNOW WHAT IT WAS BEFORE, BUT NOW, I FINALLY DO...

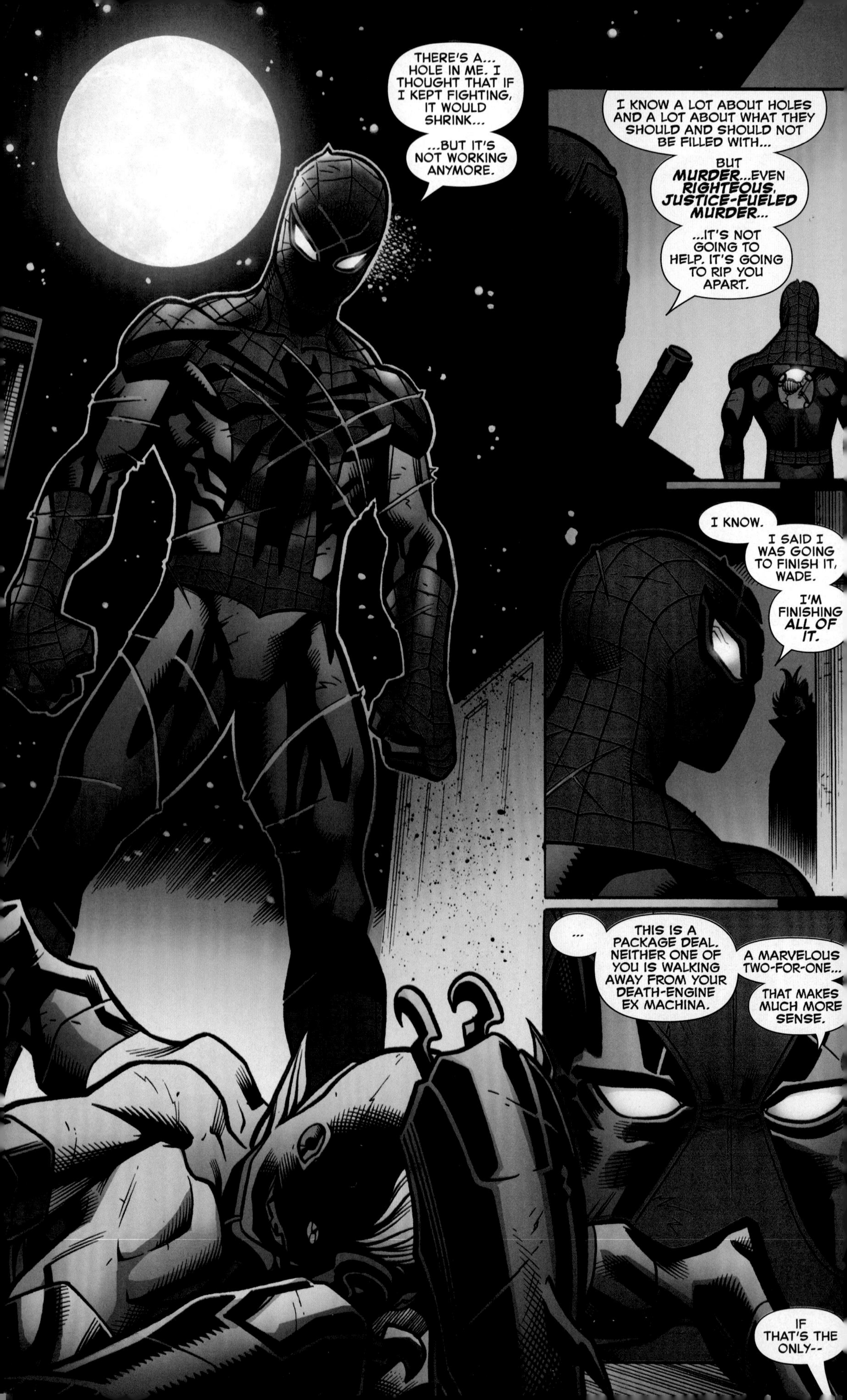
THERE'S A... HOLE IN ME. I THOUGHT THAT IF I KEPT FIGHTING, IT WOULD SHRINK...
...BUT IT'S NOT WORKING ANYMORE.
I KNOW A LOT ABOUT HOLES AND A LOT ABOUT WHAT THEY SHOULD AND SHOULD NOT BE FILLED WITH...
BUT ***MURDER***...EVEN ***RIGHTEOUS, JUSTICE-FUELED MURDER***...
...IT'S NOT GOING TO HELP. IT'S GOING TO RIP YOU APART.
I KNOW.
I SAID I WAS GOING TO FINISH IT, WADE.
I'M FINISHING ***ALL OF IT.***
...
THIS IS A PACKAGE DEAL. NEITHER ONE OF YOU IS WALKING AWAY FROM YOUR DEATH-ENGINE EX MACHINA.
A MARVELOUS TWO-FOR-ONE...
THAT MAKES MUCH MORE SENSE.
IF THAT'S THE ONLY--

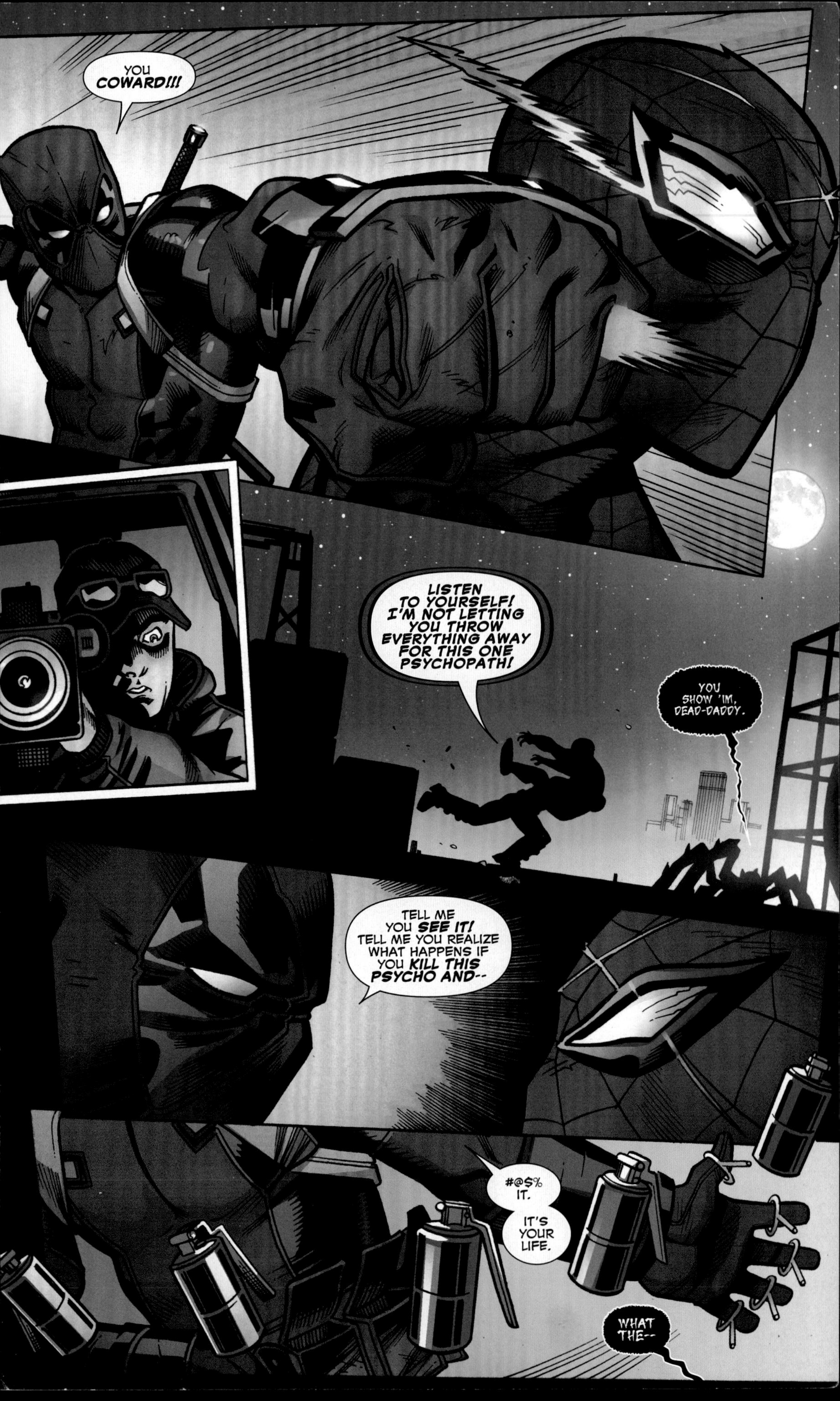
YOU COWARD!!!
LISTEN TO YOURSELF! I'M NOT LETTING YOU THROW EVERYTHING AWAY FOR THIS ONE PSYCHOPATH!
YOU SHOW 'IM, DEAD-DADDY.
TELL ME YOU SEE IT! TELL ME YOU REALIZE WHAT HAPPENS IF YOU KILL THIS PSYCHO AND--
#@$% IT.
IT'S YOUR LIFE.
WHAT THE--

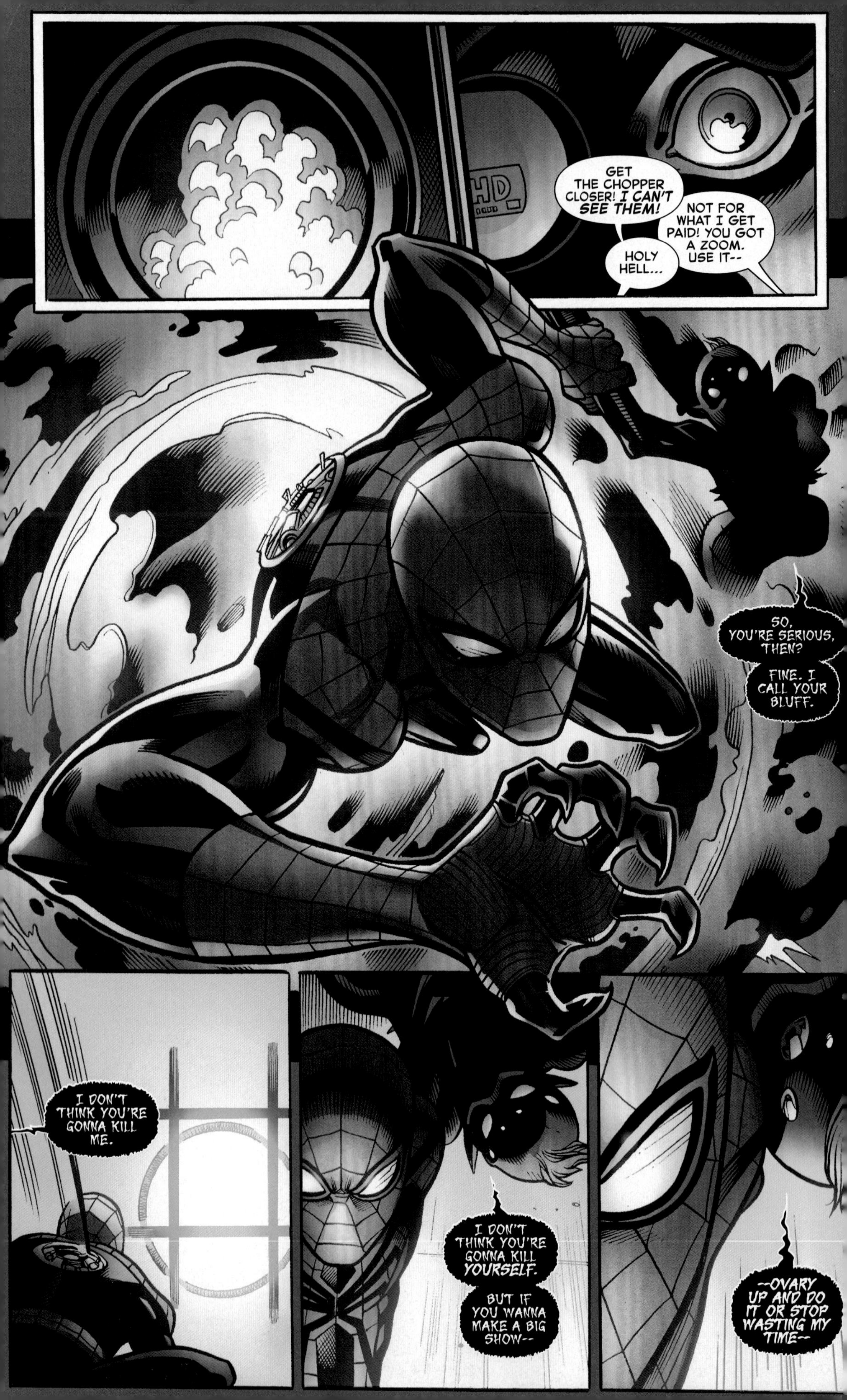
GET THE CHOPPER CLOSER! I CAN'T SEE THEM!
HOLY HELL...
NOT FOR WHAT I GET PAID! YOU GOT A ZOOM. USE IT--
HD
SO, YOU'RE SERIOUS, THEN?
FINE. I CALL YOUR BLUFF.
I DON'T THINK YOU'RE GONNA KILL ME.
I DON'T THINK YOU'RE GONNA KILL YOURSELF.
BUT IF YOU WANNA MAKE A BIG SHOW--
--OVARY UP AND DO IT OR STOP WASTING MY TIME--

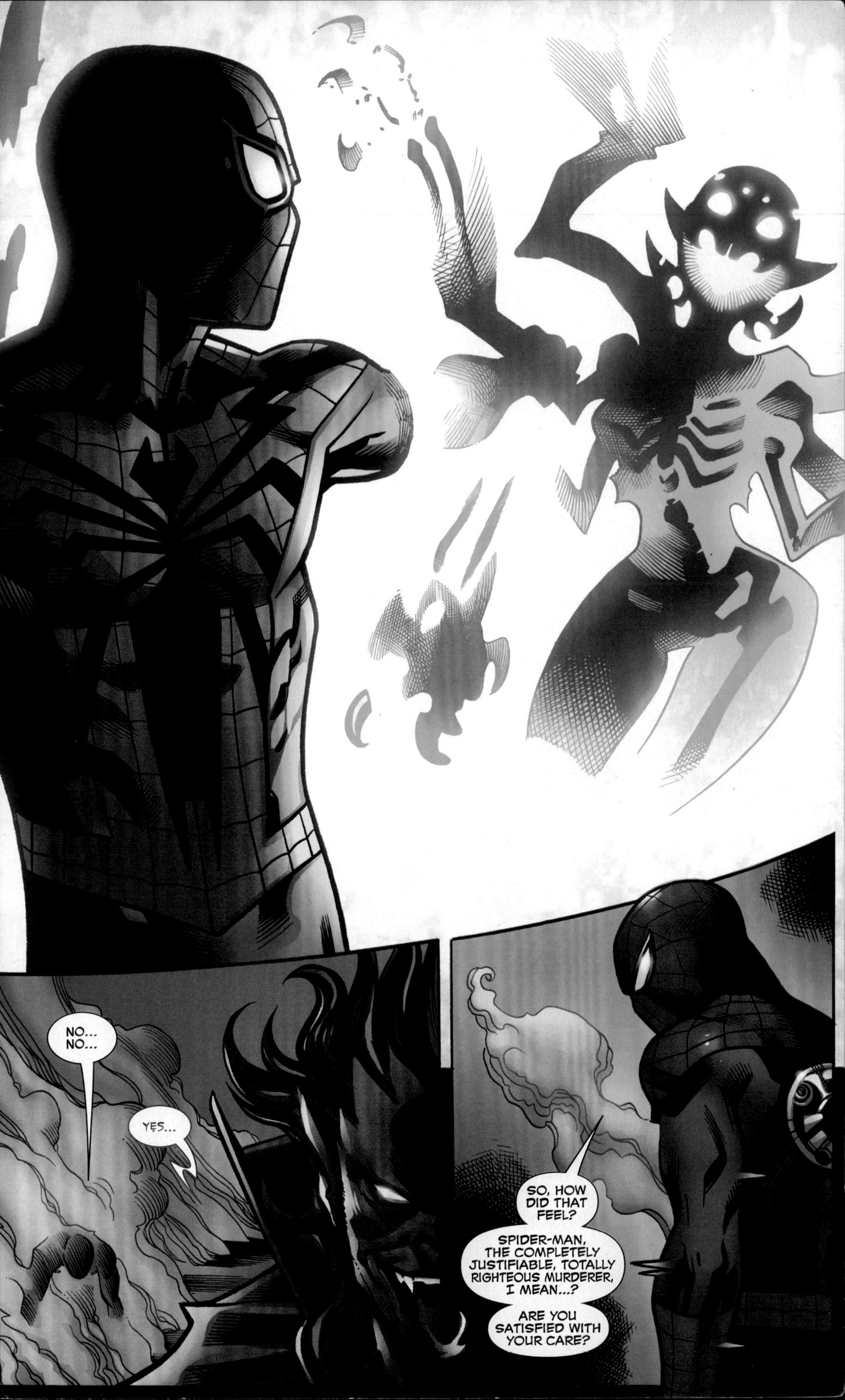
NO... NO...
YES...
SO, HOW DID THAT FEEL?
SPIDER-MAN, THE COMPLETELY JUSTIFIABLE, TOTALLY RIGHTEOUS MURDERER, I MEAN...?
ARE YOU SATISFIED WITH YOUR CARE?

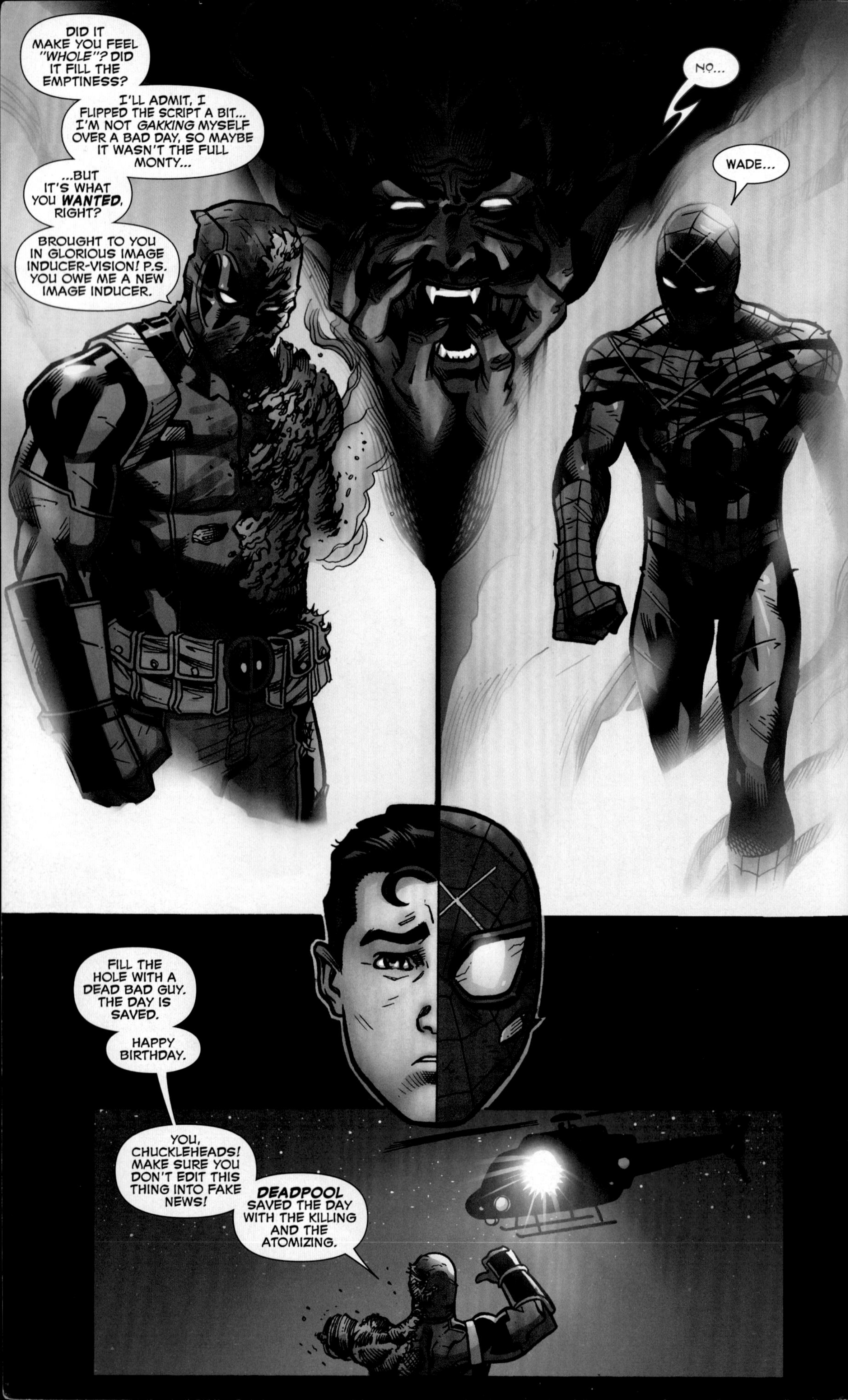
DID IT MAKE YOU FEEL "WHOLE"? DID IT FILL THE EMPTINESS?
I'LL ADMIT, I FLIPPED THE SCRIPT A BIT... I'M NOT GAKKING MYSELF OVER A BAD DAY, SO MAYBE IT WASN'T THE FULL MONTY...
...BUT IT'S WHAT YOU WANTED, RIGHT?
BROUGHT TO YOU IN GLORIOUS IMAGE INDUCER-VISION! P.S. YOU OWE ME A NEW IMAGE INDUCER.
NO...
WADE...
FILL THE HOLE WITH A DEAD BAD GUY. THE DAY IS SAVED.
HAPPY BIRTHDAY.
YOU, CHUCKLEHEADS! MAKE SURE YOU DON'T EDIT THIS THING INTO FAKE NEWS!
DEADPOOL SAVED THE DAY WITH THE KILLING AND THE ATOMIZING.

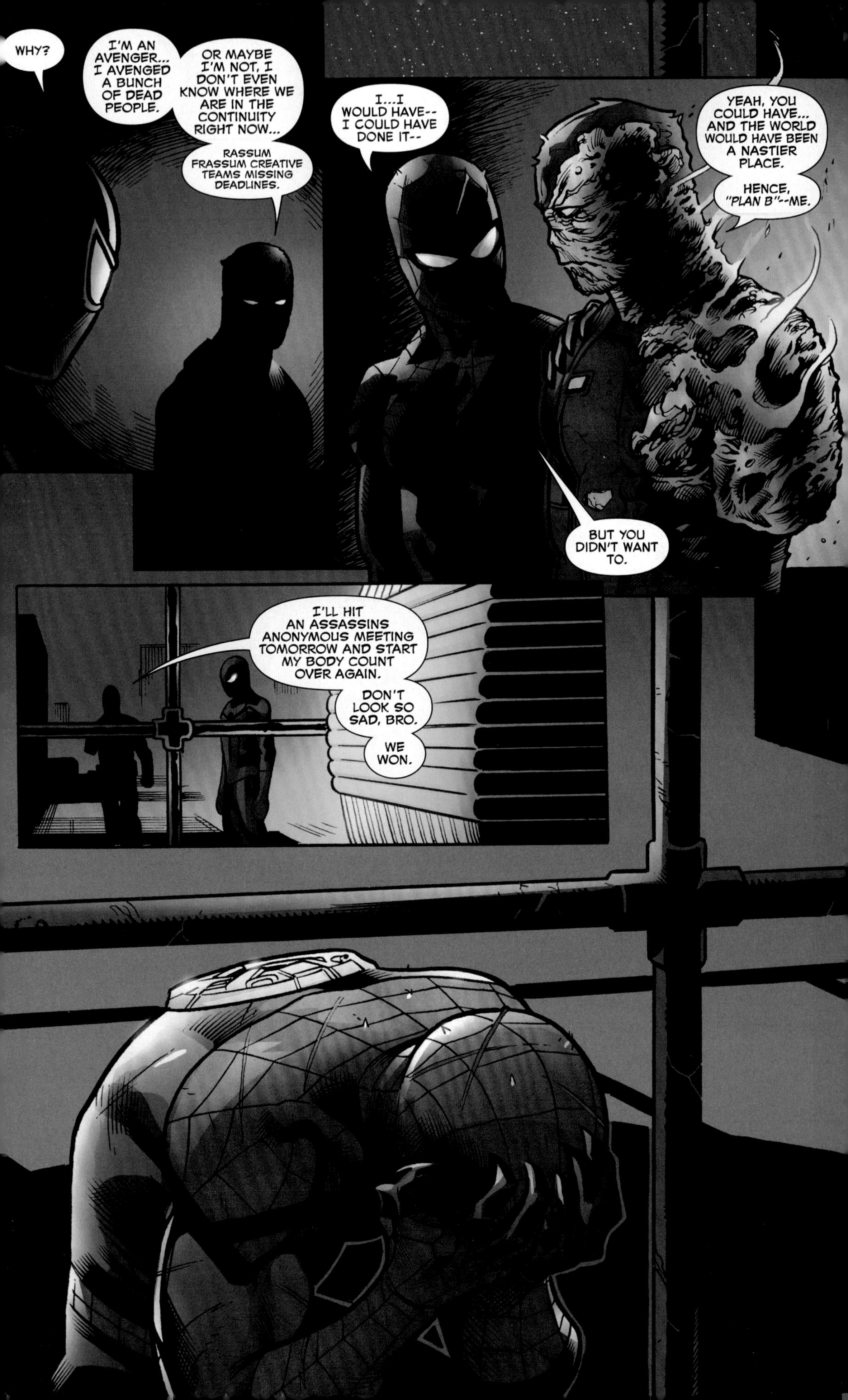
WHY?
I'M AN AVENGER... I AVENGED A BUNCH OF DEAD PEOPLE.
OR MAYBE I'M NOT, I DON'T EVEN KNOW WHERE WE ARE IN THE CONTINUITY RIGHT NOW...
RASSUM FRASSUM CREATIVE TEAMS MISSING DEADLINES.
I...I WOULD HAVE-- I COULD HAVE DONE IT--
YEAH, YOU COULD HAVE... AND THE WORLD WOULD HAVE BEEN A NASTIER PLACE.
HENCE, "PLAN B"--ME.
BUT YOU DIDN'T WANT TO.
I'LL HIT AN ASSASSINS ANONYMOUS MEETING TOMORROW AND START MY BODY COUNT OVER AGAIN.
DON'T LOOK SO SAD, BRO.
WE WON.

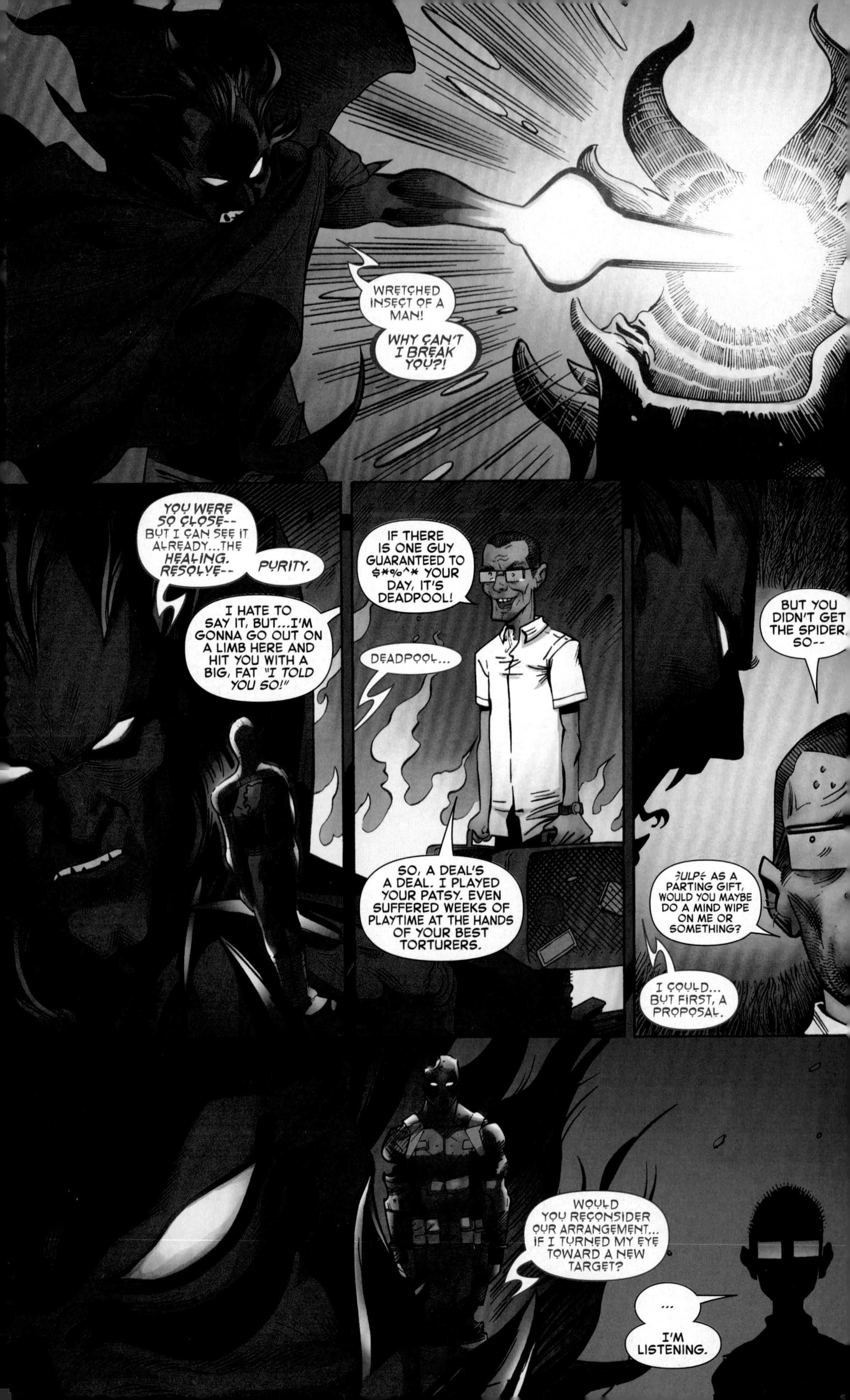
WRETCHED INSECT OF A MAN!
WHY CAN'T I BREAK YOU?!
YOU WERE SO CLOSE-- BUT I CAN SEE IT ALREADY...THE HEALING. RESOLVE--
PURITY.
I HATE TO SAY IT, BUT...I'M GONNA GO OUT ON A LIMB HERE AND HIT YOU WITH A BIG, FAT "I TOLD YOU SO!"
IF THERE IS ONE GUY GUARANTEED TO $*%^* YOUR DAY, IT'S DEADPOOL!
DEADPOOL...
SO, A DEAL'S A DEAL. I PLAYED YOUR PATSY. EVEN SUFFERED WEEKS OF PLAYTIME AT THE HANDS OF YOUR BEST TORTURERS.
BUT YOU DIDN'T GET THE SPIDER SO--
GULP AS A PARTING GIFT, WOULD YOU MAYBE DO A MIND WIPE ON ME OR SOMETHING?
I COULD... BUT FIRST, A PROPOSAL.
WOULD YOU RECONSIDER OUR ARRANGEMENT... IF I TURNED MY EYE TOWARD A NEW TARGET?
...
I'M LISTENING.

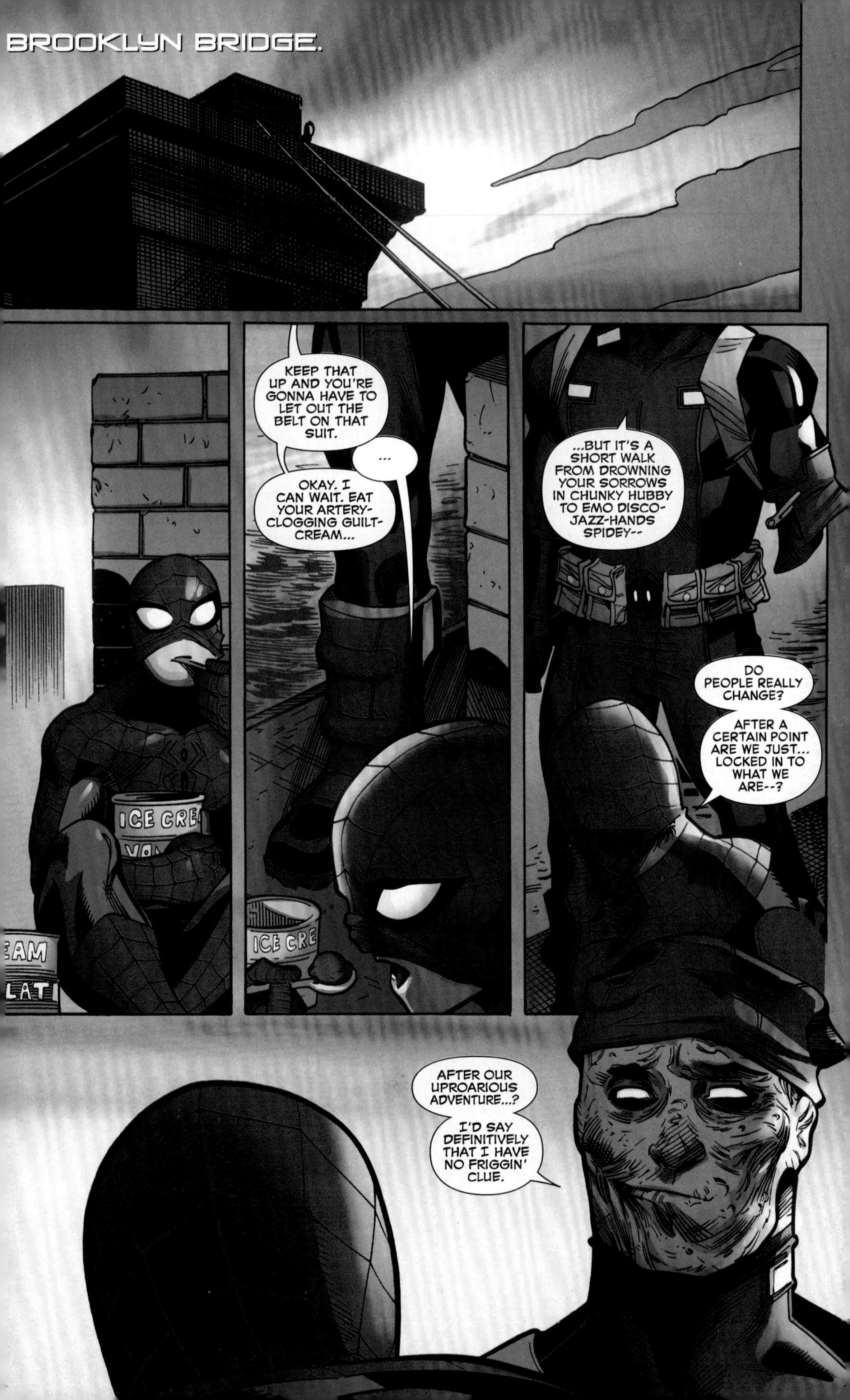
BROOKLYN BRIDGE.
KEEP THAT UP AND YOU'RE GONNA HAVE TO LET OUT THE BELT ON THAT SUIT.
...
OKAY. I CAN WAIT. EAT YOUR ARTERY-CLOGGING GUILT-CREAM...
...BUT IT'S A SHORT WALK FROM DROWNING YOUR SORROWS IN CHUNKY HUBBY TO EMO DISCO-JAZZ-HANDS SPIDEY--
DO PEOPLE REALLY CHANGE?
AFTER A CERTAIN POINT ARE WE JUST... LOCKED IN TO WHAT WE ARE--?
AFTER OUR UPROARIOUS ADVENTURE...?
I'D SAY DEFINITIVELY THAT I HAVE NO FRIGGIN' CLUE.

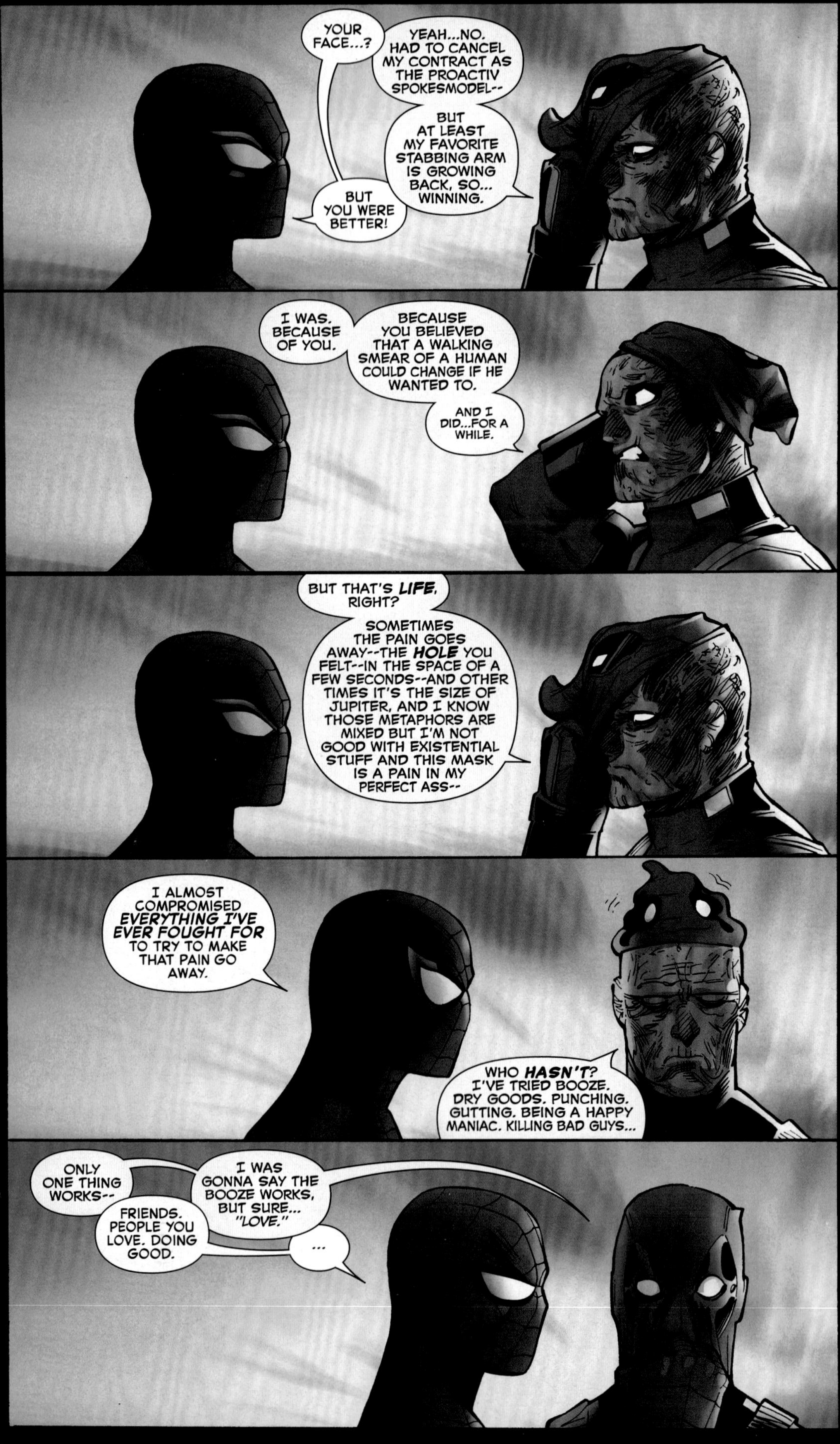
YOUR FACE...?
YEAH...NO. HAD TO CANCEL MY CONTRACT AS THE PROACTIV SPOKESMODEL--
BUT AT LEAST MY FAVORITE STABBING ARM IS GROWING BACK, SO... WINNING.
BUT YOU WERE BETTER!
I WAS. BECAUSE OF YOU.
BECAUSE YOU BELIEVED THAT A WALKING SMEAR OF A HUMAN COULD CHANGE IF HE WANTED TO.
AND I DID...FOR A WHILE.
BUT THAT'S LIFE, RIGHT?
SOMETIMES THE PAIN GOES AWAY--THE HOLE YOU FELT--IN THE SPACE OF A FEW SECONDS--AND OTHER TIMES IT'S THE SIZE OF JUPITER, AND I KNOW THOSE METAPHORS ARE MIXED BUT I'M NOT GOOD WITH EXISTENTIAL STUFF AND THIS MASK IS A PAIN IN MY PERFECT ASS--
I ALMOST COMPROMISED EVERYTHING I'VE EVER FOUGHT FOR TO TRY TO MAKE THAT PAIN GO AWAY.
WHO HASN'T? I'VE TRIED BOOZE. DRY GOODS. PUNCHING. GUTTING. BEING A HAPPY MANIAC. KILLING BAD GUYS...
ONLY ONE THING WORKS--
I WAS GONNA SAY THE BOOZE WORKS, BUT SURE... "LOVE."
FRIENDS. PEOPLE YOU LOVE. DOING GOOD.
...

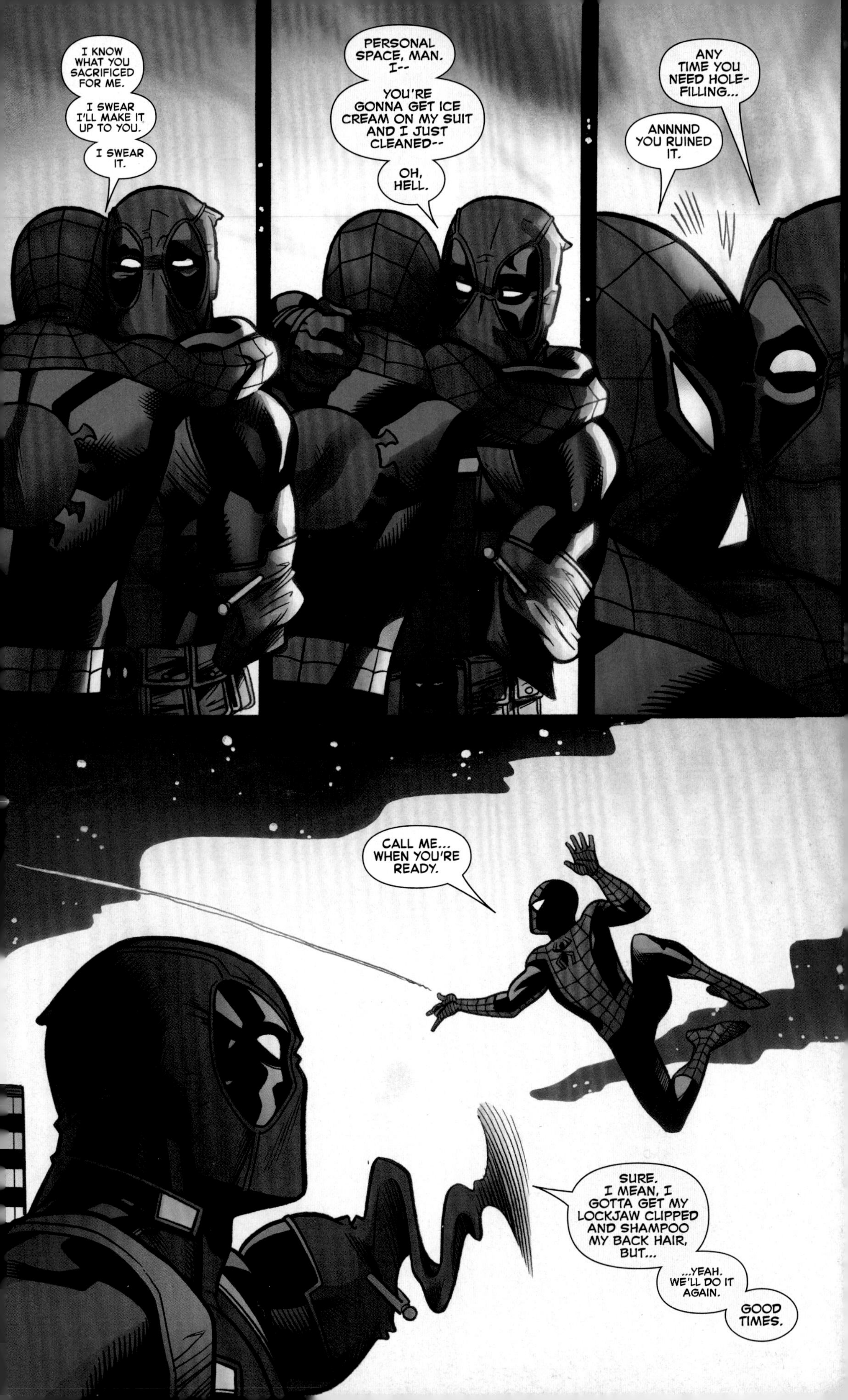
I KNOW WHAT YOU SACRIFICED FOR ME.
I SWEAR I'LL MAKE IT UP TO YOU.
I SWEAR IT.
PERSONAL SPACE, MAN. I--
YOU'RE GONNA GET ICE CREAM ON MY SUIT AND I JUST CLEANED--
OH, HELL.
ANY TIME YOU NEED HOLE-FILLING...
ANNNND YOU RUINED IT.
CALL ME... WHEN YOU'RE READY.
SURE. I MEAN, I GOTTA GET MY LOCKJAW CLIPPED AND SHAMPOO MY BACK HAIR, BUT...
...YEAH. WE'LL DO IT AGAIN.
GOOD TIMES.

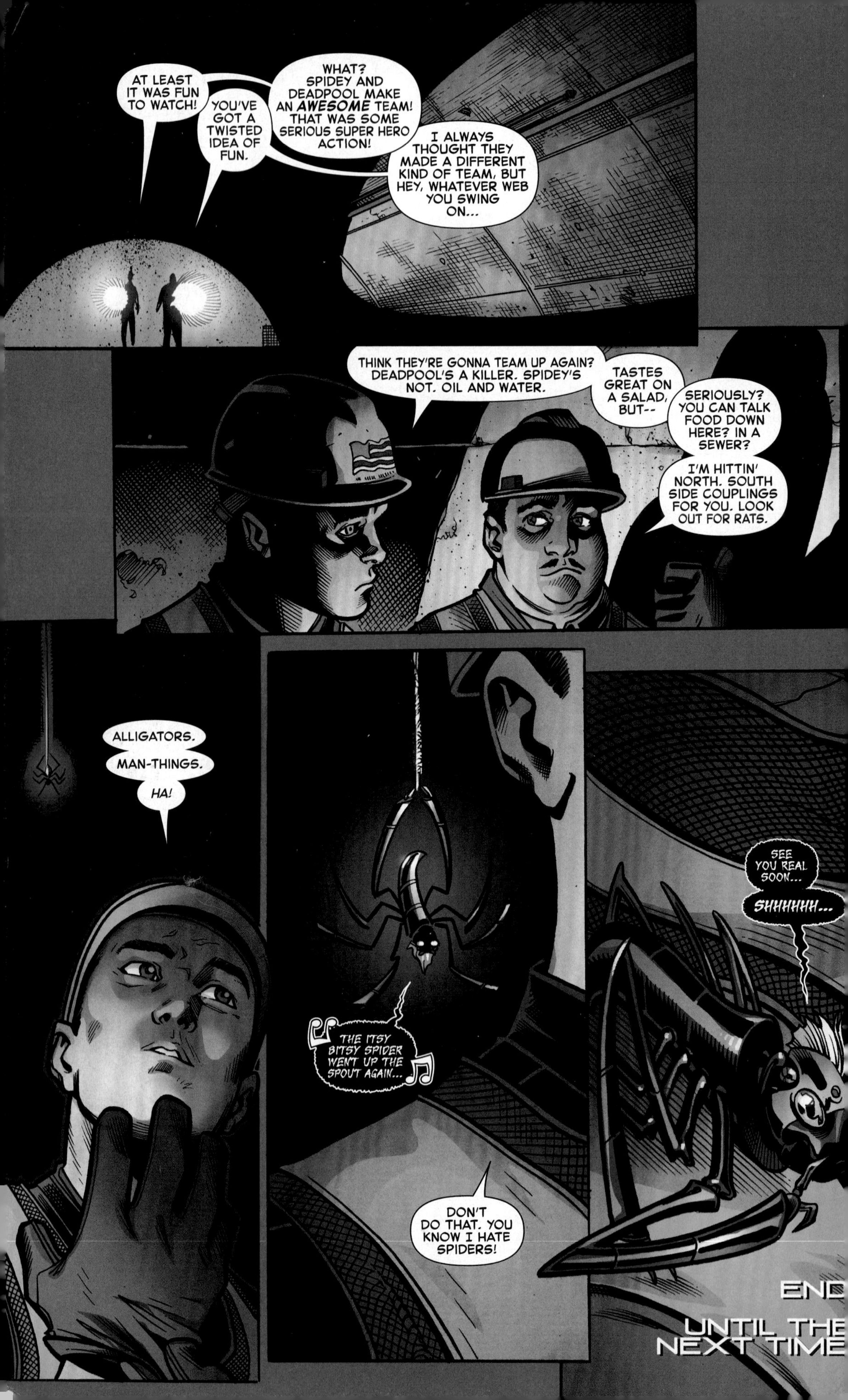
AT LEAST IT WAS FUN TO WATCH!
WHAT? SPIDEY AND DEADPOOL MAKE AN *AWESOME* TEAM! THAT WAS SOME SERIOUS SUPER HERO ACTION!
YOU'VE GOT A TWISTED IDEA OF FUN.
I ALWAYS THOUGHT THEY MADE A DIFFERENT KIND OF TEAM, BUT HEY, WHATEVER WEB YOU SWING ON...
THINK THEY'RE GONNA TEAM UP AGAIN? DEADPOOL'S A KILLER. SPIDEY'S NOT. OIL AND WATER.
TASTES GREAT ON A SALAD, BUT--
SERIOUSLY? YOU CAN TALK FOOD DOWN HERE? IN A SEWER?
I'M HITTIN' NORTH. SOUTH SIDE COUPLINGS FOR YOU. LOOK OUT FOR RATS.
ALLIGATORS.
MAN-THINGS.
HA!
THE ITSY BITSY SPIDER WENT UP THE SPOUT AGAIN...
DON'T DO THAT. YOU KNOW I HATE SPIDERS!
SEE YOU REAL SOON...
SHHHHHH...
END
UNTIL THE NEXT TIME

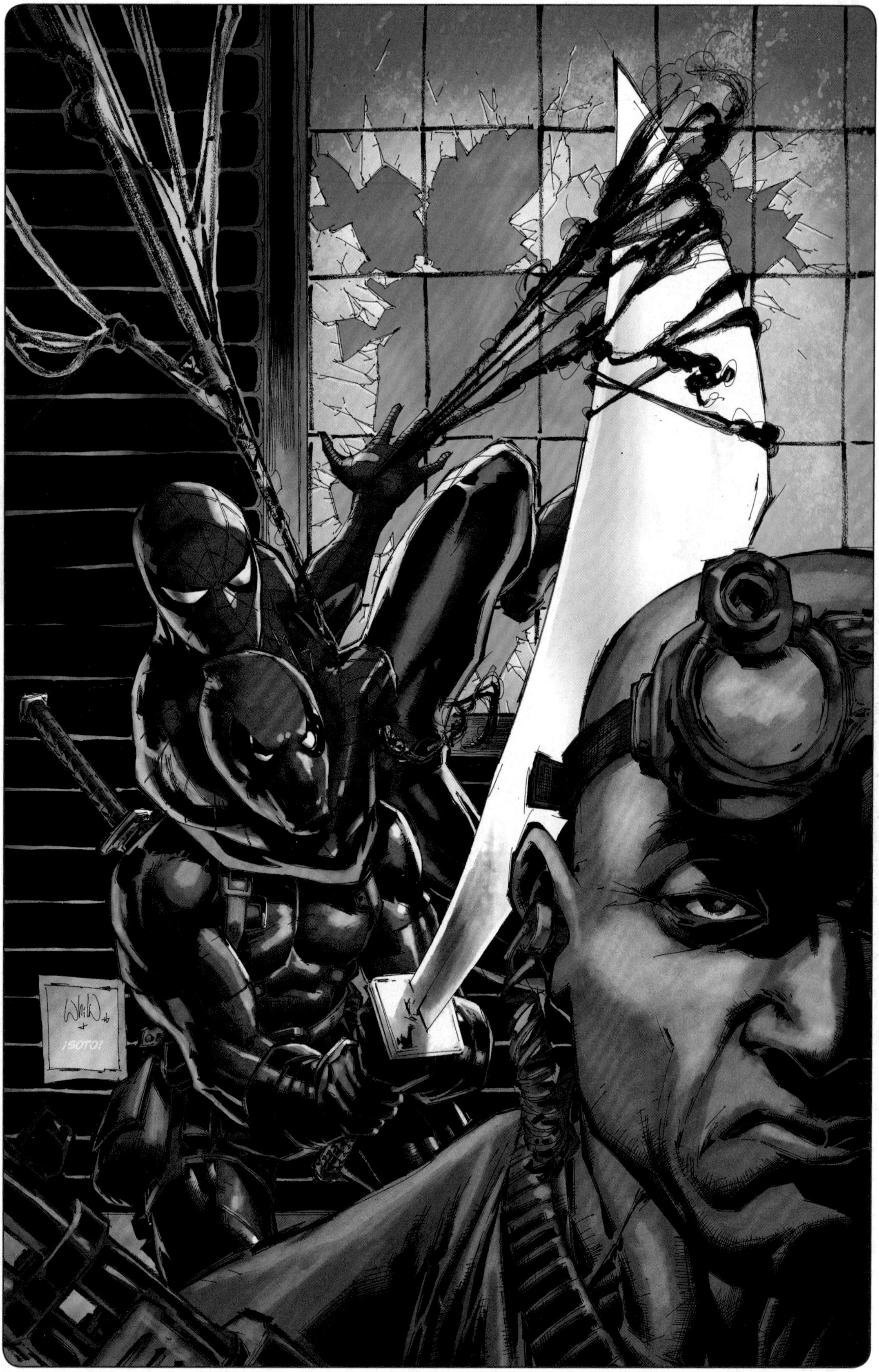

9 VARIANT BY
WHILCE PORTACIO & CHRIS SOTOMAYOR

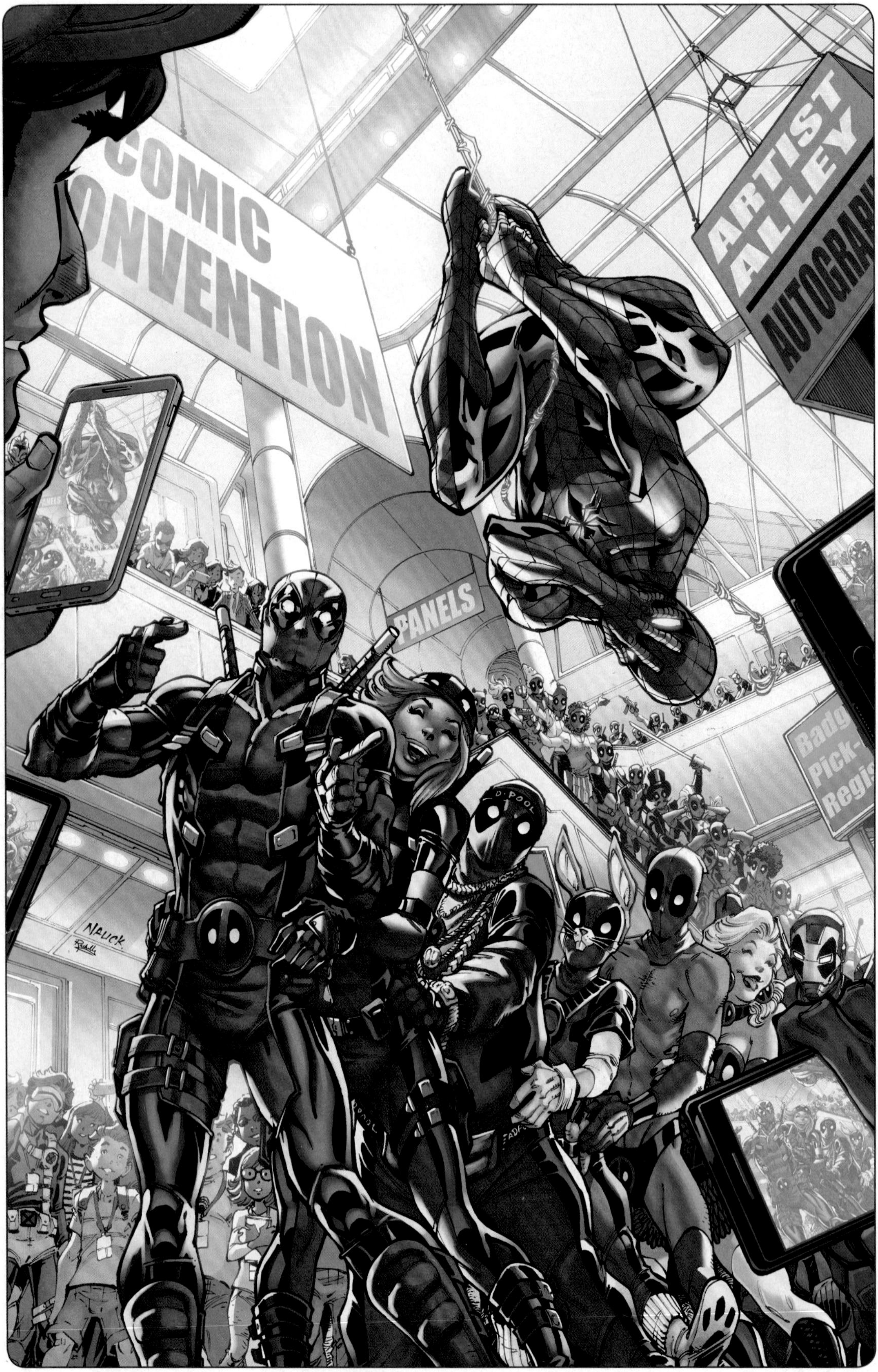
COMIC
ONVENTION
ARTIST
ALLEY
AUTOGRAP
PANELS
Badg
Pick-
Regis
D-POOL
NAUCK

14 VARIANT BY
TODD NAUCK & RACHELLE ROSENBERG